John Evans

History of all Christian Sects and Denominations

Their origin, peculiar tenets, and present condition. Fourth American Edition

John Evans

History of all Christian Sects and Denominations
Their origin, peculiar tenets, and present condition. Fourth American Edition

ISBN/EAN: 9783337148461

Printed in Europe, USA, Canada, Australia, Japan

Cover: Foto ©Lupo / pixelio.de

More available books at **www.hansebooks.com**

HISTORY

OF

ALL CHRISTIAN SECTS

AND DENOMINATIONS;

THEIR ORIGIN, PECULIAR TENETS, AND PRESENT CONDITION

WITH

AN INTRODUCTORY ACCOUNT

OF

Atheists, Deists, Jews, Mahometans, Pagans, &c.

BY JOHN EVANS, L.L.D.

FROM THE FIFTEENTH LONDON EDITION.

REVISED AND ENLARGED,

WITH THE ADDITION OF THE MOST RECENT STATISTICS RELATING TO RELIGIOUS SECTS IN THE UNITED STATES.

BY THE AMERICAN EDITOR.

The great lesson which every sect, and every individual of every sect, ought to learn from the history of the church, is Moderation. Want of genuine moderation towards those who differ from us in religious opinions seems to me the most unaccountable thing in the world.—BISHOP WATSON.

FOURTH AMERICAN EDITION.

BOSTON:
PUBLISHED BY JOSIAH P. MENDUM,
AT THE OFFICE OF THE BOSTON INVESTIGATOR.
1875.

PREFACE

TO THE FIFTEENTH LONDON EDITION.

The reader shall be detained only by the author's grateful acknowledgement of the favourable reception given by the public to his sketch of the denominations of the Christian world. Detailing the opinions of the various sects, it addresses the curiosity of Turk, Jew, Infidel, and Christian. This accounts for its unrivalled circulation. It enjoys the honour of a niche in the royal library, whilst it has descended down to the shelves of the cottage in the obscurest recesses of the country. By its translation into foreign languages, it has spread over the continent: whilst it has found its way to Calcutta, to the Cape of Good Hope, and even to Rio Janeiro in South America. Thus the little volume, like a universal missionary, proceeding silently and unostentatiously on its errand of Christian love, may be said to have traversed the four quarters of the globe.

Its professed purport is to enlighten and enlarge the understanding, by imparting accurate views of the tenets characterising the several departments of Christendom. This, in many instances, it is known to have accomplished. One singular fact may be noticed. The author entering a bookseller's shop in the country, the bookseller, taking him for a clergyman, presented him with a copy, and strongly recommended its circulation among his parishioners, for the promotion of candour, peace, and charity! He had sold, he said, many among the clergy; and added, that it had never failed to produce some good effect.

The writer can honestly declare, that having through much bodily infirmity, attained the sixtieth year of his age, and witnessed the issuing of *one hundred thousand* copies of his little book from the press, the vanity of authorship natural to early life is absorbed in the sweet heart-exhilarating consciousness of doing good to mankind. The longer he lives, the more he is convin-

With regard to the present edition, every article has been most carefully revised. The author has availed himself of the latest communications from some of the leading ministers or members of the sects. These were transmitted in reply to applications made on the subject. He has not, nor can he have, any interest in the misrepresentation of any body of Christians: —his sole object is truth and charity.

PREFACE

BY THE AMERICAN EDITOR.

From the foregoing preface of the venerable author to the fifteenth London edition of his work, some idea may be formed of the degree of favour, with which it has been received by the British public. We may add, that in reference to its adaptation to the wants of the people of the United States at the present day, numerous essential additions and improvements have been made. The object of the work being to present an accurate and impartial account of the various sects, into which the Christian world is divided, we have been careful to submit every article, in which a sketch of an existing denomination of American origin is given, to the inspection and approval of some recognised expounder of its tenets.

Among the works to which we have been largely indebted in the execution of our task of revision, are Brande's Encyclopædia; Hayward's Book of Religions; D'Aubigne's History of the Reformation; Encyclopædia Americana; Maurice's True Catholic Church; Parochial Sermons, by John Henry Newman; the Oxford Tracts; Pusey's Sermons; Puseyism no Popery, by Bishop Doane; The Churchman; &c. &c.

The condition of religious parties at the present moment is deeply interesting. All sects seem to be examining their principles, and the spirit of theological investigation was never more active. Religion cannot possibly suffer by the canvassing of its truths; and enlightened views alone are likely to be of permanent duration.

"It is more and more understood," says a celebrated divine of our own day, "that religious truth is every man's property and right, that it is committed to no order or individual, to no priest, minister, student, or sage, to be given, or kept back at will; but that every man may, and should seek it for himself; that every man is to see with his own mind as well as with his own eyes; and that God's illuminating spirit is alike promised to every honest and humble seeker after truth. This recognition of every man's right of judgment, appears in the teachings of all denominations of Christians. In all the tone of authority is giving place to that of reason and persuasion. Men of all ranks are more and more addressed, as those who must weigh and settle for themselves the grandest truths of religion.

"The same tendency to universality, is seen in the generous toleration which marks our times, in comparison with the past. Men, in general, cannot now endure to think that their own narrow church holds all the goodness on the earth. Religion is less and less regarded as a name, a form, a creed, a church, and more and more as the spirit of Christ which works under all forms and sects. True, much intolerance remains; its separating walls are not fallen; but with few exceptions, they no longer reach to the clouds. Many of them have crumbled away, till the men whom they sever can shake hands, and exchange words of fellowship, and recognize in one another's faces the features of brethren."

NEW-YORK, DEC. 1843.

CONTENTS.

CHAPTER I.
INTRODUCTORY REMARKS ON EXISTING CREEDS AT VARIANCE WITH CHRISTIANITY——ATHEISTS——PANTHEISTS——THEOPHILANTHROPISTS——PAGANS, ... 11

CHAPTER II.
JEWS——MAHOMETANS, ... 25

CHAPTER III.
CHRISTIANITY——A BRIEF VIEW OF ITS EVIDENCES, . . 40

CHAPTER IV.
TRINITARIANS——UNITARIANS, ... 52

CHAPTER V.
THE GREEK CHURCH——ROMAN CATHOLICS, . . 64

CHAPTER VI.
THE REFORMATION——ORIGIN OF THE TERM PROTESTANT——LUTHERANS——CALVINISTS——HUGUENOTS——ARMINIANS——BAXTERIANS——ANTINOMIANS——MATERIALISTS——NECESSARIANS, . . 71

CHAPTER VII.
DIFFERENT MODES OF CHURCH GOVERNMENT——THE EPISCOPALIAN, PRESBYTERIAN, AND CONGREGATIONAL OR INDEPENDENT SYSTEMS——MEMBERS OF THE CHURCH OF ENGLAND, OR EPISCOPALIANS——TRACTARIANS, OR PUSEYITES, ... 96

CHAPTER VIII.
WESLEYAN, OR EPISCOPAL METHODISTS——WHITEFIELD METHODISTS——PROTESTANT AND INDEPENDENT METHODISTS——MORAVIANS, ... 116

CONTENTS.

CHAPTER IX.

PRESBYTERIANISM—ITS ORIGIN AND PREVALENCE—THE KIRK OF SCOTLAND—AMERICAN PRESBYTERIANS—DIVISION INTO OLD AND NEW SCHOOLS—CUMBERLAND PRESBYTERIANS—DUTCH REFORMED CHURCH—GERMAN REFORMED CHURCH, . . . 130

CHAPTER X.

BAPTISM—PÆDOBAPTISTS—ANABAPTISTS—BAPTISTS—SABBATARIANS, OR SEVENTH DAY BAPTISTS—MENNONITES—DUNKERS—FREE COMMUNION BAPTISTS, ... 143

CHAPTER XI.

QUAKERS—GEORGE FOX AND WILLIAM PENN—HICKSITES—SHAKERS, ... 155

CHAPTER XII.

UNIVERSALISTS—RESTORATIONISTS—SWEDENBORGIANS, . 177

CHAPTER XIII.

DISCIPLES OF CHRIST, OR CAMPBELLITES—BEREANS—CHRISTIAN CONNECTION—COME-OUTERS—SANDEMANIANS—DALEITES, 197

CHAPTER XIV.

HUTCHINSONIANS—MILLENARIANS—MILLERITES—FOLLOWERS OF JOANNA SOUTHCOTT—WHIPPERS—WILKINSONIANS—MYSTICS—MORMONITES, OR LATTER DAY SAINTS, . . . 216

CHAPTER XV.

ARMENIANS—NESTORIANS—PELAGIANS—PAULIANS—ORIGENISTS—QUIETISTS—MANICHEISTS—MOLINISTS—GNOSTICS, . . 241

CHAPTER XVI.

SAINT SIMONIANS—HUMANITARIANS—MOMIERS, . . 255

CHAPTER XVII.

CONCLUDING REFLECTIONS ON CHRISTIAN MODERATION, . 264

INDEX.

	PAGE		PAGE
American Presbyterians	134	Dutch Reformed Church	138
Anabaptists	142		
Andover Creed	81	Edwards, Jonathan	80, 95
Antinomians	89	England, Church of	97
Apostles' Creed	100	Episcopalians	96
Arians	55	Episcopal, U. S. Church	103
Arius	"	Erasmus	73
Armenians	241	Evangelical, The term	136
Arminian Creed, The	85, 120		
Arminians, The	78, 85	Five Points, The	79
Armenius	"	Fox, George	156
Athanasian Creed	53	Free Communion Baptists	154
Atheists	11	Free-will Baptists	149
Augsburg, Confession of	75, 76, 126	Friends	155
Bacon, Lord, on Atheism	12	German Reformed Church	141
Baptism	110, 142, 161	Gnostics	253
Baptists	143	Grant, Dr. A., On the present	
" John Milton on	148	state of the Jews	30, 34
" Free Communion	154	Greek Church	64, 70
" Free Will	149		
" Seventh Day	150	Henry the Eighth	97
" Six Principle	151	Hicksites	163
Baxterians	87	Holland, Church of	138
Baxter, Richard	87, 88, 287	Hopkinsonian Calvinists	80
Bereans	202	Hopkins, Samuel	"
Bishops, succession of the	102	Huguenots	84
Brownists	96	Humanitarians	257
		Hutchinsonians	216
Calvinism	84, 133		
Calvinists	77, 138	Immersion, Modes of	145, 146
Calvin, John	58, 75	Independents	96
Chalmers, Rev. Dr.	134	Indulgences, Sale of	71
Channing, Rev. Wm. E.	63		
Chesterfield, Lord, on Atheism	14	Jewish Confession of Faith	27
Christianity	40	Jews	25
" Brief view of its evidences	45		
Christian Connection	206	Kant, Emanuel, Quotation from	16
Christian moderation	264	" His letter on Swedenborg	184
Church government, Modes of	96	Knox, John	130
Clarke, Dr., on Deism	18		
Coleridge, Quotations from	17	Latin Church	65
Come-outers	212	Latter Day Saints	232
Concluding reflections	264	Lee, Anne	165
Congregationalists	96, 137	Luther, Martin	72
Cranmer	98, 109, 112	Lutherans	76
Cumberland Presbyterians	138		
		Mahometans	35
Daleites	211	Mahometan Creed	37
Deists	18	Manicheists	251
Disciples of Christ	197	Martyr, Justin	61
Dort, Synod of	78, 86, 141	Materialists	90
Dunkers	152	Melancthon	73

INDEX.

	PAGE
Mennonites	151
Messiah, Meaning of the word	26
Methodists	116
" Episcopal	"
" Whitefield	121
" Protestant	123
" New	"
Millenarians	217
Millerites	220
Milton John, his Arianism	56
" On Baptism	148
Missions	129, 149
Molinists	252
Momiers	263
Moravians	125
Mormonites	232
Mystics	229
Nantz, Edict of	84
Necessarians	90, 93
Nestorians	243
New England, Settlers of	137
New Jerusalem Church	181
New Methodists	123
Newman, Rev. Mr.	110, 111, 114
Nicene Creed	99
Noetians	60
Nonjurors	98
Origen	177, 246
Origenists	"
Orthodox Calvinists	81
Pædobaptists	143
Pagans	20
Paley, on Christianity	49
Pantheists	17
Papists	115
Paulians	245
Pelagians	"
Penn, William	157
Plato, on Atheism	12
Pope Leo X.	71
Pope Pius's Creed	67
Presbyterianism	130
Presbyterians	96
" American	134
" Cumberland	138
" New School	"
" Old School	"
" Scottish	133
Priestly, Dr.	90
Protestants, Origin of the term	75
Protestant Methodists	123
Puritans	137
Puseyites	104
Pusey Rev. Dr.	111, 113
Quakers	155

	PAGE
Quietists	250
Reformation, The	71
" Its moral effects	76
Restorationists	179
Roman Catholics	65
Romanism	114
Sabbatarians	150
Sabellians	59
Sabellius	60
Saint Simonians	255
Sandemanians	210
Schelling, Pantheism of	18
Scotland, Kirk of	131
" Seceders from the	134
Servetus, Michael	58
Seventh Day Baptists	150
Shakers	164
Sharp, Archbishop, Murder of	134
Socinus, Faustus	57
Socinians	58
Southcott Joanna	224
Spinoza	12
Strauss	22
Sublapsarians	83
Supralapsarians	"
Swedenborg, Emanuel	181
Swedenborgians	"
Talmud, The	26
Taylor, Bishop on the Trinity	54
Theists	17
Theophilanthropists	23
Thirty-Nine Articles	98
Tillotson, Archbishop	14
Tractarians	104
Transubstantiation	66, 111
Trent, Council of	67
Trinitarians	52
Trinity	"
Unitarians	55
Universalists	177
Vanini, Lucilio	12
Watts, Dr. on the Trinity	54
Wesley, John	116
Wesleyan Methodists	"
Westminster Confession of Faith	133
Whippers	228
Whitefield, George	121
Whitefield Methodists	"
Williams, Roger	149
Wilkinsonians	229
Zinzendorf, Count	125
Zuinglius	7

HISTORY OF ALL CHRISTIAN SECTS
AND DENOMINATIONS.

CHAPTER I.

INTRODUCTORY REMARKS ON EXISTING CREEDS AT VARIANCE WITH CHRISTIANITY——ATHEISTS——PANTHEISTS—DEISTS—THEOPHILANTHROPISTS——PAGANS.

ATHEISTS.

Before entering upon an acccount of the various sects and denominations, into which the Christian world is divided, it will be interesting to glance at the opinions of those, who reject all revealed religion, and to review the present condition of Judæism and Mahommedanism. Indeed, a complete survey of the interesting field we propose to examine could not well be taken, without departing so far from our main subject as to include these topics.

To delineate the nature, point out the foundation, and calculate the tendency of every individual creed, would be an endless task. Our design is simply to enumerate the leading tenets of the several parties, which attract our notice; and, in accomplishing this purpose, it will be our earnest endeavor to avoid all uncharitable reflections and prejudiced misrepresentations.

As the idea of a Supreme Being is the foundation of all religion, we will first consider the opinions of those, who reject or profess to reject this idea, and who are consequently without any religion. The term *atheist* is derived from two Greek words, ἀ, *without*, and θεος, God; and signifies one who denies the existence of a God, or a Providence; and in this sense the appellation occurs in the New Testament, Ephes. ii. 12:—" Without God (or Atheist) in the world."

Plato distinguishes three sorts of Atheists: such as deny absolutely that there are any Gods; others, who admit the existence of the Gods, but deny that they concern themselves with human affairs, and so disbelieve a Providence; and lastly, such as believe in the Gods and a Providence, but think that they are easily appeased, remitting the greatest crimes for the slightest supplication.

It is evident that direct Atheists are few. Some persons question the reality of such a character; and others insist that pretensions to Atheism have their origin in pride, or are adopted as a cloak to licentiousness, while in not a few instances the motive is merely an affectation of eccentricity. In the seventeenth century, Benedict Spinoza was a noted defender of what comes under Plato's classification of Atheistic notions. Spinoza was a Jew of Amsterdam, born in 1634. In his work on ethics, he undertakes to deduce by mathematical reasoning from a few axioms, the principles, " that there can be no substance but God; whatever is is in God, and nothing can be conceived without God." Hence his scheme is called with justice Pantheistic, from the Greek words πᾶν, *the whole*, and θεος, *God*.

In 1619, Lucilio Vanini, an Italian, of eccentric character, was burned at Toulouse, for his Atheistical tenets. Being pressed to make public acknowledgment of his crime, and to ask pardon of God, the king, and justice, he replied, that he did not believe there was a God; that he never offended the king; and as for justice, he wished it at the devil! He confessed that he was one of the twelve who parted in company from Naples to spread their doctrines in all parts of Europe.

Lord Bacon, in his Essays, justly remarks, that " a *little* philosophy inclineth a man's mind to Atheism, but depth in philosophy bringeth men's minds about to religion: for while the mind of man looketh upon second causes scattered, it may rest in them and go no farther; but when it beholdeth the chain of them confederated and linked together, it must needs fly to Providence and Deity." And Dean Sherlock remarks, respecting the origin of Atheism, that " The universal Deluge and the confusion of languages, had so abundantly convinced mankind of a Divine power and Providence, that there was no such person as an Atheist till their ridiculous idolatries had tempted some men of wit and thought rather to own no God than such as the Heathens worshipped."

Dr. Priestley, in one of his Fast sermons, observes, that when he visited France, in 1774, " All her philosophers and men of letters were absolute infidels; and that he was represented by one of them in a mixed strain of censure and compliment, as the only man of talent he had met with, who had any faith in the Scriptures. Nay, Voltaire himself, who was then living, was considered by them as a weak-minded man, because, though an unbeliever in revelation, he believed in a *God !*"

Atheism, being purely negative, is not a religion, nor have Atheists ever associated as a body for religious worsh p—the wisest do not attempt to prove this negative, but require proofs of the Deists, and other spiritual worshippers—they usually take the name of Materialists, and attempt to account for mental phenomena by the properties and combination of matter, admitting with all men, that much in nature is beyond the powers of humanity to comprehend.

THE GOLDEN VERSES OF THE PYTHAGOREANS.

TRANSLATED FROM THE GREEK BY NICHOLAS ROWE, ESQ.

First to the Gods thy humble homage pay;
The greatest this, and first of laws obey:
Perform thy vows, observe thy plighted troth,
And let religion bind thee to thy oath.
The heroes next demand thy just regard,
Renown'd on earth, and to the stars preferr'd,
To light and endless life their virtue's sure reward.
Due rites perform and honors to the dead,
To ev'ry wife, to ev'ry pious shade,
With lowly duty to thy parents bow,
And grace and favor to thy kindred show:
For what concerns the rest of human-kind,
Choose out the man to virtue best inclin'd;
Him to thy arms receive, him to thy bosom bind.
Possess'd of such a friend, preserve him still;
Nor thwart his counsels with thy stubborn will;
Pliant to all his admonitions prove,
And yield to all his offices of love:
Him, from thy heart, so true, so justly dear,
Let no rash word nor light offences tear.
Bear all thou canst, still with his failings strive,
And to the utmost still, and still forgive;
For strong necessity alone explores
The secret vigor of our latent pow'rs,
Rouses and urges on the lazy heart.
Force, to itself unknown before, t' exert.
By use thy stronger appetites assuage,
Thy gluttony, thy sloth, thy lust, thy rage:
From each dishonest act of shame forbear;
Of others, and thyself, alike beware.
Let rev'rence of thyself thy thoughts control,
And guard the sacred temple of thy soul.
Let justice o'er thy word and deed preside;
And reason ev'n thy meanest actions guide:
For know that death is man's appointed doom,
Know that the day of great account will come,
When thy past life shall strictly be survey'd,
Each word, each deed, be in the balance laid,
And all the good and all the ill most justly be repaid.
For wealth the perishing, uncertain good,
Ebbing and flowing like the fickle flood,
That knows no sure, no fix'd abiding place,

But wand'ring, loves from hand to hand to pass;
Revolve the getter's joy and loser's pain,
And think if it be worth thy while to gain.
Of all those sorrows that attend mankind,
With patience bear the lot to thee assign'd;
Nor think it chance, nor murmur at the load;
For know what man calls fortune is from God,
In what thou mayest from Wisdom seek relief,
And let her healing hand assuage thy grief;
Yet still whate'er the righteous doom ordains,
What cause soever multiplies thy pains,
Let not those pains as ills be understood,
For God delights not to afflict the good.
 The reas'ning art to various ends apply'd,
Is oft a sure, but oft an erring guide.
Thy judgment therefore sound and cool preserve,
Nor lightly from thy resolution swerve;
The dazzling pomp of words does oft deceive,
And sweet persuasion wins the easy to believe.
 When fools and liars labor to persuade,
Be dumb, and let the babblers vainly plead.
 This above all, this precept chiefly learn,
This nearly does, and first thyself concern:
Let no example, let no soothing tongue,
Prevail upon thee with a syren's song,
To do thy soul's immortal essence wrong.
Of good and ill by words or deeds express'd,
Choose for thyself, and always choose the best.
Let wary thought each enterprise forerun,
And ponder on thy task before begun,
Lest folly should the wretched work deface,
And mock thy fruitless labors with disgrace.
Fools huddle on, and always are in haste,
Act without thought, and thoughtless words they waste
But thou in all thou dost, with early cares
Strive to prevent at first a fate like theirs;
That sorrow on the end may never wait,
Nor sharp repentance make thee wise too late.
 Beware thy meddling hand in aught to try,
That does beyond thy reach of knowledge lie;
But seek to know, and bend thy serious thought
To search the profitable knowledge out.
So joys on joys for ever shall increase,
Wisdom shall crown thy labors, and shall bless
Thy life with pleasure, and thy end with peace.
 Nor let the body want its part, but share
A just proportion of thy tender care;
For health and welfare prudently provide,
And let its lawful wants be all supplied.

Let sober draughts refresh, and wholesome fare
Decaying nature's wasted force repair;
And sprightly exercise the duller spirits cheer.
In all things still which to this care belong,
Observe this rule, to guard thy soul from wrong.
  By virtuous use thy life and manners frame,
Manly and simply pure, and free from blame.
  Provoke not Envy's deadly rage, but fly
The glancing course of her malicious eye.
  Seek not in needless luxury to waste
Thy wealth and substance, with a spendthrift's haste;
Yet flying these, be watchful, lest thy mind,
Prone to extremes, an equal danger find,
And be to sordid avarice inclin'd.
Distant alike from each, to neither lean,
But ever keep the happy Golden Mean.
  Be careful still to guard thy soul from wrong,
And let thy thought prevent thy hand and tongue.
  Let not the stealing god of sleep surprise
Nor creep in slumbers on thy weary eyes,
E'er ev'ry action of the former day
Strictly thou dost and righteously survey.
With rev'rence at thy own tribunal stand,
And answer justly to thy own demand.
Where have I been? in what have I transgress'd?
What good or ill has this day's life express'd?
Where have I fail'd in what I ought to do?
In what to God, to man, or to myself I owe?
Inquire severe whate'er from first to last,
From morning's dawn till evening's gloom is past.
If evil were thy deeds, repenting mourn,
And let thy soul with strong remorse be torn.
If good, the good with peace of mind repay,
And to thy secret self with pleasure say,
Rejoice, my heart, for all went well to-day.
These thoughts, and chiefly these, thy mind should move·
Employ thy study, and engage thy love.
These are the rules which will to Virtue lead,
And teach thy feet her heav'nly paths to tread.
This by his name I swear, whose sacred lore
First to mankind explain'd the mystic four,
Source of eternal nature and almighty pow'r.
  In all thou dost first let thy pray'rs ascend,
And to the gods thy labors first commend,
From them implore success, and hope a prosp'rous end.
So shall thy abler mind be taught to soar,
And Wisdom in her secret ways explore;
To range thro' heav'n above and earth below,
Immortal gods and mortal men to know.

So shalt thou learn what pow'r does all control,
What bounds the parts, and what unites the whole:
And rightly judge, in all this wondrous frame,
How universal nature is the same.
So shalt thou ne'er thy vain affections place
On hopes of what shall never come to pass.
Man, wretched man, thou shall be taught to know,
Who bears within himself the inborn cause of woe.
Unhappy race! that never yet could tell
How near their good and happiness they dwell.
Depriv'd of sense, they neither hear nor see;
Fetter'd in vice, they seek not to be free,
But stupid to their own sad fate agree.
Like pond'rous rolling stones, oppress'd with ill,
The weight that loads 'em makes 'em roll on still,
Bereft of choice, and freedom of the will.
For native strife in ev'ry bosom reigns,
And secretly an impious war maintains:
Provoke not this, but let the combat cease,
And ev'ry yielding passion sue for peace.
Wouldst thou, great Jove, thou father of mankind,
Reveal the Demon for that task assigned,
The wretched race an end of woes would find.

 And yet be bold, O man, divine thou art,
And of the gods celestial essence part.
Nor sacred nature is from thee concealed,
But to thy race her mystic rules revealed.
These if to know thou happily attain,
Soon shalt thou perfect be in all that I ordain,
Thy wounded soul to health thou shalt restore,
And free from every pain she felt before.

 Abstain, I warn, from meats unclean and foul,
So keep thy body pure, so free thy soul;
So rightly judge; thy reason so maintain;
Reason which Heaven did for thy guide ordain,
Let that best reason ever hold the rein.

 Then if this mortal body thou forsake,
And thy glad flight to the pure ether take,
Among the gods exalted shalt thou shine,
Immortal, incorruptible, divine:
The tyrant Death securely shalt thou brave,
And scorn the dark dominion of the grave.

PANTHEISTS.

In metaphysical theology, Pantheism is the theory which identifies nature or the τὸ πᾶν of the universe in its totality with God. This doctrine differs from Atheism in the greater distinctness with which it asserts the unity and essential vitality of nature, parts of which all animated beings are. The most ancient Greek philosophers were Pantheists in this sense, Anaxagoras being the first, who distinctly stated the co-existence with nature of a reasonable Creator—"a mind, the principle of all things." In this sense, too, Spinoza may be called a Pantheist.

The Pantheism of Schelling, and many modern German philosophers, is of a different stamp. According to these thinkers, God is conceived as the absolute and original Being, revealing himself variously in outward nature, and in human intelligence and freedom. It is not easy to see how Pantheism in this sense differs from the Christian view of God, as expressed in the sublime language of St. Paul, "In whom we live, and move, and have our being." The world is, indeed, conceived to be animated by the presence and agency of the Deity; but His distinctness and independent subsistence are definitely laid down as the condition and ground of all phenomenal existence, and of reason itself.

DEISTS.

DEISM, or Theism (Latin, Deus; Greek θεος, God,) is a belief in the existence and attributes of God, coupled with disbelief in any express revelation of His will. There exist various shades of opinion among Deists; but general usage has assigned this word a meaning synonymous with *sceptic* or *freethinker;* hence it is regarded as a term of reproach. In its original acceptation, *theist* was directly opposed in meaning to *atheist;* but these terms are now frequently, though very incorrectly, employed without distinction to designate an unbeliever in Christianity.

Dr. Clarke, in his learned work on the *Attributes,* divides Deists into four classes, according to the number of articles comprised in their creed: "The First are such as profess to believe the existence of an eternal, infinite, independent, intelligent Being; and who, to avoid the name of Epicurean Atheists, teach also that the Supreme Being made the world; though at the same time they agree with the Epicureans in this that they fancy God does not at all concern himself in the government of the world, nor has any regard to, or care of, what is done therein, agreeably to the reasoning of Lucretius, the Epicurean poet—

> 'For whatsoe'er's divine must live at peace,
> In undisturb'd and everlasting ease;
> Nor care for us, from fears and dangers free,
> Sufficient to its own felicity!
> Nought here below, nought in our pow'r it needs,
> Ne'er smiles at good, nor frowns at wicked deeds.'

"The Second sort of Deists are those who believe not only the being, but also the providence of God with respect to the *natural* world, but who, not allowing any difference between moral good and evil, deny that God takes any notice of the morally good or evil actions of men, these things depending, as they imagine, on the arbitrary constitution of human laws.

"A Third sort of Deists there are, who, having right apprehensions concerning the natural attributes of God and his all-governing providence, and some notion of his moral perfections also, yet being prejudiced against the notion of the immortality of the soul, believe that men perish entirely at death, and that one generation shall perpetually succeed another without any further restoration or renovation of things.

"A Fourth, and the last sort of Deists, are such as believe the existence of a Supreme Being, together with his providence in the government of the world; also all the obligations of natural religion, but so far only as these things are discoverable by the light of nature alone, without believing any divine revelation."

These, the learned author observes, are the only true Deists; but as their principles would naturally lead them to embrace the Christian revelation, he concludes there is now no consistent scheme of Deism, in the world.*

The term *Deist* is applied to the rejecters of revelation, because the existence of a God is the principal article of their belief. The name was first assumed by a number of gentlemen in France and Italy, who were willing to cover their opposition to the Christian revelation by a more honorable name than that of Atheists. Viret, a divine of eminence among the first reformers, appears to have been the first author who expressly mentions them; for in the Epistle Dedicatory prefixed to the second volume of his Instruction Chretienne, published in 1563, he speaks of some persons at that time, who called themselves by a new name, that of "Deists." Deists are also often called Infidels, from the Latin word infidelis, on account of their want of faith or belief in the Christian religion. Some, indeed, have censured the application of the term infidelity to unbelievers, contending that in our language it is used solely in a particular sense, implying the want of conjugal fidelity.

The advocates for Deism on the continent are Bayle, Voltaire, Frederick II. King of Prussia, Helvetius, Diderot, Rousseau, Condorcet, D'Alembert, Mirabeau, &c with other disciples of the new philosophy. In Great Britain the Deistical writers are Lord Herbert, Hobbes, Toland, Mandeville, Wollaston, Collins, Shaftsbury, Bolingbroke, Chubb, Tindal, Morgan, Blount, Hume, Gibbon, and Thomas Paine, of political celebrity. In the writings of these men it is evident that reason is extolled at the expense of revelation: but, as it has been beauti-

---

* Paganism is the corruption of natural religion, and is little else than the worship of idols and false gods. These were either men, as Jupiter, Hercules, Bacchus, &c.; or fictitious persons, as Victory, Fame, Fever, &c.; or beasts, as in Egypt, crocodiles, cats, &c.; or, finally, inanimate things, as onions, fire, water, &c. Upon the propagation of Christianity, Paganism declined. Julian, the apostate, made an ineffectual attempt to revive it; and it is now degenerated into gross and disgustful idolatry. The chief Sects of Paganism now existing, are the Sabians, Magians, Hindoos, and Chinese, together with that of the Grand Lama of Tartary.

fully remarked :—" These lights of reason and revelation fall upon our path in rays so blended, that we walk like the summer-evening traveller, who, enjoying at the same time the full orb of the moon and the sun's solstitial twilight, is unable to ascertain the proportion in which he is indebted to each of these heavenly luminaries; and some of us, alas, are such incompetent philosophers, as, because the greater is below the horizon, to attribute all to the less!"

Lord Herbert of Cherbury was the first Deist who excited public notice in England. Dr. Brown's recent edition of Leland's View of the Deistical writers, Tindal, Morgan, Chubb, Bolingbroke, &c. together with many other valuable treatises, affords information concerning their principles, and contains a refutation of their objections against revealed religion.

Mr. Belsham has thus assigned the principle causes of modern infidelity, in his reply to Mr. Wilberforce :— " First, The first and chief is an unwillingness to submit to the restraints of religion, and the dread of a future life, which leads men to overlook evidence, and to magnify objections. Second, The palpable absurdities of creeds generally professed by Christians, which men of sense having confounded with the genuine doctrines of revelation, they have rejected the whole at once, and without inquiry. Third, Impatience and unwillingness to persevere in the laborious task of weighing arguments and examining objections. Fourth, Fashion has biased the minds of some young persons of virtuous characters and competent knowledge, to resist revelation, in order o avoid the imputation of singularity, and to escape the ridicule of those with whom they desire to associate. Fifth, Pride, that they might at an easy rate attain the character of philosophers, and superiority to vulgar prejudice. Sixth, Dwelling upon difficulties only, from which the most rational system is not exempt, and by which the most candid, inquisitive, and virtuous minds are sometimes entangled.

" The mass of mankind, who never think at all, but

who admit, without hesitation, 'all that the nurse and the priest have taught,' can never become sceptics. Of course the whole class of unbelievers consist of persons who have thought more or less upon the subject; and, as persons of sense seldom discard at once all the principles in which they have been educated; it is not wonderful that many who begin with the highest orthodoxy, pass through different stages of their creed, dropping an article or two every step of their progress, till at last, weary of their labor, and not knowing where to fix, they reject it altogether. This, to a superficial and timid observer, appears to be an objection to freedom of inquiry; for no person beginning to inquire, can or ought to say where he will stop. But the sincere friend to truth will not be discouraged—for, without inquiry, truth cannot be ascertained—and, if the Christian religion shrinks from close examination, in this bold and inquisitive age, it must and it ought to fail; but of this issue I have not the smallest apprehension. Genuine Christianity can well bear the fiery trial through which it is now passing, and while the dross and the rubbish are consumed, the pure gold will remain uninjured, and will come forth from the furnace with increased lustre."

Indeed, the objections which some Deists have made to revelation, affect not so much the religion of Jesus Christ, laid down in the New Testament, as certain absurd doctrines and ridiculous practices which have been added to it by the weakness and wickedness of mankind. Reiterated accusations, therefore, of unfairness have been brought against the generality of Deistical writers; and with this palpable injustice, Bolingbroke, Voltaire, and Thomas Paine, stand particularly charged. Paine's Age of Reason, has been ably answered by many writers, especially by the late Bishop Watson, in his Apology for the Bible. By far the ablest attack upon the Christian system is that of Strauss, a German writer, born in 1808, which was published at Tubingen in 1837. It not only surpasses all its predecessors in learning, acuteness and research, but it is marked by a serious and earnest spirit. He denounces with vehemence the opinion that the Gospels were written to deceive. The work derives its importance from the fact that it is a concentration of objections to historical Christianity.*

THEOPHILANTHROPISTS.

(FOUNDED BY T. PAINE.)

This title was assumed by a society formed at Paris during the first French revolution. It is a compound word, derived from the Greek ($\theta\varepsilon o\varsigma$, God, and $\varphi\iota\lambda\alpha\iota\theta\rho\omega\pi o\varsigma$, a lover of men), and implies a profession of adoration towards God and love for mankind.

The object of the founders of this sect was to establish a new religion in the place of Christianity, which had been formally abolished in France by the Convention, and had lost its power over the minds of large classes of the people. The Directory granted these philosophical sectarians the use of ten parish churches in Paris, where they held meetings for religious service; at first on the Decadi, or revolutionary holiday, afterwards on Sunday. Their system of belief was a pure Deism; their service a

* See Leland's View of Deistical Writers—Sermons at Boyle's Lecture—Halyburton's Natural Religion Insufficient—Leslie's Short Method with the Deists—Bishop Watson's Apology for the Bible—Fuller's Gospel of Christ its own Witness—Bishop Porteus's Charge to the Clergy, for 1794, and his Summary of the Evidences of Christianity.

simple liturgy, with some emblematical ceremonies. The following inscriptions were placed upon their altar:

FIRST INSCRIPTION.—We believe in the existence of a God, in the immortality of the soul.

SECOND INSCRIPTION.—Worship God, cherish your kind, render yourselves useful to your country.

THIRD INSCRIPTION.—Good is every thing which tends to the preservation or the perfection of man.

Evil is every thing which tends to destroy or deteriorate him.

FOURTH INSCRIPTION.—Children, honor your fathers and mothers. Obey them with affection. Comfort their old age.

Fathers and mothers, instruct your children.

FIFTH INSCRIPTION.—Wives, regard in your husbands the chiefs of your houses.

Husbands, love your wives, and render yourselves reciprocally happy.

"The temple most worthy of the divinity, in the eyes of the Theophilanthropists," said one of their number, "is the universe. Abandoned sometimes under the vaults of heaven to the contemplation of the beauties of nature, they render its author the homage of adoration and gratitude. They nevertheless have temples erected by the hands of men, in which it is more commodious for them to assemble and listen to lessons concerning his wisdom Certain moral inscriptions, a simple altar on which they deposit, as a sign of gratitude for the benefits of the Creator, such flowers or fruits as the season affords, and a tribune for lectures and discourses, form the whole of the ornaments of their temples."

The attempt on the part of the Theophilanthropists to found a new religion was a failure. In 1802 they were forbidden the use of the churches of Paris by the consuls, and then ceased to exist.

PAGANS.

The term Pagan (Latin, paganus; from pagus, *a village*), among the Romans, was applied to all who lived in villages in contradistinction to the inhabitants of cities. In its present signification Paganism is a general appellation for the religious worship of the whole human race, except of that portion which has embraced Christianity, Judæism, or Mahommedanism.

That in the most ancient times one God, sole, eternal, indivisible, the Creator of the universe, was acknowledged and worshipped, has been proved by the most profound investigators of antiquity. The existence of this belief may not only be traced in the tradition of all people, but is expressly affirmed by some of the greatest philosophers of the heathen world. Nothing, indeed, could exceed the contempt with which some of them regarded the gods of the vulgar, though fear of danger or some other cause often taught them to conceal the sentiment.

The causes of idolatry were manifold, and were mostly of oriental growth. A great king regarded it as below his dignity to enter into the minute details of administration: he placed vicars or ministers over provinces and cities, over the great departments of national polity. If the onerous charge was inapplicable to an earthly, it was still more so to the celestial Sovereign; hence the subordinate deities which we perceive in the religious systems of all nations—the presiding genii of the Chaldæans, the numerous gods of Greece and Rome. The worship due to the Supreme alone was soon transferred to those imaginary entities, which, from functionaries, were transferred into so many independent chiefs, until the simple primeval notion of the divine unity was lost.

At the present day, many of the Pagan nations go to immense expense in the support of their religious worship. In China there are upwards of a thousand temples dedicated to Confucius, where above sixty thousand animals are annually offered.

The Dalai-Lama or Grand Lama is honored as the representative of divinity, or rather as a real divinity dwelling on the earth, by various tribes of Tartaric descent. This personage resides at Lassa in Thibet, and pilgrimages are made to his residence by the inhabitants of many distant regions of Tartary. He is now chiefly dependent, in a political sense, on the Chinese empire. When the actual Dalai-Lama dies, his spirit is supposed to seek another body in which to be born again; and the new Dalai-Lama can only be discovered by a certain favored class among the priests.

The festival of Juggernaut is annually held on the sea-coast of Orissa, where there is a celebrated temple, and an idol of the god.

The Pagans worship an immense variety of idols, both animate and inanimate, and very frequently make to themselves gods of objects that are contemptible even among brutes. In Hindoo, the *monkey* is a celebrated god. A few years since, the rajah of Nudeeya expended $50,000 in celebrating the marriage of a pair of those mischievous creatures, with all the parade and solemnity of a Hindoo wedding.

The North American Indians, besides their First Being, or Great Spirit, believe in an infinite number of genii, or inferior spirits, both good and evil, who have all their peculiar form of worship.

They ascribe to these beings a kind of immensity and omnipresence, and constantly invoke them as the guardians of mankind. But they never address themselves to the evil genii, except to beg of them to do them no hurt.

They believe in the immortality of the soul, and say that the region of their everlasting abode lies so far westward, that the souls are several months in arriving at it, and have vast difficulties to surmount. The happiness which they hope to enjoy is not believed to be the recompense of virtue only. To have been a good hunter, brave in war, &c., are the merits which entitle them to this paradise, which they, and the other American aborigines, figure as a delightful country, blessed with perpetual spring, where the forests abound with game, the rivers swarm with fish, where famine is never felt, and uninterrupted plenty shall be enjoyed without labor or toil.

CHAPTER II.

JEWS—MAHOMETANS, OR MOHAMMEDANS.

JEWS.

A COMPLETE system of the religious doctrines and rites of the Jews is contained in the five books of Moses, their great lawgiver, who was raised up to deliver them from their bondage in Egypt, and to conduct them to the possession of Canaan, the promised land. The Jewish economy is so much directed to temporal rewards and punishments, that it has been questioned whether the Jews had any knowledge of a future state. This opinion has been defended with vast erudition by Warburton, in his "Divine Legation of Moses;" but it has been controverted by Dr. Sykes, and other authors of respectability.

The principal sects among the Jews, in the time of our Savior, were the Pharisees, who placed religion in external ceremony—the Sadducees, who were remarkable for their incredulity—and the Essenes, who were distinguished by an austere sanctity. Some accounts of these sects will be found in the last volume of Prideaux's "Connection," in Harwood's "Introduction to the Study of the New Testament," in Milman's "History of the Jews," and in Marsh's improved edition of "Michaelis." See likewise two ingenious and learned volumes, entitled, "Ecclesiastical Researches," and also the sequel by the Rev. J. Jones.*

The Pharisees and Sadducees are frequently mentioned in the New Testament; and an acquaintance with their principles and practices serves to illustrate many passages in the Sacred History. At present the Jews have two sects: the Caraites, who admit of no rule of religion but the law

---

* The author contends that *Josephus* and *Philo* were Christians, and introduces striking passages from their writings, happily tending to confirm the truth and illustrate the genius of Primitive Christianity.

of Moses; and the Rabbinists, who add to the laws the tradition of the Talmud. The dispersion of the Jews took place upon the destruction of Jerusalem by Titus, the Roman Emperor, A. D. 70.

The expectation of a Messiah is the distinguishing feature of their religious system. The word Messiah, signifies one anointed, or installed into office by unction. The Jews used to anoint their kings, high-priests, and, sometimes, prophets, at their entering upon office. Thus Saul, David, Solomon, and Joash, kings of Judah, received the royal unction. Thus, also, Aaron and his sons received the sacerdotal, and Elisha, the disciple of Elijah, the prophetic unction.

Christians believe that Jesus Christ is the Messiah, in whom all the Jewish prophecies are accomplished. The Jews, infatuated with the idea of a temporal Messiah, who is to subdue the world, still wait for his appearance. According to Buxtorf, (a professor of Hebrew, and celebrated for rabbinical learning,) some of the modern rabbins believe that the Messiah is already come, but that he will not manifest himself on account of the sins of the Jews. Others, however, have had recourse to the hypothesis of two Messiahs, who are to succeed each other—one in a state of humiliation and suffering—the other in a state of glory, magnificence and power. Be it, however, remembered, that in the New Testament, Jesus Christ assures us, in the most explicit terms, that HE is the Messiah. In John iv. 25, the Samaritan woman says to Jesus, "I know that Messiah cometh which is called Christ: when he is come, he will tell us all things." Jesus saith unto her, "I that speak to thee am HE." According to the prediction of Jesus Christ, several impostors would assume the title of Messiah; and accordingly such persons have appeared. A history of "false Messiahs" has been written in Dutch. Barcochab was the first who appeared, in the time of Adrian; the second, in 1666, was Sabbethai Levi, who turned Mahometan; and the last was Rabbi Mordecai, who flourished in 1682.

The Talmud is a collection of the doctrines and morality

of the **Jews**. They have two works that bear this name: the first is called the "Talmud of Jerusalem," and the other the "Talmud of Babylon," but the former is shorter and more obscure than that of Babylon, and is of an older date. The Talmud compiled at Babylon the Jews prefer to that of Jerusalem, and it is clearer and more extensive.

The most remarkable periods in the history of the Jews are the call of Abraham, the giving of the law by Moses, their establishment in Canaan under Joshua, the building of the temple by Solomon, the division of their tribes, their captivity in Babylon, their return under Zerubbabel, and the destruction of their city and temple by Titus, afterwards emperor, A. D. 70.

Maimonides, an illustrious rabbi, drew up for the Jews, in the eleventh century, a confession of faith, which all Jews admit. It is as follows:

"1. I believe, with a true and perfect faith, that God is the Creator, whose name be blessed, Governor, and Maker, of all creatures, and that he hath wrought all things, worketh, and shall work forever.

"2. I believe, with a perfect faith, that the Creator, whose name be blessed, is *one*, and that such a unity as in him can be found in none other, and that he alone hath been our God, is, and forever shall be.

"3. I believe, with a perfect faith, that the Creator, whose name be blessed, is not corporeal, nor to be comprehended with any bodily property, and that there is no bodily essence that can be likened unto him.

"4. I believe with a perfect faith, the Creator, whose name be blessed, to be the first and the last, that nothing was before him, and that he shall abide the last forever.

"5. I believe, with a perfect faith, that the Creator, whose name is blessed, is to be worshipped, and none else

"6. I believe, with a perfect faith, that all the words of the prophets are true.

"7. I believe, with a perfect faith, the prophecies of Moses, our master,—may he rest in peace;—that he was the father and chief of all wise men that lived before him, or ever shall live after him.

"8 I believe with a perfect faith, that all the law which at this day is found in our hands, was delivered by God himself to our master, Moses. God's peace be with him.

"9. I believe, with a perfect faith, that the same law is never to be changed, nor another to be given us of God, whose name be blessed.

"10. I believe, with a perfect faith, that God, whose name be blessed, understandeth all the works and thoughts of men, as it is written in the prophets. He fashioneth their hearts alike; he understandeth all their works.

"11. I believe with a perfect faith, that God will recompense good to those that keep his commandments, and will punish them who transgress them.

"12. I believe, with a perfect faith, that the Messiah is yet to come; and although he retard his coming, yet I will wait for him till he come.

"13. I believe with a perfect faith, that the dead shall be restored to life, when it shall seem fit unto God the Creator, whose name be blessed, and memory celebrated, world without end. AMEN."

For about eighteen hundred years, this wonderful people have maintained their peculiarities of religion, language, and domestic habits, among Pagans, Mahometans, and Christians, and have suffered a continued series of reproaches, privations and miseries, which have excited the admiration and astonishment of all who have reflected on their condition.

The siege and destruction of Jerusalem by Titus, the Roman general, was one of the most awful and distressing scenes that mortals ever witnessed; and the details, as given by Josephus, are enough to make humanity shudder. During the siege, which lasted nearly five months, upwards of eleven hundred thousand Jews perished; and many thousands were taken captive to be exposed in the amphitheatre to fight as gladiators, or to be devoured by wild beasts.

A small portion of the crushed and ruined nation were suffered to remain and re-establish themselves in Judea;

but in consequence of a general revolt under the Emperor Adrian, in 134, they were a second time slaughtered in multitudes and driven to desperation. Bither, the place of their greatest strength, was compelled to surrender, and Barochba, their leader, who pretended to be the Messiah, was slain, and five hundred and eighty thousand fell by the sword, or perished by famine, fire and disease.

In all succeeding times, the scattered remnants of this people have been exposed to the heaviest persecutions Monarchs and subjects, Pagans, Mahometans, and Christians, disagreeing in so many things, have united in the design of exterminating this fugitive and wretched race, but have not succeeded. They have been banished, at different times, from France, Germany, Spain, Bohemia, Hungary, and England; and from some of these kingdoms they have been banished and recalled many times in succession.

The Romans and Spaniards have probably done more than any other nations to oppress and destroy this people; and the inquisition has doomed multitudes of them to torture and death.

At different times, they were accused of poisoning wells, rivers, and reservoirs of water, and, before any proof of these strange and malicious charges was produced, the populace in many parts of Germany, Italy, and France, have fallen upon them with merciless and wondrous severity. At one time, the German emperor found it necessary to issue an edict for their banishment, to save them from the rage of his exasperated and unrestrained subjects.

As the Jews have generally been the *bankers* and *brokers* of the people among whom they have resided, and have made a show of much wealth, this has tempted their avaricious adversaries to impose upon them enormous taxes and ruinous fines.

Muley Archy, a prince of one of the Barbary states, by seizing the property of a rich Jew, was enabled to dispossess his brother of the throne of Morocco.

The English parliament of Northumberland, in 1188,

for the support of a projected war, assessed the Jews with 60,000 pounds, while only 70,000 were assessed upon the Christians; which proves either that the Jews were immensely rich, or that the parliament was extremely tyrannical.

The English king John was unmercifully severe upon this afflicted people. In 1210, regardless of the costly freedom he had sold them, he subjected them all, as a body, to a fine of 66,000 marks. The ransom required by this same unfeeling king, of a rich Jew of Bristol, was 10,000 marks of silver; and on his refusing to pay this ruinous fine, he ordered one of his teeth to be extracted every day; to which the unhappy man submitted seven days, and on the eighth day he agreed to satisfy the king's rapacity. Isaac of Norwich was, not long after, compelled to pay a similar fine. But the king, not satisfied with these vast sums extorted from these injured Israelites, in the end confiscated all their property, and expelled them from the kingdom.

About the beginning of the 16th century, the Jews in Persia were subjected to a tax of two millions of gold.

"During my residence in Ooroomiah in 1840," says Dr. Grant, "a Jew was publicly burned to death in that city by order of the governor, on an allegation of killing the children of the Gentiles to obtain their blood to mingle with the bread of the Passover. Naptha was freely poured over him, the torch was applied, and the miserable man was instantly enveloped in flames. In Meshed, another city of Persia, the same accusation was last year (1839) brought against the Jews of that place: a Mohammedan child having been missing, no one knew how, it was charged upon the poor Jews, and their entire extermination was at once resolved upon! Fifteen of these unhappy people were thus murdered in cold blood, when the remainder, to escape the same fate, embraced the only alternative—the religion of the Koran. And who has not mourned over the fate of those sons of Israel, whose blood has still more recently stained the streets of Damascus!"

The history of this people certainly forms a striking evidence of the truth of divine revelation. They are a living and perpetual miracle, continuing to subsist as a distinct and peculiar race for upwards of three thousand years, and even in the midst of other nations, flowing forward in a full and continued stream, like the waters of the Rhone, without mixing with the waves of the expansive lake through which the passage lies to the ocean of eternity!

In France and the United States, the Jews are admitted to equal rights with all other citizens; which cannot be said of any other nations in Christendom. In the United States, they have acquired this freedom, of course, with all other citizens of this free country. In France, they were admitted to it by Bonaparte; and afterwards, in 1807, by his directions, they convened a Grand Sanhedrim, consisting, according to ancient custom, of seventy members, exclusive of the president. The number and distinction of the spectators of this Sanhedrim greatly added to the solemnity of the scene. This venerable assembly passed and agreed to various articles respecting the Mosaic worship, and their civil and ecclesiastical concerns.

The number of Jews in the United States is estimated at from fifty to sixty thousand. They have synagogues in Newport, R. I., the cities of New York, Philadelphia, Charleston, S. C., and in other parts of the country. A writer in Blackwood's Magazine says: "The statistics of the Jewish population are among the most singular circumstances of this most singular of all people. Under all their calamities and dispersions, they seem to have remained at nearly the same amount as in the days of David and Solomon—never much more in prosperity, never much less after ages of suffering. Nothing like this has occurred in the history of any other race; Europe in general having doubled its population within the last hundred years, and England nearly tripled hers within the last half century; the proportion of America being still more rapid, and the world crowding in a constantly increasing ratio Yet the Jews seem to stand still in this vast and increasing ratio. The population of Judea, in its most palmy days, probably did not exceed, if it reached, four millions. The numbers who entered Palestine from the wilderness, were evidently not much more than three; and their census, according to the German statists, who are generally considered to be exact, is now nearly the same as that of the people under Moses—about three millions."

In reference to these observations, a Jewish writer says: "We apprehend there is some error in the above statistics, and that the number of Jews throughout the world may be estimated at the present time (1843) at nearer six millions than three. There are more than a million in Poland and Russia; in all Asia, there are full two millions; half a million in Austria; in the Barbary States and Africa, a million; in all Europe, two millions and a half. We do not think, during the most splendid periods of Jewish history, that they ever exceeded four millions; but then their colonies and countries held tributary in Europe and Asia, amounted to many millions more. For example, at one period all Spain paid tribute to King Solomon; and all Spain and Portugal, at this day, are descendants of the Jews and Moors; and there are many thousands of Jews, in both those countries, now adhering in secret to the ancient faith of their fathers, while outwardly professing the Catholic religion. All the familiar Spanish and Portuguese names—Lopez, Mendez, Carvalho, Fonseca, Rodrigues, Peirara, Azavedo, Montefiores, &c. &c.—are of Jewish origin. Their numbers, therefore, will never be accurately known until the restoration, when thousands who, from convenience and pride, and some from apprehension, conceal their religion, will be most eager to avow it, when their nation takes rank among the governments of the earth."

Dr. Grant, in his work on "The Nestorians, or the Lost Tribes," says: "The present is an interesting moment for the Jews, and it may prove an important crisis in their history. With 'a trembling heart, and failing of eyes, and sorrow of mind,' they have looked for the long-promised Messiah, till 'all faces are turned into paleness.'

As a cordial to their fainting spirits, they have been assured, by calculations made by their learned rabbis, that their expected deliverer would make his appearance within a certain definite period, or during a particular year. That period (1840) has now expired, but it has brought them no deliverance! And where is Messiah their king! Many of the Jews in Poland, as we learn by a letter from the Rev. Mr. Brown, of St. Petersburgh, have openly avowed, that if he did not make his appearance before the end of this year, they were shut up to the conclusion that Jesus of Nazareth was the Messiah. The day that I left Constantinople, a learned Jew called upon the Rev. Mr. Goodell, and told him that there were then forty Jews in that city, who were accustomed to meet for religious worship on the first day of the week, having come to the deliberate conclusion that they could look no longer for a Messiah to come after the end of the present year (ending October, 1840), but must believe in Jesus of Nazareth as the promised Saviour. On my way to Smyrna, one of my fellow passengers in the steamer was an intelligent Christian Jew, who informed me that in that city there was the same general state of feeling regarding the Messiah, and that numbers were entertaining a secret belief in Christ as the Saviour, and that some fifteen heads of families were instructing their children in the same belief. In Persia, the belief that Christ was to come in the year 1840 has been entertained for a considerable time, and I understand the same is true of the Jews throughout the East. This hope is now torn away, and the effect will be either to harden them in infidelity, or awaken serious and anxious inquiry on the subject of Christianity."

MAHOMETANS.

Mahometanism, or Mohammedanism, one of the most celebrated systems of religion in the world, was so called from Mahomet or Mohammed, its author and founder, who was born at Mecca in Arabia, in May, 571. This founde of a new religion, and of a political power, which, even in his life-time, extended over his native country, and which, under his successors, threatened to embrace the empire of the world, traced his genealogy in a direct line through eleven descents from Koreish, who again was affirmed to be in direct descent from Ishmael, the son of Abraham.

The future prophet sprang, therefore, from the noblest tribe of the Ishmaelitish Arabs; and yet his early life was spent in comparative dependence. Upon his father's death, five camels and an Ethiopian female constituted the entire property left for the support of the mother and her infant son. Under his uncle Abu-Taled he was employed in commercial pursuits, and became acquainted with Asia, Syria, Palestine, and Egypt. He afterwards married a rich widow, and raised himself to an equality with the most opulent citizens of Mecca. Fifteen years of his life were passed in the obscurest retirement, in a lonely cave, where his scheme of a new religion was no doubt planned, and which he afterwards so ably executed. His system is a compound of Paganism, Judæism and Christianity; and the Alcoran, or Koran, which is the Bible of the Mahometans, is held by them in great reverence. It is replete with absurd representations, and is supposed to have been written by a Jew. The most eloquent passage is allowed to be the following, where God is introduced bidding the waters of the deluge to cease :—" Earth, swallow up the waters; heaven draw up those thou hast poured out: immediately the waters retreated, the command of God was obeyed, the ark rested on the mountains, and these words were heard—' Wo to the wicked !' "

There is no way of accounting for the great progress which this new religion made, by the conversion of the eastern nations to the Mahometan faith, unless on the ground of this imposter holding forth the unity of God, and the promise of sensual enjoyments in Heaven to those who obeyed his laws. The first commandment was taken from the Bible; it runs thus in the Mahometan code: I BELIEVE IN ONE GOD ONLY. This struck at the root of the polytheism of the east, and was one great cause of the reception of his doctrines.

It is remarkable that the Koran was dealt out slowly and separately during the long period of twenty-three years. It was communicated, says Mahomet, by the ministration of the angel Gabriel, who appears to have been liberal to him on these occasions. His angel of death, whose province it is at the hour of dissolution to free the departing spirit from its prison of flesh, and his vast ideal balance, in which at the last day the actions of all men shall be weighed, have in them a sort of romantic sublimity calculated to impress the fervid imagination of the eastern nations. And his sensual paradise hereafter, must, in their opinion, have imparted to it the highest degree of perfection. " The meanest in Paradise will have seventy-two wives, besides the wives he had in this world ; he shall have a tent also assigned him of pearls, hyacinths, and emeralds !"

Gibbon, in his Roman History, gives the following curious specimen of Mahometan divinity ; for the prophet propagated his religion by force of arms :—" The sword," saith Mahomet, " is the key of heaven and of hell ; a drop of blood shed in the cause of God, or a night spent in arms, is of more avail than two months of fasting and prayer. Whosoever falls in battle, his sins are forgiven at the day of judgment ; his wounds shall be resplendent as vermillion, and odoriferous as musk ; the loss of his limbs shall be supplied by the wings of angels and cherubims !"

The following specimen of the young Mussulman's creed is extracted from a catechism, said to have been printed at Constantinople :—

" I believe in the books which have been delivered from Heaven and the prophets. In this manner was the Koran given to Mahomet, the Pentateuch to Moses, the Psalter to David, and the Gospel to Jesus.

" I believe in the prophets, and the miracles they have performed. Adam was the first prophet, and Mahomet was the last.

" I believe that for the space of fifty thousand years the

righteous shall repose under the shade of the terrestrial paradise, and the wicked shall be exposed naked to the rays of the sun.

"I believe in the bridge Sirat, which passes over the bottomless pit of hell! It is as fine as a hair and as sharp as a sabre. All must pass over it, and the wicked shall be thrown off.

"I believe in the water-pools of paradise. Each of the prophets has in paradise a basin for his own use; the water is whiter than milk, and sweeter than honey. On the ridges of the pool are vessels to drink out of, and they are bordered with stars.

"I believe in heaven and hell. The inhabitants of the former know no want, and the houris who attend them are never afflicted with sickness. The floor of paradise is musk, the stones are silver, and the cement gold. The damned are, on the contrary, tormented with fire and by voracious and poisonous animals!"

Mahometanism distributes itself into two general parts, Faith and Practice; the former containing six branches:— Belief in God—in his angels—in his scriptures—in his prophets—in the resurrection and final judgment—in the divine decrees; the latter relating to prayer with washing —alms—fasting—pilgrimage to Mecca—and circumcision.

As to the negative precepts and institutions of this religion, the Mahometans are forbidden the use of wine, and are prohibited from gaming, and the eating of swine's flesh, and whatever dies of itself, or is strangled, or killed by a blow, or by another beast. They are said, however, to comply with the prohibition of gaming, (from which chess seems to be excepted), much better than they do with that of wine, under which all strong and inebriating liquors are included, for both the Persians and Turks are in the habit of drinking freely.

The Mahometans have an established priesthood and a numerous body of clergymen: their spiritual head, in Turkey, whose power is not inferior to that of the Pope, or the Grecian Patriarch, is denominated the *Mufti*, and is regarded as the oracle of sanctity and wisdom. Their houses of worship are denominated mosques, many of which are very magnificent, and very richly endowed The revenues of some of the royal mosques are said to amount to the enormous sum of 60,000 pounds sterling. In the city of Fez, the capital of the emperor of Morocco, there are near one thousand mosques, fifty of which are built in a most magnificent style, supported by marble pillars. The circumference of the grand mosque is near a mile and a half, in which near a thousand lamps are lighted every night. The Mahometan priests, who perform the rites of their public worship, are called *Imams;* and they have a set of ministers called *Sheiks,* who preach every *Friday,* the Mahometan Sabbath, much in the manner of Christian preachers. They seldom touch upon points of controversy in their discourses, but preach upon moral duties, upon the dogmas and ceremonies of their religion, and declaim against vice, luxury, and corruption of manners.

The Mahometan religion is established in, or prevails throughout, the Turkish dominions in Europe, Asia, and Africa. It has, likewise, numerous proselytes in various other countries, as in China, Persia, &c. The number of those professing the Mahometan religion at the present day has been estimated at about one hundred and forty millions.

The grossly sensual character of Mahomet's paradise, constitutes, perhaps, the greatest blemish in his religious system, and has exerted a debasing influence over all the countries where it has acquired an ascendancy. If we needed anything to prove its corrupt human origin, this single feature would be sufficient for our purpose. How immeasurably inferior does it seem, in this point of view, to the sublime, spiritual morality, which the founder of Christianity enforced by precept and example!

CHAPTER III.

CHRISTIANITY AND ITS EVIDENCES.

CHRISTIANITY.

CHRISTIANITY, to which Judæism was introductory, is the last and most entire dispensation of revealed religion with which God has favored the human race. It was instituted by Jesus Christ, the son of God, who made his appearance in Judea near two thousand years ago. He was born at Bethlehem, brought up at Nazareth, and crucified at Jerusalem. His lineage, birth, life, death, and sufferings, were minutely predicted by a succession of the Jewish prophets, and his religion is now spread over a considerable portion of the globe.

The evidences of the Christian religion are comprised under historical testimony, prophecies, miracles, the internal evidence of its doctrines and precepts, and the rapidity of its first propagation among the Jews and the Gentiles. Though thinking Christians have in every age differed widely respecting some of the doctrines of this religion, yet they are fully agreed in a belief in the divinity of its origin, and the benevolence of its tendency.

The believers in this religion, who had been denominated by the Jews, Nazarines or Galileans, and, by one another, disciples, brethren or saints, were first called Christians at Antioch, A.D. 43. Upon this, Doddridge remarks: " With pleasure let us reflect upon this honorable name, which the disciples of Jesus wore at Antioch ; and would to God, no other, no dividing name, had ever prevailed among them! As for such distinguishing titles, though they were taken from Apollos or Cephas, or Paul, let us endeavor to exclude them out of the Church as fast as we can, and while they continue in it let us take care that they do not make us forget our most ancient and most glorious title! Let us take heed that we do not so remember our difference from each other in smaller matters as to forget our mutual agreement in embracing the gospel of Christ."

As to the progress of Christianity, it suffered during the first three centuries some grievous persecutions, under which, however, it flourished after a wonderful manner, till the conversion of Constantine, A.D. 314, when it became the established religion of the Roman empire. The principal persecutions were those under Nero, A.D. 64; Domitian, 93; Trajan, 104; Hadrian, 125; Marcus Aurelius, 151; Severus, 197; Maximin, 235; Decius, 250; Valerian, 257; Aurelian, 272; Numerian, 283; Dioclesian, and Maximian, and Licinius, 303—313. It was relative to these persecutions that an ecclesiastical historian observes, that, " the blood of the martyrs became the seed of the church!" From the sixth to the sixteenth century was little else than one black record of ignorance, superstition, and tyranny.

The history of the fortunes of Christianity, in respect of its geographical extension, presents remarkable periods of advance and decline. After the conversion of Constantine, and the gradual decay of Paganism, Christianity continued to spread, but chiefly in the direction of east and south, for more than three centuries, the barbarian conquerers of the Roman provinces soon adopting it. About the middle of the seventh century, Christendom comprehended Europe, south and west of the Rhine and Danube; Africa north of the great desert; Abyssinia; parts of Nubia; Asia to the Euphrates; Armenia, and part of Arabia; and that small colony in Southern India which subsists to this day. The Saracen power rose by conquest from this extensive empire.

In little more than a century, Christendom was deprived of nearly all its Asiatic provinces, of which the faithful inhabitants were reduced to a tributary condition; of the whole of northern Africa, in which they were exterminated or converted; and of Spain. Sicily, the latest conquest of the Saracens, was occupied by them about 830. But just at the same epoch, or that of the lowes' decline, Charlemagne began to extend the limits of Christendom in the North; and the second period of advance extends through the ninth, tenth, and eleventh centuries, in which the reign of the gospel and the church was extended over the North: Bulgaria, Hungary, Bohemia, Saxony, Denmark, Norway, Sweden and Russia. From that time to the sixteenth century, Christianity gradually reconquered Spain on the one hand; while, on the other, the newly arisen power of the Turks wrested from it the remainder of its Asiatic territories and the European provinces of the Greek empire.

Since that period no important changes have taken place in the relative extent of Christendom and Ismalism; but the vast continent of America, as far as it has been colonised, has been added to the former, and the rapid increase of its communities in numbers and civilization has greatly enhanced their comparative importance. The number of Christians inhabiting Europe and America, and scattered in the other parts of the globe, may perhaps be estimated conjecturally as follows:—

Roman Catholic Church,	144,000,000
Reformed Churches,	60,000,000
Greek and other Oriental Churches	66,000,000
	270,000,000

With regard to the divisions among Christians, Bishop Gibson observes: "It will appear that the several denominations of Christians agree both in the substance of religion and in the necessary enforcements of the practice of it; that the world and all things in it were created by God, and are under the direction and government of his all-powerful hand and all-seeing eye; that there is an essential difference between good and evil, virtue and vice; that there will be a state of future rewards and punishments, according to our behaviour in this life; that Christ was a teacher sent from God, and that his apostles were divinely inspired; that all Christians are bound to declare and profess themselves to be his disciples; that not only the exercise of the several virtues, but also the belief in Christ, is necessary in order to their obtaining the pardon of sin, the favor of God, and eternal life; that the worship of God is to be performed chiefly by the heart in prayers, praises, and thanksgivings; and as to all other points, that they are bound to live by the rules which Christ and his apostles have left to them in the Holy Scriptures. Here, then, is a fixed, certain, and uniform rule of faith and practice, containing all the most necessary points of religion, established by a divine sanction, embraced as such by all denominations of Christians, and in itself abundantly sufficient to preserve the knowledge and practice of religion in the world."

The late Mr. Clarke, in his answer to the question, " Why are you a Christian ?" replies: " Not because I was born in a Christian country, and educated in Christian principles; not because I find the illustrious Bacon, Boyle, Locke, Clarke, and Newton, among the professors and defenders of Christianity; nor merely because the system itself is so admirably calculated to mend and exalt human nature---but because the evidence accompanying the gospel has convinced me of its truth. The secondary causes assigned by unbelievers, do not, in my judgment, account for the rise, progress, and early triumphs of the Christian religion. Upon the principles of scepticism, I perceive an effect without an adequate cause. I therefore stand acquitted to my own reason, though I continue to believe and profess the religion of Jesus Christ. Arguing from effects to causes, I think I have philosophy on my side. And, reduced to a choice of difficulties, I encounter not so many in admitting the miracles ascribed to the Saviour, as in the arbitrary suppositions and conjectures of his enemies.

" That there once existed such a person as Jesus Christ; that he appeared in Judea in the reign of Tiberius; that he taught a system of morals superior to any inculcated in the Jewish schools; that he was crucified at Jerusalem; and that Pontius Pilate was the Roman Governor, by whose sentence he was condemned and executed, are facts which no one can reasonably call in question. The most inveterate deists admit them without difficulty. And, indeed, to dispute these facts, would be giving the lie to all history. As well might we deny the existence of Cicero as of a person of the name of Jesus Christ. And with equal propriety might we call in question the orations of the former as the discourses of the latter. We are morally certain that the one entertained the Romans with his eloquence, and that the other enlightened the Jews with his wisdom. But it is unnecessary to labor these points, because they are generally conceded. They who affect to despise the Evangelists and Apostles, profess to reverence Tacitus, Suetonius, and Pliny. And these eminent Romans bear testimony to several particulars which relate to the person of Jesus Christ, his influence as the founder of a sect, and his crucifixion. From a deference to human authority, all, therefore, acknowledge that the Christian religon derived its name from Jesus Christ. And many are so just to its merits, as to admit that he taught better than Confucius, and practised better than Socrates or Plato. But I confess my creed embraces many more articles. I believe that Jesus Christ was not only a teacher of virtue, but that he had a special commission to teach I believe that his doctrines are not the works of human reason, but of divine communication to mankind. I believe that he was authorised by God to proclaim forgiveness to the penitent, and to reveal a state of immortal glory and blessedness to those who fear God and work righteousness. I believe, in short, the whole Evangelical history, and of consequence, the divine original of Christianity, and the sacred authority of the gospel. Others may reject these things as the fictions of humor, art, or policy; but I assent to them from a full conviction of their truth. The objections of infidelity have often shocked my feelings, but have never yet shaken my faith.

"To come then to the question—'Why are you a Christian?' I answer, because the Christian religion carries with it internal marks of its truth, because not only without the aid, but in opposition to the civil authority, in opposition to the wit, the argument, and insolence of its enemies, it made its way, and gained an establishment in the world; because it exhibited the accomplishment of some prophecies, and presents others, which have been since fulfilled; and because its author displayed an example and performed works, which bespeak not merely a superior, but a divine character. Upon these several facts I ground my belief as a Christian. And till the evidence on which they rest can be invalidated by counter evidence, I must retain my principles and my profession."

A BRIEF VIEW OF THE EVIDENCES OF CHRISTIANITY.

The external evidences of the authenticity and divine authority of the Scriptures have been divided into direct and collateral. The direct evidences are such as arise from the nature, consistency, and probability of the facts; and from the simplicity, uniformity, competency, and fidelity of the testimonies by which they are supported. The collateral evidences are, either the same occurrences supported by heathen testimonies, or others which concur with and corroborate the history of Christianity. Its internal evidences arise either from its exact conformity with the character of God, from its aptitude to the frame and circumstances of man, or from those supernatural convictions and assistances which are impressed on the mind by the immediate operation of the divine spirit. We shall here chiefly follow Dr. Doddridge, and endeavor to give some of the chief evidences which have been brought forward, and which every unprejudiced mind must confess are unanswerable.

First. Taking the matter merely in theory, it will appear highly probable that such a system as the gospel should be indeed a divine revelation. First, The case of mankind is naturally such as to need a divine revelation, 1 John v. 19; Rom. i.; Ephes. iv. Second, There is from the light of nature considerable encouragement to hope, that God would favor his creatures with so needful a blessing as a revelation appears. Third, We may easily conclude, that if a revelation were given, it would be introduced and transmitted in such a manner as Christianity is said to have been. Fourth, That the main doctrines of the gospel are of such a nature as we might in general suppose those of a divine revelation would be,—rational, practical, and sublime. Heb. xi. 6; Mark, xii. 20; 1 Tim. ii. 5; Matt. v. 48; Matt. x. 29, 30; Phil. iv. 8; Rom. ii. 6.

Secondly. It is, in fact, certain that Christianity is indeed a divine revelation; for, the books of the New Testament, now in our hands, were written by the first preachers and publishers of Christianity. In proof of this observe:—First, That it is certain that Christianity is not a new religion, but that it was maintained by great multitudes, quickly after the time in which Jesus is said to have appeared. Second, That there was certainly such a person as Jesus of Nazareth, who was crucified at Jerusalem, when Pontius Pilate was governor there. Third, The first publishers of this religion wrote books which contained an account of the life and doctrine of Jesus their master, and which went by the name of those that now make up our New Testament. Fourth, That the books of the New Testament have been preserved, in the main, uncorrupted to the present time in the original language in which they were written. Fifth, That the translation of them, now in our hands, may be depended upon as, in all things most material, agreeable to the original.

Now, *Third*, From allowing the New Testament to be genuine according to the above proof, it will certainly follow that Christianity is a divine revelation; for, in the first place, it is exceedingly evident that the writers of the New Testament certainly knew whether the facts were true or false, John i. 3; John xix. 27, 35; Acts xxvii. 7, 9. Second, That the character of these writers, so far as we can judge by their works, seems to render them worthy of regard, and leaves no room to imagine they intended to deceive us. The manner in which they tell their story is most happily adapted to gain our belief. There is no air of declamation and harangue; nothing that looks like artifice and design; no apologies, no encomiums, no characters, no reflections, no digression, but the facts are recounted with great simplicity, just as they seem to have happened; and those facts are left to speak for themselves. Their integrity, likewise, evidently appears in the freedom with which they mention those circumstances, which might have exposed their master and themselves to the greatest contempt, amongst prejudiced and inconsiderate men, such as they knew they must generally expect to meet with. John i. 45, 46; John vii. 52; Luke ii. 4, 7; Mark vi. 3; Matt. viii. 20; John vii. 48. It is certain that there are in their writings the most genuine traces, not only of a plain and honest, but a most pious and devout, a most benevolent and generous disposition, as every one must acknowledge who reads their writings. Third, The apostles were under no temptation to forge a story of this kind, or to publish it to the world knowing it to be false. Fourth, Had they done so, humanly speaking, they must quickly have perished in it, and their foolish cause must have died with them, without ever gaining any credit in the world. Reflect more particularly on the nature of those grand facts—the death, resurrection, and exaltation of Christ, which formed the great foundation of the Christian scheme, as first exhibited by the apostles. The resurrection of a dead man, and his ascension into an abode in the upper world, were such strange things, that a thousand objections would immediately have been raised against them, and some extraordinary proof would have been justly required as a balance to them. Consider the manner in which the apostles undertook to prove the truth of their testimony to these facts; and it will evidently appear that, instead of confirming their scheme, it must have been sufficient utterly to have overthrown it, had it been itself the most probable imposture that the wit of man could ever have contrived. See Acts iii. 9, 14, 19, &c. They did not merely assert that they had seen miracles wrought by Jesus, but that he had endowed them with a variety of miraculous powers; and these they undertook to display, not in such idle and useless tricks as slight of hand might perform, but in such solid and important works as appeared worthy of divine interposition and entirely superior to human power. Nor were these things undertaken in a corner, in a circle of friends or dependents; nor were they said to be wrought, as might be suspected, by any confederates in the fraud; but they were done often in the most public manner. Would imposters have made such pretensions as these? or, if they had, must they not immediately have been exposed and ruined? Now if the New Testament be genuine, then it is certain that the apostles pretend to have wrought miracles in the very presence of those to whom their writings were addressed; nay, more, they profess likewise to have conferred those miraculous gifts in some considerable degrees on others, even on the very persons to whom they write, and they appeal to their consciences as to the truth of it. And could there possibly be room for delusion here? Fifth, It is, likewise, certain that the apostles did gain early credit, and succeeded in a most wonderful manner. This is abundantly proved by the vast numbers of churches established in the early ages at Rome, Corinth, Ephesus, Colosse, &c. Sixth, That, admitting the facts which they testified concerning Christ to be true, then it was reasonable for their contemporaries, and is reasonable for us, to receive the gospel which they have transmitted to us as a divine revelation. That great thing they asserted was, that Jesus was the Christ, and that he was proved to be so by prophecies accomplished in him, and by miracles wrought by him, and by others in his name. If we attend to these, we shall find them to be no contemptible arguments; but must be forced to acknowledge, premises being established, the conclusion most easily and necessarily follows; and this conclusion, that Jesus is the Christ, taken in all its extent, is an abstract of the gospel revelation, and therefore is sometimes put for the whole of it, Acts viii. 37; Acts xvii. 18. Seventh, The truth of the gospel has also received further and very considerable confirmation from what has happened in the world since it was first published. And here we must desire every one to consider what God has been doing to confirm the gospel since its first publication, and he will find it a further evidence of its divine original. We might argue at large from its surprising propagation in the world; from the miraculous powers with which not only the apostles, but succeeding preachers of the gospel, and other converts, were endowed; from the accomplishment of prophecies recorded in the New Testament; and from the preservation of the Jews, as a distinct people, notwithstanding the various difficulties and persecutions through which they have passed.

"What is clear in Christianity," says Paley, "we shall find to be sufficient and to be infinitely valuable. What is dubious, unnecessary to be decided, or of very subordinate importance, and what is most obscure, will teach us to bear with the opinions which others may have formed upon the same subject. We shall say to those who the most widely dissent from us, what Augustine said to the worst heretics of his age—They rail against us, who know not with what labor Truth is found and Error to be avoided!"

There is one argument to prove the authority of the word of God, which cannot be overturned by all the Deists in the world. If the Bible be not the word of God, it must have been written, or invented, either by good men, or wicked men; but if it can be proved that it was neither written, nor invented, either by good men, or wicked men, it must be the word of God. That it was not written, or compiled by wicked men, will appear from its own evidence, for if it is to be judged, we must suffer that evidence to appear in its defence. Can any Deist be so weak as to suppose that wicked men, who were in the love and practice of evil, would frame laws to punish their own vices in this world, and condemn themselves to everlasting punishment by declaring, *the wicked shall be turned into hell, with all the nations that forget God?* And again, *Thou shalt not covet:* this reaches the thoughts and desires of the heart. These restrictions and declarations are opposite to those things, which are con tained in the religious books of the Mahometan and Pagan nations, which are the production of men, in which permission is given to indulge in sensuality. This, so far, is a certain proof of the divine origin of the Bible.

It is no less evident, that good men could not be the authors of the Bible. For had it been compiled by good men, the same good men neither could nor would have given a lie to their profession by calling it *the word of God*, as it would only have been the word of men: consequently the Bible must be the word of God, inspired by him, and thus given to man.

It must be allowed that God created the first man; this being admitted, as it cannot be denied, we cannot doubt that he would give him a law, or rule of life. Now whether the divine author of our being condescended to *speak* it with an audible voice,—to write it on the heart, as is said in scripture, or whether he commissioned man by that spoken law, or from that writing on the heart, to write it in a book for the instruction of posterity, it amounts to the same; for the law, or word of God, first spoken, or written on the heart, and from thence written in a book, still remains to be the *word of God*, first given by him.

The possibility of such inspiration must necessarily be allowed, for certainly it was no more wonderful for God to inspire man to write his will in a book, than it was to *inspire* him, or *enable* him to receive by continual *influx*, a regular train of ideas.

The question has long been asked by Deists, how shall we know that the Bible is the word of God? first, by being convinced from the Bible, that the precepts therein contained are worthy of God; that the pure spirit which runs through the whole, inculcates nothing but LOVE TO GOD AND CHARITY TO ALL MANKIND, viz. 'Thou shalt love the Lord thy God with all thy heart.' Deut. vi. 5. 'Thou shalt love thy neighbour as thyself.' Levit. xix. 18. Matt. vii. 12. Luke x. 27. These are the two great commandments which pervade every page of the Bible, and which on this account is truly called *sacred:* these are sacred duties. For the recorded wickedness of the Jews, or of any other nation mentioned in the Bible, makes no part of the word of God, any farther than as it shows that a departure from those precepts of true religion recorded therein, necessarily draws after it that train of fatal consequences, which is the result of that disobedience to the divine command, when the whole sum and substance of true religion contained in those two great propositions, *Thou shalt love the Lord thy God with all thy heart, and thy neighbour as thyself,* are not manifested in the life of man.

Secondly, from the accomplishment of those things foretold by the prophets, beginning with Moses, and which, to the astonishment of every impartial man, have been fulfilling from their times to the present day. Now as it must be evident, that none but God could open to man those scenes of futurity, which have been realising for the space of 3300 years, and as those precepts of morality contained in the Bible could never be gathered from the book of nature, as man must have been totally ignorant in a savage state; and as it is clear that he could not have been reformed or civilized without a knowledge of those precepts; they must have been given by the Creator: consequently, as far as demonstration can make truth appear, it is undeniable proof that the sacred scripture is the WORD OF GOD

CHAPTER IV.

TRINITARIANS AND UNITARIANS.

In the first ages of Christianity, there were various sects, which have long ago sunk into oblivion, and whose names therefore exist only in the pages of ecclesiastical history It does not accord with our object to describe these ancient denominations. We shall merely notice those which at the present day attract our attention. The primary divisions, which appear in contemplating the Christian church, are those of Trinitarians and Unitarians

TRINITARIANS.

The name of Trinitarians is applied to all the numerous sects, comprising more than nine-tenths of the Christians of the present day, who profess to believe the doctrine of the Trinity, in opposition to Arians and Socinians, who are called Unitarians and Anti-Trinitarians.

The word *Trinity* is not to be found in the Bible. It is a scholastic term, derived from the Latin word *trinitas*, denoting a three-fold unity. According to the best authorities, it was introduced into the church during the second century. The doctrine of the Trinity, as generally professed, accords with that of Athanasius, whose scheme made the Supreme Deity to consist of three persons, the same in substance, equal in power and glory. The first of those three persons, and fountain of divinity to the other two, it makes to be the Father. The second person is called the Son, and is said to be descended from the Father, by an eternal generation of an ineffable and incomprehensible nature in the essence of the Godhead. The third person is the Holy Ghost, derived from the Father and the Son, but not by generation, as the Son is derived from the Father, but by an eternal and incomprehensible procession. Every one of these three persons is very and eternal God, as much as the Father himself; and yet, though distinguished in this manner, they do not make three Gods, but one God.*

The Unitarians believe that there is but one person in the Godhead, and that this person is the Father, and they insist that the Trinitarian distinction of persons is contradictory and absurd. The *unity* of God is a doctrine, which both parties consider the foundation of all true religion.

Although the doctrine of the Trinity is ostensibly the main subject of dispute between Trinitarians and Unitarians, yet it is in reality respecting the character of Christ. Those who believe in his proper deity very easily dispose of all the other difficulties in the Trinitarian system; while anti-Trinitarians find more fault with this doctrine than any other in the Trinitarian creed; and the grand obstacle to their reception of the Trinitarian faith is removed, when they can admit that Jesus Christ is God, as well as man; so that the burden of labor, on both sides, is either to prove or disprove the proper deity of the Son of God.

In proof this doctrine, the Trinitarians urge many declarations of the Scripture, which, in their opinion, admit of no consistent explanation upon the Unitarian scheme; they there find that offices are assigned to Christ, and to

---

* It is thus expressed in the Athanasian creed :—" Now, the Catholic faith is this—that we worship one God in Trinity, and Trinity in Unity. Neither confounding the persons, nor dividing the substance. For one is the person of the Father, another of the Son, another of the Holy Ghost. But the Godhead of the Father, and of the Son, and of the Holy Ghost, is all one, the glory equal, the majesty co-eternal. Such as the Father is, such is the Son, and such is the Holy Ghost. The Father is uncreated, the Son is uncreated, and the Holy Ghost is uncreated. The Father is incomprehensible, the Son is incomprehensible, and the Holy Ghost is incomprehensible. The Father eternal, the Son eternal, and the Holy Ghost eternal. And yet they are not three Eternals, but one Eternal."

Modern divines seem generally to assent to the judgment of Waterland, who considers the Athanasian creed to have been written by Hilary. Archbishop Tillotson, in writing to Burnet, the historian, says of this creed, "I wish we were well rid of it." The episcopal church in America rejects it. Its damnatory clauses are very exceptionable, and have given just offence to many.

the Holy Spirit, which none but God can perform; particularly the creation of the world, and the grand decisions of the day of judgment. As they read the Scriptures, the attributes of *omnipotence, omniscience, omnipresence, unchangeableness,* and *eternity,* are ascribed to Jesus Christ; and they infer that a being to whom all these perfections are ascribed must be truly God, co-equal and co-eternal with the Father. (See Deut. 6 : 4. 2d Kings 19 : 15. Ps. 19 : 1; 83 : 18; 139 : 7. Isa. 6 : 3, 9; 9 : 6; 11 : 3; 14 : 5, 23, 25. Jer. 17 : 10; 23 : 6. Ezek. 8 : 1, 3. Matt. 3 : 16, 17; 9 : 6; 18 : 20; 23 : 19. Luke 1 : 76; 24 : 25. John 1 : 1; 2 : 1; 5 : 19, 23; 10 : 30; 16 : 10, 15. Acts 5 : 4; 28 : 23, 25. Rom. 1 : 5; 9 : 5; 14 : 12, 19. 1 Cor. 2 : 10; 8 : 6. 2 Cor. 13 : 14. Phil. 2 : 5, 6, 7, &c.; 3 : 31. Heb. 1 : 3, 6, 10, 11, 12; 9 : 14; 13 : 8. 1 John 5 : 7, 20. Rev. 1 : 4, 5, 6, 8; 3 : 14; 5; 13, &c.)

The Unitarians, on the other hand, contend that some of these passages are interpolations, and that the others are either mistranslated or misunderstood. The passage in John, in particular, respecting the *three* that bear record, &c., has been deemed an interpolation. Dr. Tomline gives it up in his " Elements of Theology"; and Porson, the eminent Greek scholar, also rejects it.

Bishop Taylor remarks, with great good sense, that " He who goes about to speak of the mystery of the Trinity, and does it by words and names of man's invention, talking of essences and existences, hypostaces and personalities, priorities in-co-equalities, and unity in pluralities, may amuse himself and build a tabernacle in his head, and talk something he knows not what; but the good man, who feels the power of the Father, and to whom the Son has become wisdom, sanctification, and redemption, and in whose heart the love of the spirit of God is shed abroad— this man, though he understands nothing of what is unintelligible, yet he alone truly understands the Christian doctrine of the Trinity."

Dr. Watts has written an "Essay on the Impotence of any Human Schemes to explain the Doctrine of the Trinity." This essay shows, first, that no such scheme of explication is necessary to salvation; secondly, that it may yet be of great use to the Christian church; and thirdly, that all such explication ought to be proposed with modesty to the world, and never imposed on the conscience.

The excellent Stillingfleet, in the preface to his Vindication of the Doctrine of the Trinity, says, "Since both sides yield that the matter they dispute about is above their reach, the wisest course they can take is, to assert and defend *what is revealed*, and not to be *peremptory* and quarrelsome about that which is acknowledged to be above our comprehension; I mean as to the *manner* how the *three persons* partake of the *divine nature*."

UNITARIANS.

Those who confine the Godhead to a single person are called Unitarians. This general sense of the term may be taken to represent the Arians and Socinians, as well as the sect which is more strictly denominated Unitarian.

The Arian Unitarians are so named from Arius, a presbyter of the church of Alexandria, who published his opinions at the beginning of the fourth century; which so disturbed the church that a grand council was, in the year 325, convened at Nice, of nearly all the bishops of Asia, Africa, and Europe. Arius maintained that the Son was totally and essentially distinct from the Father; that he was the first and noblest of all those beings, whom God the Father had created out of nothing; the instrument, by whose subordinate operation the Almighty Father formed the universe, and therefore inferior to the Father, both in nature and in dignity. He added, that the Holy Spirit was of a different nature from that of the Father and of the Son; and that he had been created by the Son. The ancient Arians, however, were divided among themselves upon these subjects, and torn into factions, which regarded one another with the bitterest aversion. Though they denied that Christ was the Eternal God, yet they agreed in contending for his pre-existence. His pre-existence they founded on the two following passages, among many others:—" Before Abraham was I am." And the prayer of Jesus—" Glorify me with that glory which I had with thee before the world began." These, and other texts of a similar kind, were, in their opinion, irrefragable proofs that Christ did actually exist in another state before he was born of the Virgin Mary in the land of Judea. It was also urged by the advocates of Arianism, that the pre-existent dignity of Christ, accounts for that splendid apparatus of prophecies and miracles with which the mission of the Messiah was attended. Some of them believed Christ to have been the creator of the world; but they all maintained that he existed previous to his incarnation, though in his pre-existent state they assign him different degrees of dignity. Hence the appellations High and Low Arian.

A work by John Milton was found among the State Papers at Whitehall after having lain concealed one hundred and fifty years, from which it appears that the author of "Paradise Lost" was imbued with Arian notions. This work, which was translated from the Latin by Dr. Sumner, prebendary of Canterbury, by the express order of his Majesty, George IV., is entitled "A Treatise on Christian Doctrine, compiled from the Holy Scriptures alone, by John Milton." This truly interesting work, divided into two books,—*on the knowledge of God, and on the service of God*—is expressly Arian respecting the person of Christ. Bishop Newton has pronounced, that Milton " was generally truly orthodox;" though Wharton says, that in " Paradise Lost," not a word is said there of the Son of God but what a Socinian, or at least an Arian, would allow.

In this new work, according to its translator, it is asserted, that " the Son existed in the beginning, and was the first of the whole creation, by whose delegated power all things were made in heaven and earth; begotten, not by natural necessity, but by the decree of the Father, within the limits of time, endued with the divine nature and substance, but *distinct from and inferior to the Fa-*

ther—one with the Father in love and unanimity of will, and receiving every thing in his *filial* as well as in his *mediatorial* character—from the Father's gift. This summary will be sufficient to show that the opinions of Milton were nearly Arian, ascribing to the Son as high a share of divinity as was compatible with the denial of his self-existence and eternal generation, but not admitting his co-equality and co-essentiality with the Father. That he entertained different views at other periods of his life is evident from several expressions scattered through his works." The volume abounds with a constant reference to Scripture, even to profusion. And in an admirable prefatory address, alike indicative of his sincerity and piety, he declares: "It was a great solace to me to have compiled, by God's assistance, *a precious aid for my faith*, or rather to have laid up for myself a *treasure*, which would be a provision for my future life, and would remove from my mind all grounds for hesitation, as often as it behoved me to render an account of the principles of my belief."

The reviver of the Unitarian doctrines in Europe was Faustus Socinus, an inhabitant of Sienna in Tuscany, who proclaimed his opinions in 1531. There were an uncle and nephew of the same name, and celebrated for the same opinions concerning the nature of Christ. The nephew, Faustus, was the principal founder of the sect, called after him Socinians. After publishing a treatise upon the nature of the Saviour, he desired to be admitted into a society of Unitarians already existing in Poland. Their opinions do not appear to have corresponded precisely with his, and admission was refused him; nor did he effect, during his life-time, the institution of any distinct congregation; but the views which he disseminated in his writings were gradually referred to and adopted by many ministers and religious communities, especially in Poland, where Crellius, Wolgozenius, and others, published a Socinian system of theology.

Since the death of Socinus, the theologians who have asserted the mere humanity of Christ have been generally denominated Socinians. The doctrines, however, to which that appellation can with strictness be applied, are not precisely equivalent to those of the modern Unitarians. The Socinian denies the existence of Christ previous to his birth of the Virgin Mary; he allows, however, that that birth was miraculous, and considers the Saviour as an object of peculiar reverence and an inferior degree of worship. By the term Mediator, as applied to Christ, he understands that in establishing the new covenant he was the medium between God and men; and of his sacrifice he says, that as the Jewish sacrifices were not made for the payment of sins, but for the remission of them, so also the death of Christ was designed for the remission of sins through God's favour, and not for the satisfaction of them as an equivalent.

Among the followers, who distinguished themselves in the controversy which Socinus had raised, was Michael Servetus, a Spanish physician. Eager to publish his Arian opinions on religion, he sent three questions to Calvin on the Divinity of Christ, on Regeneration, and on the Necessity of Baptism, and, when answered with civility, he reflected on the sentiments of his correspondent with arrogant harshness. This produced a quarrel, and ended in the most implacable hatred, so that Calvin, bent on revenge, obtained, by secret means, copies of a work in which his antagonist was engaged, and caused him to be accused before the archbishop as a dangerous man. Servetus escaped from prison; but, on his way to Italy, he had the imprudence to pass in disguise through Geneva, where he was recognised by Calvin, and immediately seized by the magistrate as an impious heretic. Forty heretical errors were proved against him by his accusers; but Servetus refused to renounce them, and the magistrates, at last yielding to the loud representations of the ministers of Basle, Berne, and Zurich, and especially of Calvin, who demanded the punishment of a profane heretic, ordered the unhappy man to be burnt.

On the 27th October, 1553, the wretched Servetus was conducted to the stake, and as the wind prevented the flames from fully reaching his body, two long hours elapsed before he was freed from his miseries. This cruel treatment deservedly called down the general odium on the head of Calvin, who ably defended his conduct and that of the magistrates. Servetus published various works against the Trinity, which were burnt in disgrace at Geneva and other places. The circumstance of his death is an ineffaceable stain upon the memory of his persecutor.

The *Sabellian* Unitarians were followers of Sabellius, who flourished in the third century, and whose system was an attempt to explain the doctrine of the trinity by representing the father as the sole person, and the Son and Spirit as attributes or emanations from him. Thus they compared the Divinity to the sun; of which the Father would be analogous to the substance, the Son to the light, and the Holy Ghost to the heat. This scheme has been known in later times as that of the Modal Trinity; and some divines of the orthodox English church have found themselves entangled in it, when attempting to explain accurately the mysterious doctrine to which it refers. On the other hand, their opponents have been led, inadvertently, in some cases to make too formal a distinction of the three Persons, and have thereby subjected themselves to the charge of Tritheism, or a belief in three gods.

The Sabellians supposed that the union between the divine *Logos* and the man Christ Jesus was only temporary. For they held that this divine efflux, which like a beam of light from the sun, went out of God, and was attached to the person of Christ, to enable him to work miracles while he was on earth, was drawn into God again, when he ascended into heaven, and had no more occasion to exert a miraculous power on the earth. Some of these professors went so far as to teach that since this ray was properly divine—an emanation from the father—Christ, who had this divine ray within him might be called God, but by no means different from the Father. Thus they arrived at the belief that the Father, being in Christ, suffered and died in him also; and from this, they received the name of Patripassians.

Sabellius taught that as man, though composed of body and soul, is but one person; so God, though he is Father Son, and Holy Ghost, is but one person. The Sabellians differed from the followers of Noetius in this particular: Noetius was of opinion, that the person of the Father had assumed the human nature of Christ; but Sabellius maintained, that a certain energy only, proceeding from the Supreme Parent, or a certain portion of the divine nature, was united to the Son of God, the man Jesus. He considered, in the same manner, the Holy Ghost as the efflux of the Deity.

The reader will find it interesting to compare these views of the Sabellians in regard to Christ, with those of Emanuel Swedenborg upon the same subject.

Modern Unitarians differ as widely as the ancient in their opinions touching the nature of Christ; but by far the greater number believe in the sole, exclusive, and incommunicable divinity of God; deny the personal existence of the Holy Spirit, and on this ground declare it to be contrary to scripture and reason to worship any other being than the one supreme Jehovah, who is the only object of prayer and adoration. They ascribe neither *attributes*, nor *works*, nor *honours* to Christ, which reason and revelation appropriate to God. Not believing in the pre-existence of Christ, they declare that all the benefits we derive from him consist in the bright example he set before us. These professors are in the strictest sense *Unitarians*, because they maintain the Unity of God to the total exclusion of Christ, and acknowledge him only as a prophet of God, a mortal man, but "the most complete character that was ever exhibited to the world."

These opinions were propagated in the early ages of the church by the Ebionites, by the Carpocratians in the second century, in the third century by the followers of Paul of Samosata, who were called Samosatanians, and in the fourth century by Photenius a bishop of Galatia.

The Unitarians acknowledge no other rule of faith and practice than the Holy Scriptures. They reject all creeds of human device, and hold in less esteem than many other sects nice theological subtleties concerning the precise rank of Jesus Christ, and the nature of his relation to God. They believe that the Holy Ghost is not a distinct person in the Godhead, but *that power of God, that divine influence,* by which Christianity was established through miraculous aids, and by which its spirit is still shed abroad in the hearts of men. They advocate the most perfect toleration. They believe that sin is its own punishment, and virtue its own rewarder; That the moral consequences of a man's good or evil conduct go with him into the future life, to afford him remorse or satisfaction; That God will be influenced in all his dealing with the soul by mercy and justice, punishing no more severely than the sinner deserves, and always for a benevolent end. Indeed, the greater part of the denomination are Restorationists, or believe in the final restoration of men to virtue and consequent felicity.

Unitarians consider, that besides the Bible, all the Ante-Nicene Fathers—that is, all Christian writers for three centuries after the birth of Christ—give testimony in their favor, against the " modern" popular doctrine of the Trinity. As for *antiquity*, it is their belief that it is really on their side.

In the *First Epistle of Clement to the Corinthians,* which was written towards the close of the first century, —and the evidence for the genuineness of which, they maintain, is stronger than for that of any other of the productions attributed to the apostolical fathers,—the supremacy of the father is asserted and implied throughout, and Jesus is spoken of in terms mostly borrowed from the Scriptures. He is once called the " sceptre of the majesty of God"; and this highly figurative expression is the most exalted applied to him in the whole Epistle.

Justin Martyr, the most distinguished of the ancient fathers of the church, who flourished in the former part of the second century, and whose writings (with the exception of those attributed to the *apostolic* fathers) are the earliest Christian records next to the New Testament, expressly says, " We worship God, the Maker of the universe, offering up to him prayers and thanks. But assigning to Jesus, who came to teach us these things, and for this end was born, the '*second place*' after God, we not without reason honor him."

The germ and origin of the doctrine of the Trinity, the Unitarians find in the speculations of those Christianized philosophers of the second century, whose minds were strongly tinctured with the Platonic philosophy, combined with the *emanation system*, as taught at Alexandria, and held by Philo. From this time they trace the gradual formation of the doctrine, through successive ages down to Anthanasius and Augustine; the former of whom, A. D. 362, was the first to insist upon the equality of the Holy Ghost with the Father and the Son; and the latter about half a century afterwards, was the first to insist upon their numerical unity.

In all ages of the church, there have been many learned and pious men who have rejected the Trinity as unscriptural and irrational. The first attempt at the council of Nice, to establish and make universal the Trinitarian creed, caused disturbances and dissensions in the church, which continued for ages, and produced results the most deplorable to every benevolent mind which exalts *charity* over faith.

The following proof-texts are some of those upon which the Unitarians rest their belief in the inferiority of the Son to the Father:—John 8: 17, 18. John 17: 3. Acts 10: 38. 1 Tim. 2: 5. 1 John 4: 14. Rom. 8: 34. 1 Cor. 11: 3. John 10: 29. John 14: 28. Matt. 19: 17. John 17: 21. John 20: 17. 1 Cor. 8: 5, 6. John 10: 25; 7: 16, 17; 8: 28; 5: 19, 20; 8: 49, 50. Matt. 20: 23. John 6: 38, 57; 5: 30. Mark 13: 32. Luke 6: 12. John 11: 41, 42. Matt. 27: 46. Acts 2: 22—24. Phil. 2: 11. Col. 1: 15. Rev. 3: 14. Heb. 3: 3. Matt. 12: 18. Luke 2: 52.

In England, the number of Unitarians was considerable, according to Strype, as early as 1548; and in 1550, he represents the Unitarian doctrine as spreading so fast that the leading Churchmen were alarmed, and "thought it necessary to suppress its expression by rigid measures." These "rigid measures," such as imprisonment and burning, were successful for a time. But afterwards, the "heresy" gained new and able supporters, such as Biddle, Firmin, Dr. S. Clarke, Dr. Lardner, Whiston, Emlyn, Sir Isaac Newton, &c., and has been spreading to this day; when, according to Brande's Encyclopœdia, the number of their congregations in England is stated at something more than two hundred; " but they are principally composed of persons of the educated classes." In Geneva, the pulpits of the established church are mostly occupied by the professors of these opinions.

The late Dr. William Ellery Channing, an American, was, perhaps, the most distinguished of modern Unitarian divines. Since the days of Addison, no writer of English prose has acquired a more enduring celebrity. But his was a still higher praise. "From his youth," says the Rev. Mr. Dewey, " Channing strove to give birth to his own glowing idea of the true Christian man. He could not bear that a shallow morality, or a mere worldly decency, or a vulgar fanaticism, or any distorted peculiarity of any religious class, should usurp the honors of Christian virtue. Of this great achievement, virtue—the end to him and the explanation of everything in humanity and in the human lot—his views were at once large and generous on the one hand, and on the other, strict and solemn. No preacher ever demanded a higher purity, ever set forth a loftier model."

It is estimated that there are about four hundred churches and congregations of the Unitarian denomination in the United States, and about that number of ministers.

In the city of Boston, it is one of the most numerous and influential classes of Christians, having eighteen societies, most of which are large and flourishing. In the Middle, Southern and Western States, their congregations are fewer, but gradually multiplying.

CHAPTER V

THE GREEK CHURCH—ROMAN CATHOLICS.

THE GREEK CHURCH.

The Greek Church comprises the great bulk of the Christian population of Russia and Greece, Moldavia and Wallachia, besides various congregations scattered throughout the provinces of the Turkish and Austrian empires, who acknowledge the patriarch of Constantinople as their head.

The opinions of this church bear considerable affinity to those of the Latin, or Roman Catholic. The fundamental distinction is the rejection of the spiritual supremacy of St. Peter, and the denial of any visible representative of Christ upon earth. In the view which it takes of the Holy Ghost it is also at variance, not only with the Roman Catholic church, but with Protestants.* It recognises, however, the seven sacraments; authorises the offering of prayer to the saints and Virgin; and encourages the use of pictures, though forbidding the use of images. It holds in reverence, also, the relics and tombs of holy men; enjoins strict fasting and the giving of alms, looking upon them as works of intrinsic merit; and numbers among its adherents numerous orders of monks and nuns. It allows, however, the marriage of its secular priests, and rejects auricular confession. It holds that modified form of the Roman doctrine of the eucharist, which is denominated consubstantiation; and apparently entertains some confused notions of a purgatory, in consideration of which it offers prayers for the dead. It administers baptism by immersion.

---

* The variation consists in the idea, that the Holy Ghost proceeds from the Son alone, and not from the Father and the Son.

The services of this church consist almost entirely of ceremonial observances.

Preaching and the reading of the Scriptures form but a small part of them; the former, indeed, was at one period altogether forbidden in Russia.

The origin of the separation which has now prevailed for many hundred years between two such important sections of Christendom as the Latin and Greek churches, approaching so near as they do in many of their fundamental principles, is to be attributed to the rival pretensions set up by the bishops of the two imperial cities, Rome and Constantinople, and dates almost from the foundation of the latter capital. The Roman branch continued, however, still powerful in the East, and the intrigues of the papal see were frequently successful; until in 1054, the mutual excommunications pronounced upon each other by Leo IX. and Cerularius, caused the final separation which has continued to the present day.

ROMAN CATHOLICS.

The following are the great points of Catholic belief, by which they are distinguished from other Christian societies; and these are the only real and essential tenets of their religion:—

1. They believe that Christ has established a church upon earth, and that this church is that which holds communion with the See of Rome, being one, holy, catholic, and apostolical.

2. That we are obliged to hear this church; and, therefore, that she is infallible, by the guidance of Almighty God, in her decisions regarding faith.

3. That Saint Peter, by divine commission, was appointed the head of this church, under Christ its founder; and that the Pope or Bishop of Rome, as successor to Saint Peter, has always been, and is at present, by divine right, head of this church.

4. That the canon of the Old and New Testament, as proposed to us by this church, is the word of God; as also

such traditions, belonging to faith and morals, which being originally delivered by Christ to his apostles, have been preserved, by constant succession, in the Catholic church.

5. That honour and veneration are due to the angels of God and his saints; that they offer up prayers to God for us; that it is good and profitable to have recourse to their intercession; and that the relics or earthly remains of God's particular servants are to be held in respect.

6. That no sins ever were, or can be, remitted, unless by the mercy of God, through Jesus Christ; and, therefore, that man's justification is the work of divine grace.

7. That the good works which we do, receive their whole value from the grace of God; and that by such works, we not only comply with the precepts of the divine law; but that we thereby likewise merit eternal life.

8. That by works, done in the spirit of penance, we can make satisfaction to God, for the temporal punishment, which often remains due, after our sins, by the divine goodness, have been forgiven us.

9. That Christ has left to his church a power of granting indulgences, that is, a relaxation from such temporal chastisement only as remains due after the divine pardon of sin; and that the use of such indulgences is profitable to sinners.

10. That there is a purgatory or middle state; and that the souls of imperfect Christians therein detained, are helped by the prayers of the faithful.

11. That there are seven sacraments, all instituted by Christ; baptism, confirmation, eucharist, penance, extreme unction, holy order, matrimony.

12. That, in the most holy sacrament of the eucharist, there is truly, really, and substantially, the body and blood, together with the soul and divinity, of our Lord Jesus Christ.

13. That, in this sacrament, there is, by the omnipotence of God, a conversion, or change, of the whole substance of the bread into the body of Christ, and of the whole substance of the wine into his blood, which change we call TRANSUBSTANTIATION

14. That, under either kind, Christ is received whole and entire.

15. That, in the mass, or sacrifice of the altar, is offered to God, a true, proper, and propitiatory sacrifice for the living and the dead.

16. That, in the sacrament of penance, the sins we fall into after baptism are, by the divine mercy, forgiven us.

Such is a succinct summary of the main articles of belief in the Roman Catholic church.

Mr. Pitt, in the year 1788, requested to be furnished with the opinion of the Catholic clergy and foreign universities on certain important points. Three questions sent to the universities of Paris, Louvain, Alcala, Douay, Salamanca, and Valladolid, were thus unanimously answered—First, "That the Pope, or cardinals, or any body of men, or any individual of the church of Rome, has not any civil authority, power, jurisdiction, or pre-eminence whatsoever within the realm of England. Second, That the Pope or cardinals, &c. cannot absolve or release his majesty's subjects from their oath of allegiance, upon any pretext whatsoever. Third, that there is no principle in the tenets of the Catholic faith, by which Catholics are justified in not keeping faith with heretics or other persons differing from them in religious opinions, in any transactions either of a public or a private nature."

In the history of the church, there have been seventeen general councils, and to these is attached, by Roman Catholics, infallibility. In the Council of Trent, the last of them, and which continued in session from 1545 to 1563, the tenets of their religion were embodied, and the summary is exhibited in Pope Pius's Creed, containing the substance of the decrees and canons of this council.

It may not be unacceptable to the reader to have this Creed inserted in this place. It is required to be subscribed by the members of this Church on various occasions:—

"I, N. N., with a firm faith, believe and profess all and every one of those things which are contained in that creed which the holy Roman Church maketh use of. To wit I believe in one God, the Father Almighty, Maker of

Heaven and Earth, of all things visible and invisible: And in one Lord Jesus Christ, the only begotten Son of God, and born of the Father before all ages; God of God; Light of Light; true God of the true God; begotten, not made; consubstantial to the Father, by whom all things were made. Who for us men, and for our salvation, came down from heaven, and was incarnate by the Holy Ghost of the Virgin Mary, and was made man. Was crucified also for us under Pontius Pilate; he suffered and was buried. And the third day he rose again, according to the Scriptures; sits at the right hand of the Father, and is to come again with glory to judge the living and the dead; of whose kingdom there shall be no end. And in the Holy Ghost, the Lord, and Lifegiver, who proceeds from the Father and the Son, who, together with the Father and the Son, is adored and glorified, who spoke by the Prophets. And (I believe) One, Holy, Catholic, and Apostolic Church. I confess one Baptism for the remission of sins; and I look for the resurrection of the dead, and the life of the world to come. Amen.

"I most steadfastly admit and embrace Apostolical and Ecclesiastical Traditions, and all other observances and constitutions of the same Church.

"I also admit the Holy Scriptures, according to that sense in which our holy Mother the Church has held, and does hold; to which it belongs to judge of the true sense and interpretation of the Scriptures: neither will I ever take and interpret them otherwise than according to the unanimous consent of the Fathers.

"I also profess that there are truly and properly seven sacraments of the New Law, instituted by Jesus Christ our Lord, and necessary for the salvation of mankind, though not all for every one; to wit: Baptism, Confirmation, the Eucharist, Penance, Extreme Unction, Order, and Matrimony; and that they confer Grace; and that of these, Baptism, Confirmation, and Order cannot be reiterated without sacrilege. I also receive and admit the received and approved ceremonies of the Catholic Church, used in the solemn administration of the aforesaid sacraments.

"I embrace and receive all and every one of the things which have been defined and declared in the holy Council of Trent concerning Original Sin and Justification.

"I profess, likewise, that in the Mass there is offered to God a true, proper, and propitiatory sacrifice for the living and the dead. And that in the most holy sacrament of the Eucharist, there is truly, really, and substantially the Body and Blood, together with the Soul and Divinity of our Lord Jesus Christ, and that there is made a conversion of the whole substance of the bread into the Body, and of the whole substance of the wine into the Blood; which conversion the Catholic Church calls Transubstantiation. I also confess, that under either kind alone, Christ is received whole and entire, and a true sacrament.

"I constantly hold that there is a purgatory, and that the souls therein detained are helped by the suffrages of the Faithful.

"Likewise, that the saints reigning together with Christ are to be honoured and invocated, and that they offer prayers to God for us, and that their relics are to be had in veneration.

"I most firmly assert that the Images of Christ, of the Mother of God, ever Virgin, and also of other saints, ought to be had and retained, and that due honour and veneration is to be given them.

"I also affirm that the power of indulgences was left by Christ in the Church, and that the use of them is most wholesome to Christian people.

"I acknowledge the Holy, Catholic, Apostolic Roman Church, for the Mother and Mistress of all Churches; and I promise true obedience to the Bishop of Rome, successor to St. Peter, Prince of the Apostles, and Vicar of Jesus Christ.

"I likewise undoubtedly receive and profess all other things delivered, defined, and declared by the sacred Canons and General Councils, and particularly by the holy Council of Trent. And I condemn, reject, and anathematize all things contrary thereto, and all heresies which the Church has condemned, rejected, and anathematized.

"I, N. N., do at this present freely profess, and sincerely hold, this true Catholic faith, without which no one can be saved; and I promise most constantly to retain and confess the same entire and unviolated, with God's assistance, to the end of my life."

From all this it will be seen that the Catholic believes in the immortality of the soul, and that it will be hereafter clothed with its body, which God will raise in perfection; further, that the condition of man in a future state will vary according as he has done good or evil; that the state of the good and the wicked commences immediately after death. A middle state, called Purgatory, is provided for those souls, which were not entirely estranged from the Eternal, and which, therefore, in the other world, still have a hope of ultimately becoming united with the Creator.

The Greek church also calls itself a Catholic, that is a universal church (Καθολικος, universal,) although it disowns the Roman pope. The Roman Catholic church exercised a spiritual supremacy over all Europe with the exception of Russia and Turkey, until the time of the reformation. It has more followers, at the present day, than all the Protestant sects united; and its exertions have brought nearly two millions of the adherents of the Greek ritual in Europe under the spiritual dominion of the pope. In the United States the number of Roman Catholics is variously stated at from two to four millions. The tide of emigration from Europe is constantly increasing the amount.

There are twelve Roman Catholic patriarchs in the Christian world. The sacred college of cardinals, by whom the Pope is elected, has fifty-seven members. The total number is seventy. The archbishops and bishops amount to six hundred and seventy-one. The vicars apostolic in different countries are fifty-seven in number, besides whom there are thirty-eight coadjutor-bishops, making the grand total of the Catholic episcopacy amount to seven hundred and sixty-six bishops.

CHAPTER VI.

THE REFORMATION—ORIGIN OF THE TERM PROTESTANTS—LUTHERANS—CALVINISTS—HUGUENOTS—ARMINIANS—BAXTERIANS—ANTINOMIANS—MATERIALISTS—NECESSARIANS.

Prior to that great religious epoch, known as the Reformation, the pope claimed of divine right, and exercised absolute authority over the whole Christian church, with the exception of those states and provinces in which the Eastern or Greek church was established. Not only was his authority regarded as supreme on subjects of doctrine and discipline, but his decisions were considered as infallible; and whoever ventured to question or gainsay them, was treated as a heretic, and was liable to such canonical censures and temporal penalties as the canon law determined. Of course the exercise of private judgment in religious and ecclesiastical matters, or the right of the people to peruse the bible, was peremptorily denied.

According to the doctrine of the Romish church, all the good works of the saints, over and above those necessary for their own justification, are deposited, together with the infinite merits of Jesus Christ, in one inexhaustible treasury. The keys of this treasury were committed to St. Peter and his successors, the popes, who may open it at pleasure, and by transferring a portion of this superabundant merit to any particular person for a sum of money, may convey to him either the pardon of his own sins, or a release for any one in whose happiness he is interested, from the pains of purgatory. Hence the origin, which took place in the eleventh century, of the sale of *indulgences*.

Pope Leo X., under the pretence of raising contributions towards building the church of St. Peter at Rome, granted, in 1517, the right of promulgating these indulgences in Germany, together with a share in the profits arising from the sale of them, to the archbishop of Magdeburg, who, as his chief agent for retailing them in Saxony, employed Tetzel, a Dominican friar, of dissolute morals, but of great activity and energy of character Tetzel, assisted by the monks of his order, executed the commission with great zeal, but with little discretion or decency; and by disposing of these indulgences at a very low price, carried on for some time a lucrative traffic. Princes and nobles were irritated at seeing their vassals drained of their wealth to replenish the treasury of a profuse pontiff. Men of piety regretted equally the corruptions of the church and the delusions of the people.

It was reserved for Martin Luther, formerly a monk of the Augustine order, and at that time a professor of theology at Wittenberg, effectually to expose the artifices of those who sold, and the simplicity of those who bought indulgences, and to shake the foundation of the Papal see itself. His memorable theses, ninety-five in number, against this practice, were affixed to the doors of the cathedral of Wittenberg, 31st October, 1517; while from the pulpit he inveighed bitterly against the vices of the monks, who advertised indulgences, as well as against the abuse itself.

Leo X., naturally fond of ease, paid little attention at first to the controversy, which soon raged in Germany in consequence of Luther's opposition; but at length he was roused from his apathy. After some attempts to induce Luther to recant his opinions, the pope, in June, 1520, issued a bull, condemning as heretical and offensive to pious ears, forty-one propositions extracted out of Luther's works: all persons were forbidden to read his works on pain of excommunication; those who possessed a copy of them were commanded to commit it to the flames; and he himself, if he did not within sixty days publicly recant his errors and burn his works, pronounced a heretic, excommunicated, and delivered over to Satan; and all secular princes required under pain of incurring the same censure, to seize his person, that he might be punished as his crimes deserved.

This sentence gave a fresh impulse to the spread of Luther's doctrines. In some cities the people violently obstructed the promulgation of the bull; and on the tenth of December, 1520, Luther assembled all the members of the university of Wittenberg, and, with great pomp, in presence of a vast number of spectators, cast the volumes of the canon law, together with the bull of excommunication, into the flames; and his example was imitated in several cities of Germany.

The progress of the reformed doctrines was now rapid and general, and threatened to embrace the whole of Germany, notwithstanding the Emperor Charles V. co-operated with the pope to check and destroy them. Luther, too, was, from various motives, protected not merely by the Elector of Saxony, but by many other princes; and the new views were adopted and sedulously propagated by Melancthon, Carlostadius, and other eminent men, Erasmus, too, though he did not long follow in the same course as the German reformer, and ultimately wrote against some of his views, yet discovered and exposed with great learning and ability, many errors both in the doctrine and worship of the Romish church, and may be considered as his auxiliary in the work of Reformation.

Under such circumstances it was, that the imperial diet at Worms was held, January 1521, to which the different princes were invited, to concert measures for checking the new doctrines. An attempt to condemn him in his absence was frustrated by a majority of the members of the diet; and Luther, under a safe conduct, was summoned to appear before them. He did not hesitate to attend; but nothing could induce him to retract his opinions. He was allowed to leave the city in safety; but an edict was published in the Emperor's name, after his departure, putting him under the ban of the empire. But the elector of Saxony concealed Luther in the castle of Wartburg, and the edict was not carried into effect. During his confinement his opinions continued to gain ground; and the Augustinians of Wittenberg ventured on an alteration in the established forms of public worship, by abolishing the cel ebration of private masses, and by giving the cup as well as the bread to the laity in administering the Lord's supper.

Meanwhile, an attack no less violent, occasioned by a similar cause, was made on the Romish church in Switzerland by Zuinglius, a man not inferior to Luther himself in zeal and intrepidity, and who advanced with perhaps more daring and rapid steps to overthrow the whole fabric of the established religion.

The Swiss and the German reformers were at first unacquainted with the proceedings of each other. But while they both resisted and exposed the errors and usurpations of the Romish church, and generally agreed in their sentiments, they entertained very different theological opinions; and thus were sown the seeds of those divisions, which have since agitated the reformed churches. The chief subject of dispute between the two reformers was concerning the manner in which the body and blood of Christ were really present in the Eucharist. Luther and his followers, though they rejected the papal belief of transubstantiation, were, nevertheless, of opinion that the body and blood of Christ were really present in the Lord's supper, in a way which they could not pretend to explain. Zuinglius and his adherents repudiated the doctrine, and taught that the bread and wine used at the Eucharist were no more than external symbols to excite the remembrance of Christ's sufferings in the minds of those who received it. Both parties maintained their opinions with equal obstinacy; but the dispute was not suffered long to obstruct the great work of reform.

The struggle between the Roman Catholics and the reformers still raged in Germany. At a diet held at Spires in 1529, the power, which, three years before, had been given, by the same body, to princes, of managing ecclesiastical affairs until the meeting of a general council, was revoked by a majority of votes, and every change declared unlawful that should be made in the established religion before the determination of the approaching council was known. After many ineffectual remonsrtances and arguments, six princes of the empire and thirteen imperial cities " protested" against this decision. Hence arose the denomination of PROTESTANTS; a term at first applicable only to the Lutherans, but now common to *all* who have separated from the church of Rome.

In 1530, Charles convoked a diet of the empire at Augsburg, and directed the reformers to lay before it an account of their tenets in German and Latin. The work, prepared by Luther and Melancthon, was presented to the diet; hence called the confession of Augsburg, which was read aloud by the chancellor to the assembly. It contained twenty-eight chapters, of which twenty-one were illustrative of the religious opinions of the Protestants, and the remaining seven of the errors and superstitions of the papal faith. Not only was this document rejected, but the diet published a decree condemning most of the peculiar tenets held by the Protestants, and enjoining a strict observance of the established rites; with other articles equally galling and tyrannical. But the Protestants were now too powerful a body to be easily dismayed. They assembled at Smalcalde, where they concluded a treaty of mutual defence, both religious and political, against all aggressors, and formed the Protestant states of the empire into one regular combination. Thus, in the year 1530, was the Reformation virtually established in Germany; first by the publication of the confession of Augsburg; and second, by the league of Smalcalde, which made that creed the bond of union of a powerful political confederacy

The reformed doctrines had early spread to Geneva; and John Cauvin, or Calvin, of that city, after the death of Zuinglius, carried them farther than the Swiss Protestants had done. He abolished all festivals except the Sabbath, discarded all church ceremonies, used leavened bread for the sacrament, and taught the doctrines of predestination and election in all their rigour. Calvinism thus became the third great branch of the reformation, Luther and Zuinglius being respectively at the head of the other two. The systems of Zuinglius and Calvin, however, gradually merged together, and they may now be considered as one, having the same confession of faith.

Independently of the truth or falsehood of the doctrinal and other points at issue, the Reformation was the cause of many important advantages. It burst the fetters by which the human mind had previously been bound, and restored it to liberty. It made religion an object of the understanding, and not of the eye; of the heart rather than of the memory; and it has contributed to improve even the church of Rome itself both in science and in morals.

LUTHERANS.

The religious system of Luther approaches, in some respects, nearer to Romanism than that of any other of the reformed churches. His notions upon the nature of the Eucharist are known under the name of consubstantiation, or the co-existence of the body and bread, the blood and the wine, at the same time. Lutheranism encourages, also, the private confession of sins, makes use of wafers in the administration of the Lord's Supper, and allows of images in churches. It insists, however, very strongly upon Luther's cardinal doctrine, the justification of man by faith, and not by any merit in human actions.

With respect to the divine decrees, it holds that God foreknows the dispositions of men, whether they will be good or bad, and predetermines their salvation or rejection accordingly; differing therein from the tenet of the Calvinists, which represents the Supreme Being as making his decrees by his own mere will. Upon those doctrinal points relating to the Trinity, the character of Christ, &c., it accords with the church of Rome.

The dogmas of the Lutheran church are carefully set forth in various symbolic books: the "Confession of Augsburg," the "Articles of Smalcalde," the shorter and larger catechisms of Luther, and the "Form of Concord." The principle, however, of this church, which considered Christians as accountable to God alone for their religious opinions, allows its teachers at the present day, an unbounded liberty of dissenting from these decisions.

The external affairs of the Lutheran church are directed by three judicatories, namely, a vestry of the congregation, a district or special conference, and a general synod. The synod is composed of ministers, and an equal number of Laymen, chosen as deputies by the vestries of their respective congregations. From this synod there is no appeal. The ministerium is composed of ministers only, and regulates the internal or spiritual concerns of the church, such as examining, licensing, and ordaining ministers, judging in controversies about doctrine, &c. The synod and ministerium meet annually.

Confession and absolution, in a very simple form, are practiced by the American Lutherans; also confirmation, by which baptismal vows are ratified, and the subjects become communicants. Their liturgies are simple and impressive, and the clergy are permitted to use extemporaneous prayers.

Luther, in his writings, expresses his disapprobation of attaching his name to that of a sect.

The Lutheran church predominates in the north of Germany, in Prussia, Norway, Denmark and Sweden. In the two latter countries it is the legally established religion. There are congregations of the same denomination in England, Holland and Russia. In the Prussian dominions it has been remodelled under the late king, and is called the Evangelical church. In the United States the Lutherans have about fourteen hundred churches, four hundred ministers, seventy thousand communing members, and about one hundred and forty thousand, who do not commune. The whole number of Lutherans in Europe is estimated at twenty-seven millions, embracing seventeen reigning sovereigns.

CALVINISTS.

The followers of Calvin, the second great reformer of the sixteenth century, and founder of the church of Geneva, are called Calvinists. Their distinguishing tenets refer to points both of discipline and doctrine. Calvin was the first to reject the episcopal form of church government, originally, it is said, with great reluctance, and compelled thereto by the want of regularly ordained ministers; but he afterwards maintained the exclusive establishment of the Presbyterian system, which has since obtained favour in Scotland, and among the Protestants of France, and has numerous adherents in America.

The doctrinal opinions of Calvin, however, have not been permanently received among those who have adopted his views respecting the ministry. On the contrary, in England and Geneva there are many Presbyterians Arminian in sentiment. It was at the Synod of Dort, in 1618, that the points in dispute between the Calvinists and Arminians, were most accurately distinguished and arranged under five heads, upon which the former party asserted the following opinions :—

1. Of predestination—that all men have sinned in Adam, and are become liable to the curse; but that God has by an eternal decree chosen some from the beginning, to whom he should impart faith of his free grace, and consequently salvation.

2. Of the death of Christ—that it is a sufficient sacrifice for the sins of the whole world; and that some only believe and are saved, whereas many perish in unbelief, arises not from any defect in this sacrifice, but from the perversity of the non-elect.

3. Of man's corruption—that all men are conceived in sin and born the children of wrath, and are neither willing nor able to return to God without the aid of the holy Spirit.

4. Of grace and free will—that the influence of the spirit upon our fallen natures does not force, but only quickens and corrects them, inducing them gently to turn themselves towards God by an exercise of their free will.

5. Of perseverance—that God does not wholly take away his Spirit from his own children, even in lamentable falls; nor does he permit them to fall finally from the grace of adoption and the state of justification.

These opinions, which were laid down at the Synod of Dort, represent the sentiments of the founder of this school and of the strictest among his followers.

As the Calvinists differ among themselves in the explication of these tenets, it would be difficult to give a specific account of them. Generally speaking, however, they comprehend the following propositions:—First, That God has chosen a certain number in Christ to everlasting glory, before the foundation of the world, according to his immutable purpose, and of his free grace and love, without the least foresight of faith, good works, or any conditions performed by the creature; and that the rest of mankind he was pleased to pass by, and ordain them to dishonor and wrath for their sins, to the praise of his vindictive justice. Secondly, that Jesus Christ, by his death and sufferings, made an atonement only for the sins of the elect. Thirdly, that mankind are totally depraved in consequence of the fall; and, by virtue of Adam's being their public head, the guilt of his sin was imputed, and a corrupt nature conveyed to all his posterity, from which proceed all actual transgressions; and that by sin we are made subject to death, and all miseries, temporal, spiritual, and eternal. Fourthly, that all whom God has predestinated to life, he is pleased, in his appointed time, effectually to call by his word and spirit out of that state of sin and death, in which they are by nature, to grace and salvation by Jesus Christ. Fifthly, That those whom God has effectually called and sanctified by his spirit shall never finally fall from a state of grace. Some have supposed that the Trinity was one of the five points; but this is a mistake, since both the Calvinists and Arminians, who formed the synod of Dort, where this phrase, *five points*, originated, were on the article of the Trinity, generally agreed. The prominent feature of this system is, the election of some, and the reprobation of others, from all eternity.

The Calvinists found their sentiments of election on the expression of the Saviour, respecting his having chosen his disciples out of the world; and more particularly on certain terms used by the apostle Paul in his Epistle to the

Romans. To the epistolary writers, indeed, they more frequently refer than to any other part of the New Testament. The chief advantage of this system, in the opinion of its advocates, is to produce in us a reverential awe when we look up to God, and a profound humility when we look down upon ourselves.

To the Calvinists also belongs more particularly the doctrine of atonement, or that Christ, by his death, made satisfaction to the divine justice for the elect, appeasing the anger of the divine Being, and effecting on his part a reconciliation. Thus Jesus Christ had the sin of the elect laid upon him; and in this sense, Luther said—" that Jesus Christ was the greatest sinner in the world!" This doctrine, however, is reprobated by some of their divines, who consider the death of Christ as simply a medium through which God has been pleased to exercise mercy towards the penitent.

America has produced many able Calvinistic divines. Jonathan Edwards's work on the Will is considered one of the most important contributions to this school of Theology ever published. Samuel Hopkins, who died in 1803, has made in his " System of Divinity," many additions to Edwards's views; and " Hopkinsian Calvinists" may still be found, although they no longer form a distinct sect from their brethren, the followers of the great Geneva reformer.

The following is a summary of the distinguishing tenets of the Hopkinsians: 1. "That all true virtue, or real holiness, consists in disinterested benevolence. 2. That all sin consists in selfishness. 3. That there are no promises of regenerating grace made to the doings of the unregenerate. 4. That the impotency of sinners, with respect to believing in Christ, is not natural, but moral. 5. That, in order to faith in Christ, a sinner must approve, in his heart, of the divine conduct, even though God should cast him off forever; which, however, neither implies love of misery, nor hatred of happiness. 6. That the infinitely wise and holy God has exerted his omnipotent power in such a manner as he purposed should be followed with the existence and entrance of moral evil into the system. 7. That the introduction of sin is, upon the whole, for the general good. 8. That repentance is before faith in Christ. 9. That, though men became sinners by Adam, according to a divine constitution, yet they have, and are accountable for, no sins but personal. 10. That, though believers are justified *through* Christ's righteousness, yet his righteousness is not *transferred* to them."

In New England the term *orthodox* is applied to those, who accept Calvin's doctrines in their most rigorous interpretation. The following creed, which is subscribed by every person appointed a professor in the theological institution at Andover, may be regarded as a fair exponent of the views of the " Orthodox Calvinists":—

" I believe there is one, and but one living and true GOD; that the word of GOD, contained in the Scriptures of the Old and New Testament, is the only perfect rule of faith and practice; that, agreeably to those Scriptures, GOD is a Spirit, infinite, eternal, and unchangeable, in his being, wisdom, power, holiness, justice, goodness, and truth; that in the Godhead are three Persons, the FATHER, the SON, and the HOLY GHOST; and that these THREE are ONE GOD, the same in substance, equal in power and glory; that GOD created man after his own image, in knowledge, righteousness, and holiness; that the glory of GOD is man's chief end, and the enjoyment of God his supreme happiness; that this enjoyment is derived solely from conformity of heart to the moral character and will of GOD; that ADAM, the federal head and representative of the human race, was placed in a state of probation, and that, in consequence of his disobedience, all his descendants were constituted sinners; that, by nature, every man is personally depraved, destitute of holiness, unlike and opposed to GOD; and that, previously to the renewing agency of the DIVINE SPIRIT, all his moral actions are adverse to the character and glory of GOD; that, being morally incapable of recovering the image of his CREATOR, which was lost in ADAM, every man is justly exposed to eternal damnation so that, except a man be born again, he cannot see the kingdom of GOD; that GOD, of his mere good pleasure, from all eternity, elected some to everlasting life, and that he entered into a covenant of grace, to deliver them out of this state of sin and misery by a REDEEMER; that the only REDEEMER of the elect is the eternal SON of GOD, who, for this purpose, became man, and continues to be GOD and man in two distinct natures, and one person, forever; that CHRIST, as our Redeemer, executeth the office of a Prophet, Priest, and King; that agreeably to the covenant of redemption, the SON of GOD, and he alone, by his sufferings and death, has made atonement for the sins of all men; that repentance, faith, and holiness, are the personal requisites in the gospel scheme of salvation; that the righteousness of CHRIST is the only ground of a sinner's justification; that this righteousness is received through faith; and that this faith is the gift of GOD; so that our salvation is wholly of grace; that no means whatever can change the heart of a sinner, and make it holy; that regeneration and sanctification are the effects of the creating and renewing agency of the HOLY SPIRIT, and that supreme love to GOD constitutes the essential difference between saints and sinners; that, by convincing us of our sin and misery, enlightening our minds, working faith in us, and renewing our wills, the HOLY SPIRIT makes us partakers of the benefits of redemption; and that the ordinary means by which these benefits are communicated to us, are the word, sacraments, and prayer; that repentance unto life, faith to feed upon CHRIST, love to GOD, and new obedience, are the appropriate qualifications for the Lord's supper; and that a Christian church ought to admit no person to its holy communion, before he exhibits credible evidence of his godly sincerity; that perseverance in holiness is the only method of making our calling and election sure; and that the final perseverance of the saints, though it is the effect of the special operation of GOD on their hearts, necessarily implies their own watchful diligence; that they who are effectually called, do, in this life, partake of justification, adoption, and sanctifica tion, and the several benefits which do either accompany or flow from them; that the souls of believers are, at their death, made perfect in holiness, and do immediately pass into glory; that their bodies, being still united to CHRIST, will, at the resurrection, be raised up to glory, and the saints will be made perfectly blessed in the full enjoyment of GOD to all eternity; but that the wicked will awake to everlasting contempt, and with the devils, be plunged into the lake that burneth with fire and brimstone forever and ever. I moreover believe that GOD, according to the counsel of his own will, and for his own glory, hath foreordained whatsoever comes to pass, and that all beings, actions, and events, both in the natural and moral world, are under his providential direction; that GOD'S decrees perfectly consist with human liberty, GOD'S universal agency with the agency of man, and man's dependence with his accountability; that man has understanding and corporeal strength to do all that GOD requires of him; so that nothing but the sinner's aversion to holiness prevents his salvation; that it is the prerogative of GOD to bring good out of evil, and that he will cause the wrath and rage of wicked men and devils to praise him; and all the evil which has existed, and will forever exist, in the moral system, will eventually be made to promote a most important purpose, under the wise and perfect administration of that ALMIGHTY BEING, who will cause all things to work for his own glory, and thus fulfil all his pleasure."

Among the refinements of Calvinism are to be ranked the distinctions of the SUBLAPSARIANS and the SUPRALAPSARIANS. The Sublapsarians assert that "God had only permitted the first man to fall into transgression, without absolutely predetermining his fall:" whereas the Supralapsarians maintain that "God had from all eternity decreed the transgression of Adam, in such a manner that our first parents could not possibly avoid that fatal event."

The doctrine of original sin, often set forth as peculiar to Calvin's system, is common to those of many Protestant sects. The followers of Calvin in Germany are called the reformed; but the doctrine of predestination is every day losing ground in that country. In France it is well known, most Protestants are Calvinists. Calvinism is the professed belief of the greatest part of the Presbyterians both of Europe and America; and of the Independents of every class in England and Scotland.

The great mass of the descendants of the early settlers of New England are Calvinistic Congregationalists: that is to say, they maintain the independence of every congregation or society of Christians, as to the right of electing a pastor or of governing the church. The present number of Calvinistic Congregational churches in New England is about fifteen hundred; and in the Middle and Western States there are about fourteen hundred and fifty; although the mode of church government adopted by some of them is, in some degree, modified by the " Plan of Union" with Presbyterians.

HUGUENOTS.

In French History this name was given in the sixteenth century to the Protestants or Calvinists of France. The writers of that time were not acquainted with the true derivation of this popular nickname, to which they assigned various absurd etymologies. It is undoubtedly a corruption of the German " Eidgenossen," signifying the Swiss confederates.

The Huguenots arose in the year 1560, and greatly increased to the year 1572, in the reign of Charles IX.; when at the feast of Bartholomew on the 24th of August, near eighty thousand Protestants were massacred in France, by the decree of this king. Twenty-six years afterwards, Henry IV. caused the Edict of Nantz to be passed, which enabled the Protestants to worship God agreeably to the dictates of their consciences. Their privileges were thus enjoyed by them to the time of the voluptuous and sensual reign of Louis XIV., when they were again persecuted, their churches destroyed, and thousands put inhumanly to death. From the best authorities it is said, that near one hundred thousand were driven out of their own country.

Vast numbers found an asylum in England, who brought with them the manufacture of silks, which was a great source of wealth to the government of England. Many found refuge in the United States, particularly in South Carolina; and their descendants are among the most respected of American citizens.

ARMINIANS.

The Arminians are those who hold the tenets of Arminius, a Protestant divine, born in Holland in the year 1560, and latterly a professor of divinity at Leyden.

Thinking the doctrines of Calvin in regard to free will, predestination and grace, contrary to the beneficent perfections of the Deity, Arminius began to express his doubts concerning them in the year 1591; and upon further inquiry, adopted sentiments more nearly resembling those of the Lutherans than of the Calvinists. After his appointment to the theological chair at Leyden, he thought it his duty to avow and vindicate the principles which he had embraced; and the freedom with which he published and defended them, exposed him to the resentment of those that adhered to the theological system of Geneva.*

His tenets include the five following propositions: *First*, That God has *not* fixed the future state of mankind by an absolute, unconditional decree, but determined, from all eternity, to bestow salvation on those whom he foresaw would persevere to the end in their faith in Jesus Christ, and to inflict punishment on those who should continue in their unbelief, and resist to the end his divine assistance. *Secondly*, That Jesus Christ, by his death and sufferings, made an atonement for all mankind in general, and of ev'ry individual in particular: that, however, none but those who believe in him, can be partakers of this divine benefit.

* Arminius's motto was a remarkable and a liberal one:—" A good conscience is a paradise."

Thirdly, That mankind are *not* totally depraved, and that depravity does not come upon them by virtue of Adam's being their public head, but that mortality and actual evil only are the direct consequences of his sin to posterity. *Fourthly,* That there is no such thing as irresistible grace in the conversion of sinners. And *Fifthly,* That those who are united to Christ by faith may fall from their faith, and forfeit finally their state of grace.

Thus the followers of Arminius believe that God, having an equal regard for all his creatures, sent his Son to die for the sins of the whole world; that men have the power of doing the will of God, otherwise they are not the proper subjects of approbation and condemnation; and that, in the present imperfect state, believers, if not particularly vigilant, may, through the force of temptation, fall from grace, and sink into final perdition.

The Arminians found their sentiments on the expressions of our Saviour respecting his willingness to save all that come unto him; especially on his prayer over Jerusalem, his sermon on the mount, and above all, on his delineation of the process of the last day, where the salvation of men is not said to have been procured by any decree, but because they had done the will of the Father, who is in Heaven. This last argument they deem decisive; because it cannot be supposed that Jesus, in the account of the judgment day, would have deceived them. They also say, the terms in the Romans respecting election, are applicable only to the Jews as a body, without reference to the religious condition of individuals, either in the present or future world.

The asserters of these opinions in Holland were vehemently attacked by the Calvinistic party, which was prevalent at the time; and in 1610, the Arminians addressed a petition to the States of Holland for protection, from which they derived the name of Remonstrants. In the year 1618, nine years after the death of Arminius, the synod of Dort was convened by the States General, and a hearing given to both parties. But the synod was succeeded by a shameful persecution of the Arminians. Benevelt lost his head on the scaffold; and the learned Grotius, condemned to perpetual imprisonment, escaped from his cell and took refuge in France.

Mosheim is of opinion that even before the meeting of the synod, it was agreed upon, that on account of their religious opinions, the Arminians should be regarded as enemies of their country, and punished accordingly. The storm some time after abated; and Episcopius, an Arminian minister, opened a seminary at Amsterdam, which produced able divines and excellent scholars.

There is no longer any particular sect to which the name Arminian is exclusively applied; but the opinions above stated are adopted in England, by one branch of the Methodists, who follow therein the views of their founder, Wesley, and by many individuals of the church of England, and other denominations. The articles of the English church have been represented by different parties as inclining both to Arminianism and Calvinism; and Whitby, and Taylor, bishop of Norwich, are among the most famous of her friends, who have maintained the Arminian tenets.

BAXTERIANS.

In ecclesiastical history, the name of Baxterians is applied to those theologians, who adopted the sentiments of Richard Baxter on the subject of grace and free will, forming a sort of middle way between Calvinism and Arminianism. They never formed, strictly speaking, a sect, and the name is now disused; nevertheless, similarly modified opinions are common among Presbyterians at this day.

With the Calvinist, Baxter professes to believe that a certain number, determined upon in the divine councils, will be infallibly saved; and with the Arminian he joins in rejecting the doctrine of reprobation as absurd and impious; admits that Christ, in a certain sense, died for all, and supposes that such a portion of grace is allotted to *every* man, as renders it his own fault if he does not attain eternal life.

Among Baxterians are ranked both Watts and Doddridge. Dr. Doddridge, indeed, has this striking remark: "That a being who is said not to tempt any one, and even swears that he desires not the death of a sinner, should *irresistibly* determine millions to the commission of every sinful action of their lives, and then with all the pomp and pageantry of an universal judgment condemn them to eternal misery, on account of these actions, that he may promote the happiness of others who are, or shall be, irresistibly determined to virtue, in the like manner, is of all incredible things to me the most incredible!"

Baxter, who was born in Shropshire, England, in 1615, was an extraordinary character in the religious world. He wrote about one hundred and twenty books, and had above sixty written against him. His "Saint's Rest" is a work with which every intelligent Christian, of whatever denomination he may be, should be familiar. Though he possessed a metaphysical genius, and consequently sometimes made a distinction without a difference, yet the great object of most of his productions was peace and amity. Accordingly his system was formed, not to inflame the passions and widen the breaches, but to heal those wounds of the Christian church, under which she had long languished.

As a proof of this assertion, take the following affecting declaration from the narrative of his own Life and Times: "I am deeplier afflicted at the disagreements of Christians, than when I was a young Christian; except the case of the infidel world nothing is so sad and grievous to my thoughts as the case of the divided churches! And therefore, I am the more deeply sensible of the sinfulness of those who are the principal cause of these divisions. Oh, how many millions of souls are kept by their ignorance and ungodliness, and deluded by faction, as if it were true religion. How is the conversion of infidels hindered, Christ and religion heinously dishonored! The contentions between the Greek church and the Roman, the Papists and the Protestants, the Lutherans and the Calvinists, have woefully hindered the kingdom of Christ!"

ANTINOMIANS.

The Antinomian derives his name from two Greek words, Αντι, against, and Νομος, a law; his favorite tenet being, that the law is not a rule of life to believers. It is not easy to ascertain what he means by this position. But he seems to carry the doctrine of the imputed righteousness of Christ, and of salvation by faith without works, to such lengths as to injure, if not wholly destroy, the obligation to moral obedience.

In controversial tracts, the Antinomians are sometimes denominated Solfidians, a term composed of two Latin words, *solus*, alone, and *fides*, faith; implying a contest for faith alone without the necessity of good works.

Antinomianism may be traced to the period of the Reformation, and its promulgator was John Agricola, originally a disciple of Luther. The Catholics, in their disputes with the Protestants of that day, carried the merit of good works to an extravagant length, and thus induced some of their opponents to run into the opposite extreme. Justification by faith, not necessarily productive of good works, and righteousness imputed to such a faith, are the doctrines by which the Antinomians are chiefly distinguished. This sect sprang up in England during the protectorate of Oliver Cromwell, and extended their system of libertinism much further than Agricola, the disciple of Luther. Cromwell himself, seems to have been strongly inclined to their doctrines. Some of their teachers expressly maintained, that, as the elect cannot fall from grace, nor forfeit the divine favour, the wicked actions they commit are not really sinful, nor are they to be considered as instances of their violation of the divine law; consequently they have no occasion either to confess their sins, or to break them off by repentance. According to them, it is one of the essential and distinctive characters of the elect, that they cannot do any thing displeasing to God, or prohibited by the law

Mosheim says of this sect: "The Antinomians are a

more rigid kind of Calvinists, who pervert Calvin's doctrine of absolute decrees to the worst purposes, by drawing from it conclusions highly detrimental to the interests of true religion and virtue."

MATERIALISTS.

Materialists are those who maintain that the soul of man is material, or that the principle of perception and thought is not a substance distinct from the body, but the result of corporeal organization. There are others called by this name, who have maintained that there is nothing but matter in the universe.

The followers of the late Dr. Priestley are considered as Materialists, or philosophical Necessarians. According to the doctor's writings, he believed,—

1. That man is no more than what we now see of him; his being commenced at the time of his conception, or perhaps at an earlier period. The corporeal and mental faculties, inhering in the same substance, grow, ripen, and decay together; and whenever the system is dissolved, it continues in a state of dissolution, till it shall please that Almighty Being, who called it into existence, to restore it to life again. For if the mental principle were, in its own nature, immaterial and immortal, all its peculiar faculties would be so too; whereas we see that every faculty of the mind, without exception, is liable to be impaired, and even to become wholly extinct, before death. Since, therefore, all the faculties of the mind, separately taken, appear to be mortal, the substance or principle, in which they exist, must be pronounced mortal too. Thus we might conclude that the body was mortal, from observing that all the separate senses and limbs were liable to decay and perish.

This system gives a real value to the doctrine of the resurrection from the dead, which is peculiar to revelation; on which alone the sacred writers build all our hope of a future life; and it explains the uniform language of the Scriptures, which speak of one day of judgment for all mankind, and represent all the rewards of virtue, and all the punishments of vice, as taking place at that awful day, and not before. In the Scriptures, the heathen are represented as without hope, and all mankind as perishing at death, if there be no resurrection of the dead.

The apostle Paul asserts, in 1 Cor. 15: 16, that "if the dead rise not, then is not Christ risen; and if Christ be not raised, your faith is vain, ye are yet in your sins: then they also who are fallen asleep in Christ are perished." And again, verse 32, "If the dead rise not, let us eat and drink, for to-morrow we die." In the whole discourse, he does not even mention the doctrine of happiness or misery without the body.

If we search the Scriptures for passages expressive of the state of man at death, we shall find such declarations as expressly exclude any trace of sense, thought, or enjoyment. (See Ps. 6: 5. Job 14: 7, &c.)

2. That there is some fixed law of nature respecting the will, as well as the other powers of the mind, and every thing else in the constitution of nature; and consequently that it is never determined without some real or apparent cause foreign to itself, i. e., without some motive of choice; or that motives influence us in some definite and invariable manner, so that every volition, or choice, is constantly regulated and determined by what precedes it; and this constant determination of mind, according to the motives presented to it, is what is meant by its *necessary determination*. This being admitted to be fact, there will be a necessary connection between all things past, present, and to come, in the way of proper cause and effect, as much in the intellectual as in the natural world; so that, according to the established laws of nature, no event could have been otherwise than it *has been*, or *is to be*, and therefore all things past, present, and to come, are precisely what the Author of Nature really intended them to be, and has made provision for.

To establish this conclusion, nothing is necessary but that throughout all nature the same consequences should invariably result from the same circumstances. For if this be admitted, it will necessarily follow that, at the commencement of any system, since the several parts of it, and their respective situations, were appointed by the Deity, the first change would take place according to a certain rule established by himself, the result of which would be a new situation; after which the same laws containing another change would succeed, according to the same rules, and so on forever; every new situation invariably leading to another, and every event, from the commencement to the termination of the system, being strictly connected, so that, unless the fundamental laws of the system were changed, it would be impossible that any event should have been otherwise than it was. In all these cases, the circumstances preceding any change are called the causes of that change; and, since a determinate event, or effect, constantly follows certain circumstances, or causes, the connection between cause and effect is concluded to be invariable, and therefore necessary.

It is universally acknowledged that there can be no effect without an adequate cause. This is even the foundation on which the only proper argument for the being of a God rests. And the Necessarian asserts that if, in any given state of mind, with respect both to dispositions and motives, two different determinations, or volitions, be possible. it can be on no other principle, than that one of them should come under the description of an effect without a cause; just as if the beam of a balance might incline either way, though loaded with equal weights And if any thing whatever—even a thought in the mind of man—could arise without an adequate cause, any thing else—the mind itself, or the whole universe—might likewise exist without an adequate cause.

This scheme of philosophical necessity implies a chain of causes and effects established by infinite wisdom, and terminating in the greatest good of the whole universe; evils of all kinds, natural and moral, being admitted, as far as they contribute to that end, or are in the nature of things inseparable from it. Vice is productive, not of good, but of evil, to us, both here and hereafter, though good may result from it to the whole system; and, according to the fixed laws of nature, our present and future happiness necessarily depends on our cultivating good dispositions.

Materialists deny any intermediate state of consciousness between death and the resurrection. Dr. Price and Dr. Priestley had a friendly correspondence on this article; and though Dr. Price was no Materialist, yet he did not believe in an intermediate state. Those who deny the existence of an intermediate state, are sometimes called Soul-sleepers. Mr. Locke suggests the idea of a certain unknown substratum, such as may be capable of receiving the properties both of matter and of mind, viz.: extension, solidity, and cogitation; for he supposes it possible for God to add cogitation to what is corporeal, and thus to cause matter to think. But, in spite of these philosophical speculations, the common man will exclaim with Sterne—"I am positive I have a soul, nor can all the books with which Materialists have pestered the world ever convince me to the contrary!"

NECESSARIANS.

That scheme which represents all human actions and feelings as links in a chain of causation, determined by laws in every respect analogous to those by which the physical universe is governed, is termed the Doctrine of Necessity. This doctrine has been attacked and defended with great zeal, in almost every period of speculative inquiry since the Reformation.

The inductive method of research, applied by Bacon and his contemporaries to the phenomena of nature, led very soon to the adoption of a similar method in reference to the phenomena of mind. The discovery, or rather the distinct re-assertion of the law of association, by Hobbes, and the ready solution which it appeared to furnish of states of consciousness, which, without it, would have seemed capricious and unaccountable, encouraged many philosophers to attempt its application to every province of the human mind. It is only in connection with this fact that the prevalence of Necessarian views in modern times can be adequately explained.

Without venturing an opinion on the merits of the question at issue, between the advocates of free will and of necessity, we are sufficiently assured of the historical fact, that the distinction between man and nature, between the actions of a self-conscious agent and the workings of blind, unintelligent powers, was considered by the great philosophers of antiquity as the groundwork of their systems of morality, and as involved in the very conception of moral science. It was natural that this distinction should be felt to be a barrier to the progress of the exclusively empirical psychology to which we have alluded. To the historians of man's nature, the necessity of his actions appeared in the light of an hypothesis which lay at the very foundation of their inquiries, precisely as the natural philosopher is compelled to assume the regular recurrence of the same outward phenomena under the same circumstances.

The psychologist considers the states of which he is conscious, merely as they are related to each other in time; and, thus considered, it seems to him a mere identical proposition to assert that all that can be known of them is the order of their succession. If their succession were arbitrary or uncertain, nothing could be known of it, and the science which he professes could no longer have an existence.

It is in this consideration, rather than in the dialectic subtleties by which the doctrine has been sometimes defended, that the real strength of the Necessarian lies. So long as he can maintain the merely phenomenal character of human knowledge, he can reduce his opponents to the dilemma of either denying the possibility of mental science altogether, or of admitting the existence of those uniform laws which are its only object.

In its relation to morality, the doctrine of necessity has been naturally considered to involve dangerous consequences. Attempts have been made by modern Necessarians to rescue it from this imputation. Sir James Mackintosh, in particular, has devoted some portion of his Dissertation to the explanation of the principal ethical terms, on the Necessarian hypothesis. Nothwithstanding the ingenuity of this effort, the student will probably find, on careful examination, that the great question at issue is left much in the same state as before.

Among the most distinguished writers on this subject are Liebnitz, the German philosopher, Jonathan Edwards, of whom we have already spoken, Lord Kaimes and Dr. Priestley.

Dr. Doddridge remarks: " Those who believe the being and perfections of God, and a state of retribution, in which he will reward and punish mankind, according to the diversity of their actions, will find it difficult to reconcile the *justice* of punishment with the *necessity* of crimes punished! And those who believe all that the Scripture says on the one hand, of the eternity of future punishments, and on the other, of God's compassion to sinners, and his solemn assurance that he desires not their death, will find the difficulty greatly increased."

The true law of necessity, so far as human conduct is concerned, is happily described by the tragic writer, Hill, in the following couplet:

"The first crime past impels us on to more;
Thus guilt proves *fate*, which was but *choice* before!"

How important, then, to shun the initiatory steps that lead to evil! What momentous consequences may hang upon what at first seems a trivial error or an amusing foible! It may be the first link to a chain which is to bind and paralyze the best impulses and energies of the immortal soul

CHAPTER VII.

DIFFERENT MODES OF CHURCH GOVERNMENT—THE EPISCOPALIAN, PRESBYTERIAN, AND CONGREGATIONAL, OR INDEPENDENT SYSTEMS—MEMBERS OF THE CHURCH OF ENGLAND, OR EPISCOPALIANS—TRACTARIANS OR PUSEYITES.

THERE are three modes of church government in Christian communities; namely, the Episcopalian, from the Greek word επισκοπος, signifying an overseer; the Presbyterian, from the Greek word πρεσβυτερος, an elder; and the Congregational, or Independent mode. Under one of these forms, or by a mixture of their several peculiarities, every Christian church is governed. The Episcopal form is the most extensive, as it embraces the Catholic, Greek, English, Methodist and Moravian churches.

Episcopalians have three orders in the ministry, namely: bishops, priests, and deacons. They have liturgies, longer or shorter; and they believe in the existence and necessity of an apostolic succession of bishops, by whom alone, regular and valid ordinations can be performed.

The Presbyterians believe that the authority of their ministers to preach the gospel and to administer the sacrament is derived from the Holy Ghost, by the imposition of the hands of the Presbytery. They affirm, however, that there is no order in the church, as established by Christ and his apostles, superior to that of presbyters; that all ministers, being ambassadors of Christ, are equal by their commission; that *presbyter* and *bishop*, though different words, are of the same import; and that prelacy was gradually established upon the primitive practice of making the moderator, or speaker of the presbytery, a permanent officer.

The Congregationalists, or Independents, formerly called Brownists from the name of their founder, are so called from their maintaining that every congregation of Christians, which meets in one house for public worship, is a complete church, has sufficient power to act and perform every thing relating to religious government within itself, and is in no respect subject or accountable to other churches.

Independents, or Congregationalists, generally ordain their ministers by a council of ministers called for the purpose; but still they hold that the essence of ordination lies in the voluntary choice and call of the people, and that public ordination is no other than a declaration of that call.

MEMBERS OF THE CHURCH OF ENGLAND, OR EPISCOPALIANS.

The term Episcopalian is generally applied to members of the church of England, although all denominations of Christians who have adopted the Episcopal system of church government, are equally entitled to the appellation. For the sake of convenience, however, we shall, in speaking of the American off-shoot from the established church of England, characterise it simply by the term Episcopalian.

The church of England broke off from the Romish church in the time of Henry the Eighth, when, as has been already related, Luther had begun the reformation in Germany. During the earlier part of his reign, Henry was a bigoted Papist. He burned William Tyndal, who made one of the first and best English translations of the New Testament. He wrote fiercely in defence of the seven sacraments against Luther, for which the Pope honoured him with the title of "Defender of the Faith." This title is retained by the kings and queens of Great Britain, even to the present day, though they are the avowed enemies of that faith, by contending for which he acquired that honourable distinction. Henry falling out with the pope, took the government of ecclesiastical affairs into his own hands; and having reformed many enormous abuses, entitled himself "Supreme Head of the Church."

The church of England was first reformed by law on the accession of Edward the Sixth; but many important points of doctrine and discipline were left untouched; and the enactments of Elizabeth, by which its whole constitution was finally settled, and it was made the established church, followed rather than preceded the expressed convictions of the nation.

The government of the church of England is episcopal, and the bishops sit in the House of Lords by virtue of the temporal baronies into which their benefices were converted by William the Conquerer. This constitution was subverted on the success of the great rebellion, and Presbyterianism established in its stead; but the Episcopal form was restored in 1660 with the return of Charles the Second. The established church of Ireland is the same as the church of England, and at the union of England and Ireland became one united church. It is governed by four archbishops and eighteen bishops. Since the Union of Ireland with Great Britain, four only of these spiritual lords sit in the house of lords, assembled at Westminster.

In Scotland, and other parts, since the Revolution, there existed a species of Episcopalians called Nonjurors, because being inflexibly attached to the Stuarts, who were then driven from the throne, they refused to take the oath of allegiance to the Brunswick family. They are, indeed, the remains of the ancient Episcopal church of Scotland, which was, after various fluctuations, abolished at the Revolution.

The church of England has produced a succession of eminent men. Among its ornaments are to be reckoned Usher, Jewell, Hall, Taylor, Stillingfleet, Cudworth, Wilkins, Tillotson, Cumberland, Barrow, Burnet, Pearson, Hammond, Whitby, Clarke, Hoadley, Jortin, Seeker, Butler, Warburton, Horne, Lowth, Porteus, Hurd, Horsley, Hooker, Sherlock, and Milman.

The articles of faith of the English church are thirty-nine in number; the substance of which was first promulgated in forty-two articles by Edward the Sixth, in 1543. Under Henry the Eighth a committee had been appointed for the formation of ecclesiastical laws, which was renewed under his successor; and in 1551. according to Style, Archbishop Cranmer " was directed to draw up a book of articles for preserving and maintaining peace and unity of doctrine in the church, that, being finished, they might be set forth by public authority."

From this and the details that follow, it seems that Cranmer composed the articles in their original form, with the assistance of Ridley and others. A great similarity in thought and expression may be traced between many of the articles, and the language of the Augsburg confession. The Eleventh Article (on justification) corresponds with what Cranmer had previously written on the subject in private memoranda.

There has been considerable question raised as to the authorities, from which the Seventeenth Article (on predestination) is derived; for while some persons have interpreted expressions in it according to the Calvinistic system, others have denied the justice of such interpretation, and have undertaken to show that Cranmer must have referred in the composition of the article to the writings and sentiments of Luther and Melancthon.

On the accession of Elizabeth these articles were remodelled by archbishop Parker, who omitted four of them, introducing four new ones, and altering seventeen. These were again revised by convocation in 1563, some alterations made, and the number reduced to thirty-eight.

The thirty-ninth was restored in a final review by Parker in 1571, and then imposed on the clergy for subscription. It is remarkable that in the manuscripts and earliest editions there is one important variation in the admission or rejection of the first clause of the Twentieth Article, the authority of which may be considered as virtually recognising and establishing it.

The following Creed, commenced by the council of Nice, A. D. 325, and completed by the second general council of Constantinople, A. D. 381, is used in the Protestant Episcopal Churches of England, and occasionally in those of the United States. It is usually called the

Nicene creed, and contains all the important points of belief, by which the church is distinguished:—

"I believe in one God, the Father Almighty, Maker of heaven and earth, of all things visible and invisible. And in one Lord Jesus Christ, the only-begotten Son of God. And born of the Father, before all ages. God of God, Light of Light, true God of true God, begotten, not made; consubstantial to the Father, by whom all things were made. Who for us men, and for our salvation, came down from heaven. And was incarnated by the Holy Ghost of the Virgin Mary; AND HE WAS MADE MAN: was crucified also under Pontius Pilate; he suffered, and was buried. And the third day he rose again, according to the Scriptures. And he ascended into heaven. Sits at the right hand of the Father. And he is to come again with glory to judge the living and the dead; of whose kingdom there shall be no end. And in the Holy Ghost, the Lord and Giver of Life, who proceeds from the Father and the Son, who, together with the Father and the Son, is adored and glorified; who spoke by the Prophets. And One, Holy, Catholic, and Apostolical Church. I confess one Baptism, for the remission of sins. And I look for the resurrection of the dead; and the life of the world to come. Amen."

The "Apostle's Creed," which is also received by Episcopalians, as "proved by most certain warrant of Holy Scripture," is as follows:

"I believe in God the Father Almighty, Creator of heaven and earth; and in Jesus Christ, his only Son, our Lord, who was conceived by the Holy Ghost, born of the Virgin Mary, suffered under Pontius Pilate, was crucified, dead, and buried; he descended into hell; the third day he rose again from the dead; he ascended into heaven, sitteth at the right hand of God the Father almighty; from thence he shall come to judge the living and the dead. I believe in the Holy Ghost; the holy Catholic church; the communion of saints; the forgiveness of sins; the resurrection of the body; and life everlasting AMEN."

It is believed by Episcopalians, that the Saviour, when upon earth, established a church, or society, of which he was the ruler and head, and with which he promised to be, till the end of the world. They believe, that, during the forty days in which he remained upon earth, after his resurrection, " speaking " to his disciples " of the things pertaining to the kingdom of God," he gave them such directions for the government and management of this society, or church, as were necessary; which directions they implicitly followed: and that, from their subsequent practice, these directions of the Saviour, whatever they may have been, are to be ascertained.

That this society might endure forever, say the advocates of this church, some provision must be made for the renewal of its officers, so that, when any were taken away, by death, their places might be supplied with suitable successors. That the Saviour made all necessary provision for these purposes, there can be no doubt; and that the organization which he directed his apostles to establish, was Episcopal, is easily susceptible of proof.

Throughout the Bible, different orders in the ministry are recognized or referred to. Under the Jewish dispensation, (which, be it remembered, was established by God himself,) there were the three orders of High Priest, Priests, and Levites. When the Saviour was upon earth, he was the visible head of the church,—the " Bishop and Shepherd of our souls,"—and the apostles and seventy disciples were the other two orders. After his ascension, the apostles became the visible heads of the church, the lower orders being Bishops, (called also Priests or Presbyters, and Elders,) and Deacons. When the apostles were called hence, their successors did not assume the name or title of apostle, but took that of Bishop, which thenceforth was applied exclusively to the highest order of the ministry, the other two orders being the presbyters (priests or elders) and deacons. Thus it has continued to the present day.

It is worthy of remark, that early writers have been careful to record the ecclesiastical genealogy or succession of the bishops, in several of the principal churches Thus, we have catalogues of the Bishops of Jerusalem, Antioch, Rome, &c.; though it does not appear that the presbyters and deacons of those churches were honoured with any similar notice. In like manner, catalogues of temporal rulers are preserved, when the names of officers subordinate to them are suffered to pass into oblivion. It is easy to trace back the line of bishops, by name, from our own day, up to the apostles themselves.

It is to be observed, that it is not only necessary that a church should preserve the true order in the ministry, but also that it retain the true faith. For a true faith and true order are both necessary to continue a church. All the heretical sects of the ancient church had the apostolic ministry; but, when they departed from the true faith, they were excluded from the communion of the church.

An external commission, conveyed by Episcopal consecration or ordination, is considered necessary to constitute a lawful ministry; and it is therefore declared, by the Church, that " no man shall be accounted or taken to be a lawful bishop, priest, or deacon, in this church, or suffered to execute any of said functions," unless he has " had Episcopal consecration or ordination;" and the power of ordaining, or setting apart to the ministry, and of laying on hands upon others, is vested in the bishops.

In the Church of England, there are Archbishops, Deans, and various other officers and titles of office; but these are of local authority, and do not interfere with the three divinely-appointed orders.

For a period of fifteen hundred years after the Apostolic age, say the advocates of this church, ordination by Presbyters was totally unknown, except in a few crooked cases, where the attempt was made, and followed by instant condemnation from the Church, and the declaration that they were utterly null and void. There was no ministry in existence, before the era of the Reformation, but that which had come down direct from the Apostles, that is, the Episcopal. This is admitted by nearly all the opponents of Episcopacy.

The Episcopal Church in the United States, agrees with that of England in doctrine, discipline, and worship, with some few unessential variations. Their Ritual, or Form of worship, is the same, except that some few parts have been omitted for the sake of shortening the service, or for other reasons. Changes became necessary in the prayers for Rulers, in consequence of the independence of the United States.

The different Episcopal parishes in every State of the United States, (except in some of the newly-settled parts of the country, where two or more states are united for this purpose,) are connected by a constitution, which provides for a convention of the clergy and lay delegates from every parish in the state or diocese. This convention is held annually, and regulates the local concerns of its own diocese, the Bishop of which is the President of the convention. The conventions of the different dioceses elect deputies to a general convention, which is held once in three years. Every Diocese may elect four clergymen and four laymen, as delegates, who, when assembled in general convention, form what is called the "House of Clerical and Lay Deputies," every order from a diocese having one vote, and the concurrence of both being necessary to every act of the convention. The Bishops form a separate House, with a right to originate measures for the concurrence of the House of clerical and lay deputies, each House having a negative upon the other, as in the Congress of the United States. The whole church is governed by canons, framed by the general convention. These canons regulate the mode of elections of Bishops, declare the age and qualifications necessary for obtaining the orders of Deacon or Priest, the studies to be previously pursued, the examinations which every candidate is to undergo, and all other matters of permanent legislation Deacon's orders cannot be conferred on any person under the age of twenty-one, nor those of Priest before that of twenty-four. A Bishop must be at least thirty years of age.

At the last general convention held in New York, there

were present twenty-one Bishops, and seventy-nine clerical and fifty-seven lay members. The whole number of clergymen at the present time is estimated at about twelve hundred.

TRACTARIANS, OR PUSEYITES.

This name has been given by their opponents to a school of theologians, members of the established Episcopal church in England, whose tenets have been set forth in a series of publications, known as the Oxford tracts, which began to appear about the year 1833—4. From one of the most able and indefatigable of the champions of the party, the Rev. Dr. Pusey, the advocates of these tenets have been also called Puseyites.

The main points, insisted on by them, according to their own accounts, are the following:

"I. The doctrine of Apostolic succession as a rule of practice; that is, First, That the participation of the Body and Blood of Christ is essential to the maintenance of Christian life and hope in each individual. Second, That it is conveyed to individual Christians, *only* by the hands of the successors of the Apostles and their delegates. Third, That the successors of the Apostles are those who are descended in a direct line from them, by the imposition of hands; and that the delegates of these are the respective presbyters whom each has commissioned.

"II. That it is sinful, voluntarily to allow the interference of persons or bodies not members of the church in matters spiritual.

"III. That it is desirable to make the church more popular, as far as is consistent with the maintenance of its Apostolic character."

The following memorandum, drawn up by Mr. Newman, one of the most distinguished members of the school, explains more fully the original intention and peculiar doctrines of the Tractarians:

"Considering, 1. That the only way of salvation is the partaking of the Body and Blood of our sacrificed Redeemer

" 2. That the mean expressly authorised by Him, for that purpose, is the Holy Sacrament of His Supper;

" 3. That the security, by him no less expressly authorised, for the continuance and due application of that Sacrament, is, the Apostolical commission of the Bishops, and, under them the Presbyters of the church;

" 4. That under the present circumstances of the Church of England, there is peculiar danger of these matters being slighted and practically disavowed, and of numbers of Christians being left or tempted to precarious and unauthorised ways of communion, which must terminate often in virtual apostacy;

" We desire to pledge ourselves, one to another, reserving our canonical obedience, as follows:

" 1. To be on the watch for all opportunities of inculcating, on all committed to our charge, a due sense of the inestimable privilege of communion with our Lord, through the successors of the Apostles; and of leading them to the resolution to transmit it, by His blessing, unimpaired to their children;

" 2. To provide and circulate books and tracts, which may tend to familiarize the imaginations of men to the idea of an Apostolical commission, to represent to them the feelings and principles resulting from that doctrine, in the purest and earliest churches, and especially to point out its fruits, as exemplified in the practice of the primitive Christians; their communion with each other, however widely separated, and their resolute sufferings for the truth's sake;

" 3 To do what lies in us towards reviving among Churchmen, the practice of daily common prayer, and more frequent participation of the Lord's Supper. And whereas there seems great danger, at present, of attempts at unauthorised and inconsiderate innovation, as in other matters, so especially in the service of our church, we pledge ourselves,

" 4. To resist any attempt that may be made, to alter the liturgy on insufficient authority; i. e., without the exercise of the free and deliberate judgment of the church on the alterations proposed:

" It will also be one of our objects to place, within the reach of all men, sound and true accounts of those points in our discipline and worship, which may appear, from time to time, most likely to be misunderstood or undervalued, and to suggest such measures, as may promise to be most successful in preserving them."

In regard to the charge of Romanism, so frequently brought against the Tractarians, we find in the first volume of the tracts, the following statement of " irreconcileable differences" with Rome :

" Be assured of this—no party will be more opposed to our doctrine, if it ever prospers and makes a noise, than the Roman party. This has been proved before now. In the seventeenth century, the theology of the divines of the English Church was substantially the same as ours is; and it experienced the fell hostility of the Papacy. It was the true Via Media: Rome sought to block up that way, as fiercely as the Puritans. History tells us this. In a few words, then, before we separate, I will state some of my irreconcileable differences with Rome, as she is; and, in stating her errors, I will closely follow the order observed by Bishop Hall, in his treatise on The Old Religion, whose Protestantism is unquestionable.

" I consider that it is unscriptural to say, with the Church of Rome, that ' we are justified by inherent righteousness.'

" That it is unscriptural to say, that ' the good works of a man justified do truly merit eternal life.'

" That the doctrine of transubstantiation, as not being revealed, but a theory of man's devising, is profane and impious.

" That the denial of the cup to the laity, is a bold and unwarranted encroachment on their privileges as Christ's people.

" That the sacrifice of masses, as it has been practised in the Roman Church, is without foundation in Scripture or antiquity, and therefore blasphemous and dangerous.

" That the honour paid to images is very full of peril in the case of the uneducated, that is, of the great part of Christians.

"That indulgences, as in use, are a gross and monstrous nvention of later times.

"That the received doctrine of purgatory is at variance with Scripture, cruel to the better sort of Christians, and administering deceitful comfort to the irreligious.

"That the practice of celebrating Divine service in an unknown tongue, is a great corruption.

"That forced confession is an unauthorised and dangerous practice.

"That the direct invocation of saints is a dangerous practice, as tending to give, often actually giving, to creatures, the honour and reliance due to the Creator alone.

"That there are seven sacraments.

"That the Roman doctrine of Tradition is unscriptural.

"That the claim of the Pope, to be universal Bishop, is against Scripture and antiquity.

"I might add other points, in which also, I protest against the church of Rome, but I think it enough to make my confession in Hall's order, and so leave it."

And Mr. Newman himself says: "Whether we be right or wrong, our theory of religion has a meaning, and that really distinct from Romanism. They maintain that faith depends upon the Church; we that the Church is built upon the faith. By Church Catholic we mean the Church Universal; they, those branches of it which are in communion with Rome. Again, they understand by the faith, whatever the Church at any time declares to be faith; we, what it has actually so declared from the beginning. Both they and we anathematise those who deny the faith; but they extend the condemnation to all who question any decree of the Roman church; we apply it to those only who deny any article of the original Apostolical creed."

Tractarians seem to insist that no vital Christianity can exist out of the pale of the Episcopal Church. "A church," says the British Critic, their principal organ in England, "is such only by virtue of that from which it obtains its *unity*—and it obtains its unity only from that in which it *centres*, viz: the Bishop. And therefore, all its teaching must be through the medium of the Episcopate, as is beautifully expressed in the act of the synod of Bethlehem, which the Eastern Church transmitted to the nonjuring Bishops.

"Therefore we declare that this hath ever been the doctrine of the Eastern Church—that the Episcopal dignity is so necessary in the Church, that without a Bishop there cannot exist any church, nor any Christian man; no, not so much as in name. For he, as successor of the Apostles, having received the grace, given to the Apostle himself of the Lord, to bind and to loose, by imposition of hands and the invocation of the Holy Ghost—by continuous succession from one to another, is a living image of God upon earth—and by the fullest communication of the virtue of that spirit who works in all ordinances, is the source of and fountain, as it were, of all those mysteries of the Catholic Church, through which we obtain salvation. And we hold the necessity of a Bishop to be as great in the Church as the breath of life is in man, or as the sun is in the system of creation. Whence, also, some have elegantly said, in praise of Episcopal dignity, that, as God himself is in the Heavenly Church the first born, and as the sun in the world, so is every Bishop in the Diocesan or particular church, inasmuch as it is through him that the flock is lightened and warmed, and made into a Temple of God. But that the great mystery and dignity of the Episcopate has been continued, by succession from one Bishop to another, to our time, is clear. For the Lord promised to be with us, even unto the end of the world; and although he be indeed with us, also, by other modes of grace and divine benefit, yet does He, in a more especial manner, through the Episcopate, as the prime source of all holy ministrations, make us his own, abide with us and render himself one with us, and us with him, through the holy mysteries of which the Bishop is the chief minister and prime worker, through the spirit."

Tractarianism has been often called a " sacramental religion," because of the extreme views of its supporters in regard to the efficacy of baptism and the administration of the Lord's supper. It must be confessed, however, that in defence of their views they quote the earliest and most revered authorities, and adduce numerous strong passages from the writings of Cranmer and Ridley, the composers of those Thirty-nine Articles, which may be said to lie at the foundation of the Protestant Episcopal church. Thus Ridley says: "As the body is nourished by the bread and wine, at the Communion, and the soul by grace and Spirit, with the body of Christ; even so, in baptism, the body is washed with the visible water, and the soul cleansed from all filth by the invisible Holy Ghost."

And Cranmer, the martyr, is quoted in behalf of the Tractarian view regarding baptism as follows: "And when you say, that in baptism we receive the spirit of Christ, and in the sacrament of his body, we receive his very flesh and blood, this your saying is no small derogation to baptism; wherein we receive, not only the Spirit of Christ, but also Christ himself, whole body and soul, manhood and Godhead, unto everlasting life. For St. Paul saith, as many as be baptised in Christ, put Christ upon them. Nevertheless, this is done in divers respects; for in baptism, it is done in respect of regeneration, and in the Holy Communion, in respect of nourishment and sustenation."

"Thus it is," says Bishop Doane of New Jersey, "that the bishops, doctors, martyrs of the Reformation, teach a 'religion of sacraments.' Such and only such, is the 'sacramental religion' which the men of Oxford preach. How can they do other, when it is written, in the words of Jesus Christ Himself, 'Verily, verily, I say unto thee, except a man be born of water and of the Spirit—he cannot enter the kingdom of God;' and again, 'He that eateth My flesh, and drinketh My blood, dwelleth in Me, and I in him?' When it is written, in the words of St. Paul, 'According to his mercy he saved us, by the washing of regeneration, and renewing of the Holy Ghost;' and again, 'the cup of blessing which we bless, is it not the communion of the blood of Christ? The bread which we break, is it not the communion of the body of Christ?'

When it is written in the words of St. Peter, 'Repent and be baptised every one of you, in the name of Jesus Christ, for the remission of sins, and ye shall receive the gift of the Holy Ghost;' and again, 'The figure whereunto even baptism doth now save us.' But let the whole subject be summed up in the words of Mr. Simeon. 'St. Peter says, 'Repent and be baptised every one of you, for the remission of sins,' and in another place, 'Baptism doth now save us.' And speaking elsewhere of baptised persons, who were unfruitful in the knowledge of our Lord Jesus Christ, he says, 'He hath forgotten that he was purged from his old sins.' Does not this very strongly countenance the idea which our Reformers entertained, that the remission of our sins, and the regeneration of our souls, is attendant on the baptismal rite.'"

"According to our church," says Dr. Pusey, "we are, by baptism, brought into a state of salvation or justification, (for the words are thus far equivalent,) a state into which we were brought by God's free mercy alone, without works, but in which, having been placed, we are to work out our own salvation with fear and trembling,' through the indwelling Spirit of 'God, working in us, to will and to do of his good pleasure.'"

And the following passage from the lectures of Dr. Pusey's celebrated co-labourer, the Rev. Mr. Newman, may be regarded as sufficient in imparting an idea of the views of the Tractarians upon the subject of justification:

"In the foregoing lectures, a view has been taken, substantially the same as this, but approaching more nearly in language to the Calvinist; namely, that CHRIST IN-DWELLING IS OUR RIGHTEOUSNESS; only what is with them a matter of words, I would wish to use in a real sense, as expressing a sacred mystery; and therefore I have spoken of it in the language of Scripture, as *the indwelling of Christ through the Spirit.* Stronger language cannot be desired, than that which the Calvinists use on the subject; so much so, that it may well be believed that many who use it, as the great Hooker himself, at the time he wrote his Treatise, meant what they say. For instance, the words of a celebrated passage, which occurs in it, taken literally, do most entirely express the doctrine on the subject, *which seems to me the scriptural and catholic view:* ' Christ hath merited righteousness for as many as are found in Him. In Him God findeth us, if we be faithful; for by faith we are incorporated into Christ. Then, although in ourselves we be altogether sinful and unrighteous, yet even the man which is impious in himself, full of iniquity, full of sin, him being found in Christ through faith, and having his sin remitted through repentance, him God beholdeth with a gracious eye, putteth away his sin by not imputing it, taketh quite away the punishment due thereto by pardoning it, and accepteth him in Jesus Christ, as perfectly righteous, as if he had fulfilled all that was commanded him in the Law; shall I say more perfectly righteous than if himself had fulfilled the whole law ? I must take heed what I say; but the Apostle saith, God made Him which knew no sin, to be sin for us; that we might be made the righteousness of God in Him. Such we are in the sight of God the Father, as is the very Son of God Himself. Let it be counted folly, or phrensy, or fury, or whatsoever, it is our comfort and our wisdom; we care for no knowledge in the world but this, that man hath sinned, and God hath suffered; that God hath made Himself the sin of man, and that men are made the righteousness of God.' "

"Justification, then," says Mr. Newman, in another place, "viewed relatively to the past, is forgiveness of sin, for nothing more can it be; but, considered as to the present and future, it is more; it is renewal, wrought in us by the Spirit of Him, who, withal by his death and passion, washes away its still adhering imperfections, as well as blots out what is past. And faith is said to justify in two principal ways:—first, as continually pleading before God; and secondly, as being the first recipient of the Spirit, the root, and therefore, the earnest and anticipation, of perfect obedience."

Upon the subject of transubstantiation, Dr. Pusey says: " We believe the doctrine of our Church to be, that in the

Communion, there is a true, real, actual, though spiritual, (or rather the more real, because spiritual,) communication of the Body and Blood of Christ to the believer through the Holy Elements; that there is a true, real, spiritual Presence of Christ at the Holy Supper; more real than if we could, with Thomas, feel Him with our hands, or thrust our hands into His side; that this is bestowed upon faith, and received by faith, as is every other spiritual gift, but that our faith is but a receiver of God's real, mysterious, precious gift; that faith opens our eyes to see what is really there, and our hearts to receive it; but that it is there, independently of our faith. And this Real, Spiritual Presence it is, which makes it so awful a thing to approach unworthily."

In defence of these views, the authority of Cranmer, the martyr, is quoted, who says: "Christ saith of the Bread, 'This is My Body;' and of the Cup He saith, 'This is My Blood.' Wherefore we ought to believe that in the Sacrament we receive truly the Body and Blood of Christ. For God is almighty, (as ye heard in the Creed.) He is able, therefore, to do all things, what He will. And, as St. Paul writeth, He called those things which be not as if they were. Wherefore, when Christ taketh Bread, and saith, 'Take, eat, this is My Body,' we ought not to doubt but we eat His very Body. And when He taketh the Cup, and saith, 'Take, drink, this is My Blood,' we ought to think assuredly that we drink His very Blood. And this we must believe, if we will be counted Christian men.

"And whereas, in this perilous time, certain deceitful persons be found, in many places, who, of very frowardness, will not grant that there is the Body and Blood of Christ, but deny the same, for none other cause but that they cannot compass, by man's blind reason, how this thing should be brought to pass; ye, good children, shall with all diligence beware of such persons, that ye suffer not yourselves to be deceived by them. For such men surely are not true Christians, neither as yet have they learned the first article of the Creed, which teacheth that

God is almighty, which ye, good children, have already perfectly learned. Wherefore, eschew such erroneous opinions, and believe the words of our Lord Jesus, that you eat and drink His very Body and Blood, although man's reason cannot comprehend how and after what manner the same is there present. For the wisdom of reason must be subdued to the obedience of Christ, as the Apostle Paul teacheth."

The Tractarians are charged with inculcating the necessity of dispensing religious truth with caution, not throwing it promiscuously before minds ill suited to receive it. What Oxford teaches may be presented, in a few words, from Dr. Pusey's Letter to the Lord Chancellor:

" In brief, then, my Lord, the meaning of our Church, (as we conceive) in these Articles, is, that the Scripture is the sole authoritative source of the Faith, *i. e.* of 'things to be believed in order to salvation;' the Church is the medium, through which that knowledge is conveyed to individuals; she, under her responsibility to GOD, and in subjection to His Scripture, and with the guidance of His Spirit, testifies to her children, what truths are necessary to be believed in order to salvation; expounds Scripture to them; determines, when controversies arise; and this, not in the character of a judge, but as a witness, to what she herself received."

" And in this view of the meaning of our Church, we are further confirmed by the Canon of the Convocation of 1571, to which we have of late often had occasion to appeal; the same Convocation which enforced subscription to the Articles.

"' They (preachers) shall in the first place be careful never to teach any thing from the pulpit, to be religiously held and believed by the people, but what is agreeable to the doctrine of the Old or New Testament, and *collected out of that very Doctrine by the Catholic Fathers and ancient Bishops.*'

" So have we ever wished to teach, ' what is agreeable to the Doctrine of the Old or New Testament:' and, as the test of its being thus agreeable, we would take, not our own private and individual judgments, but that of the Universal Church, as attested by the 'Catholic Fathers and Ancient Bishops.'"

"Nor do we, in this, nor did they, approximate to Romanism: but rather they herein took the strongest and the only unassailable position against it. Rome and ourselves have alike appealed to the authority of 'the Church;' but, in the mouth of a Romanist, the Church means, so much of the Church as is in communion with herself, in other words, it means herself: with us, it means the Universal Church, to which Rome, as a particular Church, is subject, and ought to yield obedience. With Rome, it matters not whether the decision be of the Apostolic times, or of yesterday; whether against the teachers of the early Church, or with it; whether the whole Church universal throughout the world agree in it, or only a section, which holds communion with herself: she, as well as Calvin, makes much of the authority of the Fathers, when she thinks that they make for her; but she, equally with the founder of the Ultra-Protestants, sets at naught their authority, so soon as they tell against her: she unscrupulously sets aside the judgment of all the Ancient Doctors of the Church, unhesitatingly dismisses the necessity of agreement even of the whole Church at this day, and proudly taking to herself the exclusive title of Catholic, sits alone, a Queen in the midst of the earth, and dispenses her decrees from herself. No, my Lord! they ill understand the character of Rome, or their own strength who think that she would really commit herself, as Cranmer did, to Christian Antiquity, or who would not gladly bring her to that test! What need has she of Antiquity who is herself infallible, except to allure mankind to believe her so?"

"Oh, that we knew," says Mr. Newman, "Oh, that we knew our own strength as a Church! Oh, that instead of keeping on the defensive, and thinking it much not to lose our remnant of Christian light and holiness, which is getting less and less, the less we use it: instead of being timid, and cowardly, and suspicious, and jealous, and panic-struck, and grudging, and unbelieving, we had a heart to rise, as a Church, in the attitude of the Spouse of Christ, and the Dispenser of His grace; to throw ourselves into that system of truth which our fathers have handed down, even through the worst of times, and to use it like a great and understanding people! Oh, that we had the courage, and the generous faith, to aim at perfection, to demand the attention, to claim the submission of the world! Thousands of hungry souls, in all classes of life, stand around us: we do not give them what they want, the image of a true Christian people, living in that Apostolic awe and strictness which carries with it an evidence that they are the Church of Christ! This is the way to withstand, and repel, the Romanists: not by cries of alarm, and rumours of plots, and dispute and denunciation, but by living up to the precepts and doctrines of the Gospel, as contained in the Creeds, the Services, the Ordinances, the Usages of our own Church, without fear of consequences, without fear of being called Papists; to let matters take their course freely, and to trust to God's good providence for the issue."

The Tractarians advocate a more reverential and careful observance of all the ceremonies and requirements of the church, and especially a more frequent participation of the Lord's Supper. Their peculiar views appear to have gained ground rapidly among the clergy of the established church in England; and they have, in this country, numerous adherents. Much controversy has grown, and is still likely to grow, out of the agitation of the opinions which they have revived or originated.

CHAPTER VIII.

WESLEYAN, OR EPISCOPAL METHODISTS—WHITEFIELD METHODISTS—PROTESTANT AND INDEPENDENT METHODISTS—MORAVIANS.

EPISCOPAL METHODISTS.

The body of Christians to whom the name of Methodists is chiefly applied, are the followers of the late John Wesley, the founder of this numerous sect; hence called Wesleyan Methodists. But the term bears a more extensive meaning, being applied also to several bodies or sections of Christians, who have seceded or withdrawn from the Wesleyan denomination.

The origin of the Methodist Society took place at Oxford in 1729. After the Revolution, when the principles of religious toleration were recognised amid the progress of free inquiry, the clergy of the Established Church were thought by some to have sunk into a state of comparative lukewarmness and indifference. This alleged indifference was observed with pain by John Wesley and his brother Charles, when students at the University of Oxford; and being joined by a few of their fellow-students who were intended for the ministry in the Established Church, they formed the most rigid and severe rules for the regulation of their time and studies, for reading the Scriptures, for self-examination, and other religious exercises. The ardent piety and austere observance of system in everything connected with the new opinions displayed by the Wesleys and their adherents, as well as in their college studies, which they never neglected, attracted the notice and excited the jeers of the various members of the University, and gained for them the appellation of *Methodists*; in allusion to the *Methodoci*, a class of physicians at Rome, who practiced only by theory.

In the meantime, Wesley took orders in the Established Church, and acted for a few months as assistant to his father, who was rector of Epworth, in Lincolnshire. After the death of the latter, he was induced (1735), in company with his brother Charles and two other friends, to accept of an offer to go to Georgia, in North America, to preach the gospel to the Indians. On his return to England in 1737, Wesley officiated in several of the established churches. But the higher ranks were offended at his declamatory and enthusiastic mode of preaching; and the clergy having disclaimed some of his doctrines, the churches in general were soon shut against him. It was his desire, however, to be allowed to officiate in the pulpit of his native church. His object, in truth, was to effect a reformation in the church, not to recede from connexion with it; and the rules he observed himself, and imposed upon his followers, were designed as supplementary to the established ritual, not as superseding it. But the circumstances to which we have referred threw his labours into a different and ultimately an opposite channel; and, in short, without having at first intended it, he became the founder of the most numerous class of Dissenters in Great Britain.

Being thus virtually excluded from the Established Church, he preached in dissenting chapels in London and other places where he could obtain admission. In course of time, and owing to the vast multitudes that crowded to listen to his ministrations, he adopted the expedient of officiating in the open air, and commenced field-preacher. He first formed his followers into a separate society in 1738, the year after his return from America, though he referred the establishment of Methodism to a prior date.

From this period, Wesley devoted his time and his great talents exclusively to the propagation of what he regarded the doctrines of the Gospel, and to the extension of that sect, of which he was the founder. His labours were chiefly confined to England; but he also paid visits to Scotland and Ireland, in the former of which his success was inconsiderable. But while he confined his own labours to Great Britain and Ireland, he was not inattentive to the spiritual necessities of other countries, and by means of a succession of missionaries, propagated his doctrines to a very great extent in America and many of the West India Islands.

The unparalleled success which attended his great missionary exertions was not gained without much obloquy and persecution, particularly in the United Kingdom. Owing to the intelligence and liberality of the age, neither himself nor any of his missionaries were exposed to stripes and imprisonment; but all of them met with violent opposition on the part, not merely of the clergymen, both Established and Dissenting, and the wealthier classes, but also of the people; and some of them were beset with mobs, assailed by showers of stones and other missiles, and sometimes dragged through the streets as raving enthusiasts and as disturbers of the public peace.

Finding his societies rapidly increasing, and having been refused assistance from the established clergy, Wesley was induced to have recourse to lay preachers; an expedient which he was at first exceedingly adverse to adopt, but which he afterwards found most efficient in promoting the triumph of his views. He was thus enabled to exercise superintendance over all his followers, and greatly to extend his sphere of action.

Like Luther, he knew the importance of the press, and kept it teeming with his publications. His itinerant preachers were good agents for their circulation. "Carry them with you through every round," he would say; "exert yourselves in this; be not ashamed, be not weary, leave no stone unturned." His works, including abridgments and translations, amounted to about two hundred volumes. These comprise treatises on almost every subject of divinity, poetry, music, history, natural, moral, metaphysical, and political philosophy. He wrote as he preached, *ad populum;* and his works have given to his people, especially in Great Britain, an elevated tone of intelligence as well as of piety. He may, indeed, be considered the leader in those exertions which are now being made for the popular diffusion of knowledge.

"The wonder of his character," said Robert Hall, "is the self-control by which he preserved himself calm, while he kept all in excitement around him. He was the last man to be infected by fanaticism. His writings abound in statements of preternatural circumstances; but it must be remembered that his faults in these respects were those of his age, while his virtues were peculiarly his own."

Though of a feeble constitution, the regularity of his habits, sustained through a life of great exertions and vicissitudes, produced a vigour and equanimity which are seldom the accompaniments of a laborious mind or of a distracted life. "I do not remember," he says, "to have felt lowness of spirits one quarter of an hour since I was born." "Ten thousand cares are no more weight to my mind than ten thousand hairs are to my head." "I have never lost a night's sleep in my life." His face was remarkably fine, his complexion fresh to the last week of his life, and his eyes quick, keen, and active. He ceased not his labours till death. After the eightieth year of his age, he visited Holland twice. At the end of his eighty-second, he says, "I am never tired (such is the goodness of God) either with writing, preaching, or travelling." He preached under trees which he had planted himself, at Kingswood. He outlived most of his first disciples and preachers, and stood up, mighty in intellect and labours, among the second and third generations of his people. In his later years persecution had subsided; he was every where received as a patriarch, and sometimes excited, by his arrival in towns and cities, an interest "such as the presence of the king himself would produce." He attracted the largest assemblies, perhaps, which were ever congregated for religious instruction, being estimated sometimes at more than *thirty thousand!* . Great intellectually, morally, and physically, he at length died, in the eighty-eighth year of his age and sixty-fifth of his ministry, unquestionably one of the most extraordinary men of any age.

Nearly one hundred and forty thousand members, upward of five hundred itinerant, and more than one thousand local preachers, were connected with him when he died.

Wesley objected to his adherents being called Dissenters, and required them to attend the Established church of England when they had no opportunity of hearing their own preachers. His creed is Arminian, and differs, therefore, from the system of Calvin in regard to predestination, election, and the extent of the atonement, which he maintained was for all men. He held that repentance preceded faith. He taught, that by virtue of the blood of Christ, and the operation of the Holy Spirit, it was the privilege of Christians to arrive at that maturity in grace and participation of the Divine nature which excludes sin from the heart, and fills it with perfect love to God and men. Wesley and his followers, we may here observe, continued, long after their separation from the church of England, to read the service of that church, although they adopted a system of government quite distinct; forming themselves into an independent church, under the direction of bishops, elders and preachers, according to the forms of ordination annexed to their Prayer-Book, and the regulations which are laid down in their forms of discipline.

Wesley accustomed all his congregations to his plan of itinerancy, and a frequent change of ministers. A general conference annually fix the station of the itinerant preachers, who are supported from a common fund. This "conference" is generally composed of preachers elected at previous district meetings to be their representatives; of the superintendents of the circuits, and of every minister of the denomination, who chooses to attend. From this body all authority emanates, and by them all regulations to be observed throughout the whole Methodist connexion are formed. In their name are levied all the funds required for carrying on the operations of the body; and in their name ministers are appointed to their respective stations.

The Episcopal Methodists form an extremely numerous and influential body both in England and the United States.

In 1843, their whole number of ministers in the latter country amounted to about twelve thousand; and the number of communicants was estimated at 1,068,525.

The missionary labours of this sect have been liberal and important. In 1840, the English Wesleyans had, in the West Indies, fifty missionary stations; in British North America, eighty-four stations; in Asia, twenty-two; in the South Seas, twenty-five; in Africa, thirty-one; and in Europe, forty-two stations. In all these countries, the society had two hundred and fifty-four stations, six hundred and twenty-three missionaries and teachers, seventy-two thousand seven hundred and twenty-four communicants, and fifty-six thousand five hundred and twenty-two scholars.

The U. S. Episcopal Methodist Society, in Foreign missions, have sixty-three missionaries, four thousand three hundred and seventeen church members. Domestic missions—one hundred and seventy-eight missionaries, forty-one thousand church members. Total—two hundred and forty-one missionaries, forty-five thousand three hundred and seventeen church members.

The whole amount of missionary money collected for the year ending April 20, 1842, was one hundred and five thousand two hundred and eighty-one dollars; expended, one hundred and forty-nine thousand and sixty-five dollars.

WHITEFIELD METHODISTS.

Various off-shoots have taken place from the Wesleyan Methodists at various times: among the most important of which may be reckoned the followers of Whitefield, formerly the coadjutor, and afterwards the most powerful and eloquent opponent of Wesley, and supporter of Calvinism.

George Whitefield was born in 1714 at Gloucester in England, where his mother kept the Bell Inn. He entered as servitor at Pembroke College, Oxford, and was ordained at the proper age by Benson, bishop of Gloucester

He early adopted the custom of field-preaching, which Wesley had introduced, and drew around him multitudes of hearers. In 1738, he visited America. In all his public discourses, he insisted largely on the necessity of regeneration. He maintained, that the form of ecclesiastical worship and prayer, whether taken from the Book of Common Prayer, or poured forth extemporaneously, was a matter of indifference; and accordingly made use of both forms.

During a ministry of thirty-four years Whitefield crossed the Atlantic thirteen times, and preached more than eighteen thousand sermons. Bold, fervent, and popular in his eloquence, no other uninspired man ever preached to so large assemblies, or enforced the simple truths of the gospel by motives so persuasive and awful, and with an influence so powerful on the hearts of his hearers. He died at Newburyport in Massachusetts of asthma, September 30, 1770.

Few preachers ever were more devoid of the spirit of sectarianism than Whitefield. His only object seemed to be to " preach Christ and him crucified." The following anecdote serves to illustrate this feature of his character. One day, while preaching from the balcony of the courthouse, in Philadelphia, he cried out, " Father Abraham, who have you got in heaven; any Episcopalians?" " No!" " Any Presbyterians?" " No!" " Any Baptists?" " No!" " Have you any Methodists there?" " No!" " Have you any Independents, or Seceders?" " No! No!" " Why, who have you, then?" " We don't know those names here; all that are here are Christians—believers in Christ—men who overcome by the blood of the Lamb, and the word of his testimony!" " O, this is the case? then God help me—God help us all—to forget party names, and to become Christians in deed and in truth."

It will be seen from this that the followers of Whitefield are Independents in their notions of church discipline; and that they regard as matters of small moment all forms and ceremonies. Indeed they can hardly be said to exist at the present day as a distinct sect; although the influence of Whitefield's preaching is still widely felt in the United States.

PROTESTANT METHODISTS.

In England, the " New Methodists," as they are called, separated from the original Methodists in 1797. The grounds of this separation they declare to be church government, and not doctrines, as affirmed by some of their opponents. They object to the old Methodists, for having formed a hierarchy or priestly corporation; and say, that in so doing, they have robbed the people of those privileges, which, as members of a Christian church, they are entitled to by reason and Scripture. The New Methodists have, therefore, attempted to establish every part of their church government on popular principles, and profess to have united as much as possible the ministers and people in every department of it.

In the United States, the seceders from the Methodist Episcopal church are known as Protestant Methodists. They adhere to the Wesleyan doctrines, but discard certain parts of the discipline, particularly those concerning episcopacy and the manner of constituting the general conference. They separated from the Methodist Episcopal Church in 1830, and formed a constitution and discipline of their own.

The following preamble and articles precede the constitution :—

" We, the representatives of the associated Methodist churches, in general convention assembled, acknowledging the Lord Jesus Christ as the only HEAD of the church, and the word of God as the sufficient rule of faith and practice, in all things pertaining to godliness, and being fully persuaded that the representative form of church government is the most scriptural, the best suited to our condition, and most congenial to our views and feelings as fellow-citizens with the saints, and of the household of God; and whereas, a written constitution, establishing the form of government, and securing to the ministers and members of the church their rights and privileges, is the best safeguard of Christian liberty. We, therefore, trusting in the protection of Almighty God, and acting in the name and by the authority of our constitution, do ordain and establish, and agree to be governed by, the following elementary principles and constitution:—

" 1. A Christian church is a society of believers in Jesus Christ, and is a divine institution.

" 2. Christ is the only Head of the church, and the word of God the only rule of faith and conduct.

" 3. No person who loves the Lord Jesus Christ, and obeys the gospel of God our Saviour, ought to be deprived of church membership.

" 4. Every man has an inalienable right to private judgment in matters of religion, and an equal right to express his opinion in any way which will not violate the laws of God, or the rights of his fellow men.

" 5. Church trials should be conducted on gospel principles only; and no minister or member should be excommunicated except for immorality, the propagation of unchristian doctrines, or for the neglect of duties enjoined by the word of God.

" 6. The pastoral or ministerial office and duties are of divine appointment, and all elders in the church of God are equal; but ministers are forbidden to be lords over God's heritage, or to have dominion over the faith of the saints.

" 7. The church has a right to form and enforce such rules and regulations only as are in accordance with the holy Scriptures, and may be necessary or have a tendency to carry into effect the great system of practical Christianity.

" 8. Whatever power may be necessary to the formation of rules and regulations, is inherent in the ministers and members of the church; but so much of that power may be delegated, from time to time, upon a plan of representation, as they may judge necessary and proper.

" 9. It is the duty of all ministers and members of the

church, to maintain godliness, and to oppose all moral evil.

"10. It is obligatory on ministers of the gospel to be faithful in the discharge of their pastoral and ministerial duties, and it is also obligatory on the members to esteem ministers highly for their works' sake, and to render them a righteous compensation for their labours.

"11. The church ought to secure to all her official bodies the necessary authority for the purposes of good government; but she has no right to create any distinct or independent sovereignties."

This society is rapidly increasing especially in the middle states of the Union. It has twenty-one annual conferences in as many states; nearly four hundred travelling and a large number of unstationed ministers. They have a general conference which meets once in four years, consisting of two delegates from every thousand communicants, one a minister and the other a layman. This is their legislative body. The number of communicants is about sixty-five thousand.

MORAVIANS.

This denomination assert that they are descended from the ancient stock of the old Bohemian and Moravian brethren, who were a little church sixty years before the Reformation; and so remained, without infringement, till that time, retaining their peculiar ecclesiastical discipline, and their own bishops, elders and deacons. They derive their present name from the country where they first made their appearance; but they were originally called Fratres Legis Christi, Brethren of the Law of Christ; afterwards, Unitas Fratrum, the United Brethren; and finally, the Moravian Brethren.

Count Zinzendorf, a German, was the great supporter of the opinions of this sect. Having induced several Moravian families to accompany him, he formed an establishment in Upper Lusatia, about the year 1722, to which he gave the name of Herrnhut, signifying in German, "under the Lord's protection."

This society originally observed many of the outward acts of the Apostles, such as washing one another's feet, going barefoot, and having property in common, after the manner of a sect which arose one hundred and forty years after Christ, called the Apostolici.

The Moravians profess to adhere to the Augsburgh Confession of Faith, drawn up by Melancthon. They avoid discussions, however, respecting the speculative truths of religion, and insist upon individual experience of the practical efficiency of the gospel in producing a real change of sentiment and conduct, as the only essentials in religion. They believe in justification by faith alone through *grace* or *favour;* they avoid saying any thing on particular redemption, and do not call themselves either Calvinists or Arminians. They think they are spiritually joined to the great family of those who love and fear God. The order of their church is episcopal, and they are very particular as to those who are to succeed as bishops. They think episcopal ordination perfectly consistent with the patriarchal and apostolic institutions, because it was the order in the patriarchal churches; and the Apostle says, Acts i. 20: "*For it is written in the Psalms, let his habitation be desolate, and let no man dwell therein; and his bishoprick let another take.*" Phil. i. 1: "*to all the saints of Christ Jesus, who are at Philippi, with the bishops and deacons.*" 1 Tim iii 1: "*desire the office of bishop.*"

In their deliberations, which are conducted by synods after the custom of the first Christian churches, if any thing of very considerable importance be brought forward, the result of which is doubtful, they have recourse to the ancient custom of deciding it by *lot*, which they think is consistent with the Scripture, Jonah i. 7. " And they said every one to his fellow, come, let us cast lots, that we may know for whose cause this evil is upon us; so they cast lots, and the lot fell upon Jonah." Acts i. 26. " The lot fell on Matthias."

The Moravians consider the manifestation of God in Christ as intended to be the most beneficial revelation of the Deity to the human race; and, in consequence, they make the life, merits, acts, words, sufferings, and death of the Saviour, the principal theme of their doctrine, while they carefully avoid entering into any theoretical disquisitions on the mysterious essence of the Godhead, simply adhering to the words of Scripture. Admitting the sacred Scriptures as the only source of divine revelation, they nevertheless believe that the Spirit of God continues to lead those who believe in Christ into all further truth, not by revealing new doctrines, but by teaching those who sincerely desire to learn, daily, better to understand and apply the truths which the Scriptures contain. They believe, that to live agreeably to the gospel it is essential to aim, in all things, to fulfil the will of God. Even in their temporal concerns, they endeavour to ascertain the will of God. They do not, indeed, expect some miraculous manifestation of his will, but only endeavour to test the purity of their purposes by the light of the divine word.

What characterizes the Moravians most, and holds them up to the attention of others, is their missionary zeal. In this they are superior to any other body of people in the world. "Their missionaries," as one observes, "are all of them volunteers; for it is an inviolable maxim with them to *persuade* no man to engage in missions. They are all of one mind as to the doctrines they teach, and seldom make an attempt where there are not half a dozen of them in the mission. Their zeal is calm, steady, persevering. They would reform the world, but are careful how they quarrel with it. They carry their point by address, and the insinuations of modesty and mildness, which commend them to all men, and give offence to none. The habits of silence, quietness, and decent reserve, mark their character."

Where the Moravians form separate communities, they have many peculiar ceremonies and observances. Easter morning is devoted to a solemnity of a peculiar kind. At sunrise, the congregation assembles in the graveyard; a service, accompanied by music, is celebrated, expressive of the joyful hopes of immortality and resurrection, and a solemn commemoration is made of all who have, in the course of the last year, departed this life from among them, and " gone home to the Lord"—an expression they often use to designate death.

Considering the termination of the present life no evil, but the entrance of an eternal state of bliss to the sincere disciples of Christ, they desire to divest this event of all its terrors. The decease of every individual is announced to the community by solemn music from a band of instruments. Outward appearances of mourning are discountenanced. The whole congregation follows the bier to the grave-yard, (which is commonly laid out as a garden,) accompanied by a band, playing the tunes of well-known verses, which express the hopes of eternal life and resurrection; and the corpse is deposited in the simple grave during the funeral service.

The preservation of the purity of the community is intrusted to the board of elders and its different members, who are to give instruction and admonition to those under their care, and make a discreet use of the established church discipline. In cases of immoral conduct, or flagrant disregard of the regulations of the society, this discipline is resorted to. If expostulations are not successful, offenders are for a time restrained from participating in the holy communion, or called before the committee. For pertinacious bad conduct, or flagrant excesses, the culpable individual is dismissed from the society.

The ecclesiastical church officers, generally speaking, are the bishops,—through whom the regular succession of ordination, transmitted to the United Brethren through the ancient church of the Bohemian and Moravian Brethren, is preserved, and who alone are authorised to ordain ministers, but possess no authority in the government of the church, except such as they derive from some other office, being, most frequently, the presidents of some board of elders,—the civil seniors,—to whom, in subordination to the board of elders of the Unity, belongs the management of the external relations of the society,—the presbyters, or ordained stated ministers of the communities, and the deacons. The degree of deacon is the first bestowed upon young ministers and missionaries, by which they are authorised to administer the sacraments. Females, although elders among their own sex, are never ordained; nor have they a vote in the deliberations of the board of elders, which they attend for the sake of information only.

Some of the peculiar religious tenets of the Moravians may be thus summed up: 1. They hold, that creation and sanctification ought not to be ascribed to the Father, Son, and Holy Ghost; but belongs principally to the Saviour: and to avoid idolatry, we should look singly to Jesus as the appointed channel of the Deity. 2. That Christ has not conquered as God, but as man, with precisely the same power we have to that purpose. For as his Father assisted him, he assists us. The only difference is, it was his meat and drink to do the will of his Father who is in heaven. 3. That the children of God have not to combat with their own sins, but with the kingdom of corruption in the world. For the apostle declares, that sin is condemned in the flesh, Rom. viii. 3; and our marriage with it dissolved through the body of Christ, the Lamb of God, who has undergone this conflict once for all and instead of all.

The Moravians assert, that faith consists in a joyful persuasion of our interest in Christ, and our title to his purchased salvation.

They deny the Calvinistic doctrines of particular redemption and final perseverance.

James Montgomery, one of the most distinguished of the modern poets of England, is a member of this interesting sect.

The Moravians that first visited the United States, settled at Savannah, Ga., in 1735. Their descendants form a highly respectable body, and have been peculiarly active in spreading the knowledge of christianity among the North American Indians. All the Moravian missions are on a most liberal scale, and judiciously managed.

CHAPTER IX.

PRESBYTERIANISM—ITS ORIGIN AND PREVALENCE—THE KIRK OF SCOTLAND—AMERICAN PRESBYTERIANS—DIVISION INTO OLD AND NEW SCHOOLS—CUMBERLAND PRESBYTERIANS—DUTCH REFORMED CHURCH—GERMAN REFORMED CHURCH

In the introductory portion of the preceding chapter, we have given the meaning and derivation of the term *Presbyterian*. The supporters of this system contend that we nowhere read in the New Testament of bishops and presbyters or of pastors of different rank, in the same church; that all ministers of the gospel, being ambassadors of Christ, are inherently equal; and that deacons are laymen, whose sole duty it is to take charge of the poor.

The first Presbyterian church in modern times, was founded in Geneva, by John Calvin, about 1541; and the system was thence introduced into Scotland, with some modification, by John Knox, about 1560, but was not legally established there till 1592. For about a century from this date there was a continual struggle in Scotland between presbytery and episcopacy for superiority. The latter, which was patronised by the court, predominated in 1606; but was superseded by the former, to which the great body of the people were attached, in 1538. Presbytery kept its ground from this period till the revolution in 1660, when episcopacy again obtained the ascendancy, which it maintained till 1688; soon after which it was abolished, and the national church of Scotland declared presbyterian—a form which it has since retained. The most numerous bodies of dissenters from the Scottish established church, such as the Associate and Relief Synods, are also Presbyterians; their cause of secession being that the church had relaxed the strictness of presbyterian principles.

Presbytery has never flourished greatly in England. In that country the first presbyterian church was formed at Wandsworth, Surrey, in 1572, about twenty years before presbytery was established by law in Scotland; but though the system was never palatable to the English nation generally, an attempt was made to make the established church presbyterian in the reign of Charles I. This object was signally promoted by the famous Assembly of Divines at Westminster. In 1649, presbytery was sanctioned by the English parliament, and the established church was nominally presbyterian from this date till the restoration in 1660; yet it was never generally adopted, or regularly organized, except in London and in Lancashire. Upwards of two thousand presbyterian clergy were ejected from their cures in England, in consequence of the Act of Uniformity in 1662. There are still many congregations (about one hundred and fifty) in England, particularly in the northern counties, called presbyterian; some of them in full connexion with the Scottish church, others differing materially from that polity, while not a few of them have adopted nearly the same church government with the Independents. In Ireland, chiefly in the province of Ulster, there are about four hundred and fifty presbyterian congregations. There are upwards of one hundred such congregations in the British North American possessions; and presbytery has also been introduced to a greater or less extent in the other British colonies.

In the United States of America presbytery embraces upwards of twenty-eight hundred congregations, with two thousand ministers. The same system, though somewhat modified from that which obtains in Scotland, is the established church in Holland. It still exists, though to a very limited extent, in Geneva; it prevails also less or more in several of the other Swiss cantons.

THE KIRK OF SCOTLAND.

The constitution of the church of Scotland, which has long been the most perfect and efficient model of presbytery, is as follows: The kirk session is the lowest court, and is composed of the parochial minister and of lay elders, the number of whom varies in different parishes, but is generally about twelve. The minister is moderator *ex officio*. This kirk session exercises the religious discipline of the parish; but an appeal may be made from its decisions to the presbytery, the court next in dignity.

The presbytery, from which there is a power of appeal to the synod, is composed of the ministers of a number of contiguous parishes, varying in number in different cases, with a lay elder from all respectively. A moderator, who must be a clergyman, is chosen every half year. A presbytery generally meets once a month, but it must meet at least twice a year; and it may hold especial, or extraordinary, meetings. This court takes young men on trial as candidates for licence; ordains presentees to vacant livings; has the power of sitting in judgment on the conduct of any of its members, and can depose them; and has the general superintendence of religion and education within its bounds.

The number of presbyteries is at present eighty-two. The synod, which meets twice yearly, is formed of the members, both lay and clerical, of two or more presbyteries. At every meeting a moderator is chosen, who must be a clergyman; and a sermon is preached before the court proceeds to business. The number of synods is sixteen. The general assembly is the highest ecclesiastical court, its decisions being supreme. It meets annually in the month of May, and sits for ten successive days. Unlike the inferior courts, it consists of representatives chosen by the various presbyteries, royal burghs, and universities of Scotland. The number of representatives from presbyteries depends on the number of members of which each is composed. No presbytery sends less than two ministers and one lay elder; and none more than six ministers and three elders. The total number of members of the general assembly is three hundred and eighty-six, of whom two hundred and eighteen are ministers. This supreme court has of late consisted of more than this number, as the church has admitted the ministers of *quoad sacra* parishes as constituent members of ecclesiastical courts; but the civil law has not given its sanction to this measure: indeed the question is at present under judicial consideration.

The assembly chooses a new moderator yearly, who, in recent times, is always a clergyman. A sermon is preached before the opening of the court. The assembly is honoured with the presence of a nobleman as representative of the sovereign, under the title of lord high commissioner; but this high functionary takes no part in the proceedings of the court, except in opening and closing or dissolving its sittings, and has no voice in its deliberations. The assembly before its close appoints a commission, which is equivalent to a committee of the whole house, being composed of all the members of assembly, and one minister additional, named by the moderator. The commission meets quarterly; but may hold extraordinary meetings.

The income of the clergy, which may average about £250 yearly, including manse and glebe, is regulated by the state; and they are nominated to livings by patronage. They have no liturgy, no altar, no instrumental music. The Scottish presbyterians do not kneel, but stand in time of prayer; and in singing the praises of God they sit. The sacrament of the Supper is not administered in private houses to any person under any circumstances whatever. Pluralities have been prohibited; and the residence of clergymen within their respective parishes has always been imperative. Their creed is rigid Calvinism, and may be found embodied in the " Westminster Confession of Faith," of which the Andover creed we have already quoted in our account of the Calvinists, is a faithful transcript.

Dreadful scenes took place in Scotland previous to the establishment of Presbyterianism in its present form at the Revolution, and its confirmation in 1706, by the Act of Union between the two kingdoms. During the Commonwealth, Presbyterianism was the established religion, but, 'n the Restoration, Episcopacy was introduced in its room So averse, however, were the Scotch to the Episcopalians, and so harsh were the measures of the Episcopalian party, that the whole country was thrown into confusion. Leighton, the most pious and moderate prelate amongst them, disgusted with the proceedings of his brethren, resigned his archbishopric of Glasgow, and told the king: "He would not have a hand in such oppressive measures, were he sure to plant the Christian religion in an infidel country by them; much less when they tended only to alter the form of church government." On the other hand, Sharp, Archbishop of St. Andrew's, who had been an apostate from the Presbyterians, adopted violent measures, which terminated in his death. For in 1679, nine ruffians stopped his coach near St. Andrew's, assassinated him, and left his body covered with thirty-two wounds! On the monument of this unfortunate prelate, in one of the churches of St. Andrew's, is to be seen an exact representation in sculpture of this tragical event.

There has recently been an ominous dissension in the Scottish church caused by the secession of great numbers of the clergy, who oppose all political interference in their church affairs. The celebrated Dr. Chalmers, who has long been regarded as one of the main pillars of the establishment, is one of the leaders of the seceders of the "Free Church party." In abandoning their salaries, and throwing themselves upon the precarious chances of support from the people, the seceding clergymen have given the best proof of their sincerity and disinterestedness.

AMERICAN PRESBYTERIANS.

The Presbyterian denomination began its organized existence in America about the year 1700, and is the offspring of the church of Scotland. The first church of this order was organized in Philadelphia, 1703; the first presbytery 1704, and the first synod in 1716.

The Presbyterian churches are governed by congregational, presbyterial and synodical assemblies. The church session, which is the congregational assembly of judicatory, consists of the minister, or minister and elders of a particular congregation. A presbytery consist of all the ministers and one elder from every congregation within a certain district—three ministers and three elders constitutionally convened, being competent to do business. A synod is a convention of several presbyteries. The general assembly is the highest judicatory in the Presbyterian church, and is constituted by an equal number of teaching and ruling elders, elected by every presbytery, annually, and specially commissioned to deliberate and vote and determine, in all matters which may come before that body. Every presbytery may send one bishop and one ruling elder to the assembly: every presbytery having more than twelve ministers, may send two ministers and two ruling elders, and so, in the same proportion, for every twelve ministerial members.

The doctrines of the Presbyterian church are Calvinistic; and the only fundamental principle which distinguishes it from other churches of a similar belief, is this—that God has authorized the government of his church by presbyters, or elders, who are chosen by the people, and ordained to office, by predecessors in office, in virtue of the commission which Christ gave his apostles as ministers in the kingdom of God; and that among all presbyters, there is an official parity, whatever disparity may exist in their talents or official employment.

All the different congregations, under the care of the general assembly, are considered as the one Presbyterian church in the United States, meeting, for the sake of convenience and edification, in their several places of worship. Each particular congregation of baptised people, associated for godly living, and the worship of Almighty God, may become a Presbyterian church, by electing one or more elders, agreeably to the form prescribed in the book styled the Constitution of the Presbyterian Church, and having them ordained and installed at their session.

They judge that to presbyteries the Lord Jesus has committed the spiritual government of each particular congregation, and not to the whole body of the communicants; and on this point they are distinguished from Independents and Congregationalists. If all were governors, they should not be able to distinguish overseers or bishops from all the male and female communicants; nor could they apply the command, "Obey them that have rule over you, and submit yourselves; for they watch for your souls, as they that must give account." (Heb. 13: 17.) If all are rulers in the church who are communicants, they are at a loss for the meaning of the exhortation, "We beseech you, brethren, to know them that labour among you, *and are over you in the Lord*, and admonish you; and esteem them very highly in love for their works' sake."

If an aggrieved brother should tell the story of his wrongs to every individual communicant, he would not thereby tell it to the church judicially, so that cognizance could be taken of the affair. It is to the church, acting by her proper organs, and to her overseers, met as a judicatory, that he must bring his charge, if he would have discipline exercised in such a way as God empowered his church to exercise it.

Every Presbyterian church elects its own pastor; but, to secure the whole church against insufficient, erroneous, or immoral men, it is provided that no church shall prosecute any call, without first obtaining leave from the presbytery under whose care that church may be; and that no licentiate, or bishop, shall receive any call, but through the hands of his own presbytery.

Any member of the Presbyterian church may be the subject of its discipline; and every member, if he judges himself injured by any portion of the church, may by appeal or complaint, carry his cause up from the church session to the presbytery, from the presbytery to the synod, and from the synod to the general assembly, so as to obtain the decision of the whole church, met by representation in this high judicatory.

Evangelical* ministers of the gospel, of all denomina-

---

* This general title was originally assumed by the different Protestant sects of Germany, implying their reliance on the Bible alone as the

tions, are permitted, on the invitation of a pastor, or of the session of a vacant church, to preach in their pulpits; and any person, known properly, or made known to a pastor or session, as a communicant in good, regular standing, in any truly Christian denomination of people, in most of their churches, may be affectionately invited to occasional communion. They wish to have Christian fellowship with all the redeemed of the Lord, who have been renewed by his Spirit; but in ecclesiastical government and discipline, they ask and expect the co-operation of none but Presbyterians.

Most of the first settlers of New England were Congregationalists, and established the government of individuals by the male communicating members of the churches to which they belonged, and of congregations by sister congregations, met by representation in ecclesiastical councils. A part of the ministers and people of Connecticut, at a very early period of her history, were Presbyterians in their principles of church government. Being intermixed, however, with Congregational brethren, instead of establishing presbyteries in due form, they united with their fellow-christians in adopting, in 1708, the "Saybrook Platform," according to which the churches and pastors are consociated, so as virtually to be under Presbyterian government, under another name.

The Presbyterians are found chiefly in the Middle, Western and Southern States. The number of people attached to this form of church government in the United States is supposed to exceed two millions. Within the bounds of the church there are thirteen theological seminaries, three of which are under the care of the General Assembly. They have a board of education, which has about four hundred young men in training for the ministry.

Through the foreign missions and stations established or

---

rule of faith. It more especially designates the Lutheran church; but in the United States it seems to cover all Trinitarian sects. The word is compounded of two Greek words, signifying a messenger of good tidings; a gospel preacher.

occupied by this church, it is brought in direct contact with five different heathen nations, containing two-thirds of the whole human race. The annual expenditures of the establishment are about sixty-five thousand dollars.

The Presbyterian Domestic Board of Missions employs or aids two hundred and sixty missionaries and agents, who have under their charge about twenty thousand communicants, and twenty thousand Sabbath school scholars. The annual disbursements are about thirty-five thousand dollars.

In 1837, a division arose in the United States Presbyterian church, into Old and New Schools, in consequence of some not very essential variant views of doctrine and discipline. The friends of the New School were exscinded, or cut off, from the old church, but still claim to be the General Assembly of the Presbyterian church.

The "Cumberland Presbyterians," as they are called at the West, have formed themselves into an independent presbytery, and take their name from the district of Cumberland in Kentucky, where it was constituted.

As to their doctrinal views, they occupy a kind of middle ground between Calvinists and Arminians. They reject the doctrine of eternal reprobation, and hold the universality of redemption, and that the Spirit of God operates on the world, or as co-extensively as Christ has made the atonement, in such a manner as to leave all men inexcusable.

The Cumberland Presbyterians have about five hundred and fifty churches and ministers, and about seventy thousand members. They have a college at Cumberland, Ky.

DUTCH REFORMED CHURCH.

The Dutch Reformed churches in the United States are ancient and respectable. They are Calvinistic in their doctrines, differing in nothing essentially from the great body of Presbyterians. As they were immediately descended from the church of Holland, they were, for about a century after their establishment in America, in a state of colonial dependence on the Classis of Amsterdam, and the Synod of North Holland, and were unable to ordain a minister or perform any ecclesiastical function of the kind, without a reference to the parent country and mother church.

The origin of this church will lead us back to the earliest history of the city and state of New-York; for they were first settled by this people, and by them a foundation was laid for the first churches of this persuasion, the most distinguished of which were planted at New-York, (then called New-Amsterdam,) Flatbush, Esopus, and Albany. The church at New-York was probably the oldest, and was founded at, or before, the year 1639; this is the earliest period to which its records conduct us. The first minister was the Rev. Evarardus Bogardus. But when he came from Holland, does not appear. Next to him were two ministers by the name of Megapolensis, John and Samuel.

The first place of worship built by the Dutch in the colony of New Netherlands, as it was then called, was erected in the fort at New-York, in the year 1642. The second, it is believed, was a chapel built by Governor Stuyvesant, in what is now called the Bowery. In succession, churches of this denomination arose on Long Island, in Schenectady, on Staten Island, and in a number of towns on the Hudson River, and several, it is believed, in New Jersey. But the churches of New-York, Albany, and Esopus, were the most important, and the ministers of these churches claimed and enjoyed a kind of episcopal dignity over the surrounding churches.

The Dutch church was the established religion of the colony, until it surrendered to the British in 1664; after which its circumstances were materially changed. Not long after the colony passed into the hands of the British, an act was passed, which went to establish the Episcopal church as the predominant party; and for almost a century after, the Dutch and English Presbyterians, and all others in the colony, were forced to contribute to the support of that church.

The first judicatory higher than a consistory, among this people, was a Cætus, formed in 1747. The object and powers of this assembly were merely those of advice and fraternal intercourse. It could not ordain ministers, nor judicially decide in ecclesiastical disputes, without the consent of the Classis of Amsterdam.

The first regular Classis among the Dutch was formed in 1757. But the formation of this Classis involved this infant church in the most unhappy collisions, which sometimes threatened its very existence. These disputes continued for many years, by which two parties were raised in the church, one of which was for, and the other against, an ecclesiastical subordination to the judicatories of the mother church and country. These disputes, in which eminent men on both sides were concerned, besides disturbing their own peace and enjoyment, produced unfavourable impressions towards them among their brethren at home.

In 1766, John H. Livingston, D.D., then a young man, went from New-York to Holland, to prosecute his studies in the Dutch universities. By his representations, a favourable disposition was produced towards the American church in that country; and, on his return, in full convention of both parties, an amicable adjustment of their differences was made, and a friendly correspondence was opened with the church in Holland, which was continued until the revolution of the country under Bonaparte.

The Dutch church suffered much, in the loss of its members, and in other respects, by persisting to maintain its service in the Dutch language after it had gone greatly into disuse. The solicitation for English preaching was long resisted, and Dr. Lasdlie, a native of Scotland, was the first minister in the Dutch church in North America, who was expressly called to officiate in the English language.

The religious views of the Dutch Reformed church may be regarded as having been definitely embodied and promulgated at the Synod of Dort, of which we have already made mention. This synod was an assembly of Protestant divines convoked at Dort in 1618—19, by the States-General, under the influence of Maurice, prince of Nassau; and here the tenets of the Arminians on the five points relating to election, redemption, original sin, effectual grace and perseverance, were condemned by the adherents of Calvinism. Among the members of this assembly were ecclesiastical deputies from Switzerland, England, and Scotland.

It was at this synod, that the project of translating the Bible into Dutch was originated. The execution of the task was entrusted to some of the most learned men of the time; and, after the lapse of nineteen years, their labours were given to the world in what has since been known as the Dort Bible.

GERMAN REFORMED CHURCH.

As the Dutch Reformed church in the United States is an exact counterpart of the church of Holland, so the German Reformed is of the Reformed or Calvinistic church of Germany. The people of this persuasion were among the early settlers of Pennsylvania: here their churches were first formed; but they are now to be found in nearly all the states south and west.

The German Reformed churches in the United States, remained in a scattered and neglected state until 1746, when the Rev. Michael Schlatter, who was sent from Europe for the purpose, collected them together, and placed their concerns in a more prosperous train. They have since increased to a numerous body, and are assuming an important stand among the American Presbyterians.

This denomination is scattered over the Middle, Western, and Southern States, but is most numerous in the states of Ohio and Pennsylvania. The population of the church in the United States is estimated at three hundred thousand. It has one hundred and eighty ministers; six hundred congregations, and thirty thousand communicants.

CHAPTER X.

BAPTISM—PÆDOBAPTISTS—ANABAPTISTS—BAPTISTS—FREE-WILL BAPTISTS—SABBATARIANS—MENNONITES—DUNKERS—FREE COMMUNION BAPTISTS.

The rite of initiation into the community of Christians, ordained by Christ himself, when he commissioned his apostles to go and baptise all nations in the name of the Father, the Son, and the Holy Ghost, is called baptism, from the Greek word $Bαπτω$, I dip.

It is recorded by the Evangelists, that our Saviour himself received baptism from John; and the ceremony which the baptist performed is allowed generally to have been an imitation of a rite in common practice among the Jews, who appear to have admitted proselytes by circumcision and baptism. Lustration, however, by water, as an imitatory rite, is of great antiquity and general practice, especially in the East; and Christian Baptism may be considered as an adaptation of a form, which was generally understood to have a symbolical meaning. Accordingly, it has been recognised by all Christian communities as a sacrament, although they have differed in their explanation of its nature and meaning.

It is upon this point that the question of the validity of infant baptism principally depends; the words of Scripture in that particular, not being allowed on all hands to be decisive, nor even the practice of the early church universally admitted. Those, therefore, who consider baptism to be a symbol of a covenant thereupon entered into between God and the person baptised, require the understanding of the person to accompany the act, and reject the notion of sponsors undertaking to promise on the part of infants; the more common notion, however, conceives this sacrament to have in itself a regenerative virtue, by which an infant may be received into participation in the promises made to the church, and be really and truly from that time forth put into the way of salvation.

Baptism was originally administered by immersion, which act is thought by some to be necessary to the sacrament. It is not clear, however, even from the Scripture history, that this ceremony was always adhered to. At present sprinkling is generally substituted for dipping, at least in Northern climates.

Those Christians who hold that Baptism should be administered during infancy, are, in ecclesiastical language, termed PÆDOBAPTISTS, from the Greek παις, a child. Of course, nearly the whole Christian world, except the Baptists and Friends, are Pædobaptists.

All sects, which insist upon the repetition of baptism upon admission into their communion, from a notion of the invalidity of the religious ceremonies of other denominations, may be, properly speaking, called ANABAPTISTS.

BAPTISTS.

The denominations of Christians, who deny the validity of infant baptism, and maintain the necessity of immersion, are called Baptists. Some of them entertain Calvinistic and others Arminian sentiments. The Regular, or Associated Baptists, who constitute the most numerous body of Baptists in the United States, incline to the former doctrines.

Being Independent, or Congregational in their form of church government, the ecclesiastical assemblies of the Baptists disclaim all right to interfere with the concerns of individual churches. Their public meetings, by delegation from different churches, are held for the purpose of mutual advice and improvement, but not for the general government of the whole body.

The champions of this sect maintain that the word *baptise* signifies immersion or dipping only; that John baptised in Jordan; that he chose a place where there was *much* water; that Jesus came up *out of* the water; that

Philip and the eunuch went down both *into* the water; that the terms *washing, purifying, burying in baptism*, so often mentioned in Scripture, allude to this mode; that immersion *only* was the practice of the apostles and the first christians; and that it was only laid aside from the love of novelty and the coldness of our climate.

With regard to the *subjects* of Baptism, they allege that it ought not to be administered to children or infants at all, nor to adults in general; but to those only who profess repentance for sin and faith in Christ. Our Saviour's commission to his apostles, by which Christian baptism was instituted, is to go and teach all nations, baptising them, &c.; that is, not to baptise all they meet with, but first to examine and instruct them, and whoever will receive instruction to baptise in the name of the Father, and of the Son, and of the Holy Ghost. This construction of the passage is confirmed by another passage—" Go ye into all the world, and preach the gospel to every creature; he that believeth and is baptised, shall be saved." To such persons, and to such only, say the advocates of this sect, baptism was administered by the apostles and the immediate disciples of Christ; for those who were baptised in primitive times are described as repenting of their sins, and believing in Christ. See Acts 2: 38; 8: 37, and other passages of Scripture.

They further insist that all positive institutions depend entirely upon the will and declaration of the institution; and that, therefore, reasoning by analogy from previous abrogated rites is to be rejected, and the express commands of Christ respecting the mode and subjects of baptism ought to be our only rule. See Matt. 3: 5, 6, 11, 13—16; 20: 22, 23; 21: 25; 28: 19. Mark 1: 4, 5, 8, 9, 10; 11: 30; 16: 15, 16. Luke 3: 3, 7, 12, 16, 21; 7: 29, 30; 12: 50; 20: 4. John 1: 28, 31, 33; 3: 22, 23; 4: 1, 2. Acts 1: 5, 22; 2: 38, 41,; 8: 12, 13, 36 —39; 9: 18; 10: 37, 47, 48; 13: 24; 16: 15, 33; 18: 8, 25; 19: 4, 5; 22: 16. Rom. 6: 3, 4. 1 Cor. 1: 13 —17; 10: 2; 12: 13; 15: 29. Gal. 3: 27. Eph. 4: 5 Col. 2· 12. Heb. 6: 2. Pet. 3: 21.

Thus the Baptists claim an immediate descent from the apostles, and assert that the constitution of their churches is from the authority of Jesus Christ himself, and his immediate successors.

The following account from Robinson's History of Baptism, of a mode of administering the ordinance to adults, applies to the United States, as well as to England:

"The ceremony took place on a fine morning in May. About fifteen hundred people were assembled together. The late Dr. Gifford, teacher of a Baptist congregation in London, ascended a moveable pulpit placed in a large open court-yard near the river. Round him stood the congregation. People on horseback, in coaches, and in carts, formed the outside semi-circle. Many other persons sat in the rooms of the house, the sashes being open. All were uncovered, and there was a profound silence. The doctor first gave out a hymn, which the congregation sang. Then he prayed. Prayer ended, he took out a New Testament, and read his text—'I indeed baptise you with water unto repentance.' He observed that the force of the preposition had escaped the notice of the translators, and that the true reading was—I indeed baptise or dip you in water at or upon repentance; which sense he confirmed by the forty-first verse of the twelfth chapter of Matthew, and other passages. Then he spoke as most Baptists do on these occasions, concerning the nature, subject, mode, and end of this ordinance. He closed by contrasting the doctrine of infant sprinkling with that of the believer's baptism, which, being a part of Christian obedience, was supported by divine promises on the accomplishment of which all good men might depend. After the sermon, he read another hymn and prayed, and then came down. Then the candidates for baptism retired, to prepare themselves.

"About half an hour after, the administrator, in a long black gown of fine baize, without a hat, with a small New Testament in his hand, came down to the river side, accompanied by several Baptist ministers and deacons of their churches, and the persons to be baptised. The men came first, two and two, without hats and dressed as usual, except that instead of coats, every one had on a long white baize gown, tied round the waist with a sash. Such as had no hair had white cotton or linen caps. The women followed the men, two and two, all dressed neat, clean and plain, with gowns of white linen or dimity. It was said the garments had knobs of lead at the bottom to make them sink. Every woman had a long light silk cloak hanging loosely over her shoulders, a broad ribband tied over her gown beneath the breast, and a hat on her head. They all arranged themselves around the administrator at the water-side. A great number of spectators stood on the banks of the river on both sides; some had climbed and sat on the trees, many sat on horseback and in carriages, and all behaved with a decent seriousness, which did honour to the good sense and the good manners of the assembly. First, the administrator read a hymn, which the people sang. Then he read that portion of the Scripture, which is read in the Greek church on the same occasion, the history of the baptism of the eunuch, beginning at the 23d verse and ending with the 39th. About ten minutes he stood expounding the verses, and then taking one of the men by the hand, he led him into the water, saying as he went, ' See, here is water, what doth hinder? If thou believest with all thy heart, thou mayest be baptised.' When he came to a sufficient depth, he stopped, and with the utmost composure, placing himself on the left hand of the man, his face being towards the man's shoulder, he put his right hand between his shoulders behind, gathering into it a little of the gown for a hold: the fingers of the left hand he thrust into the sash before, and the man putting his thumbs into that hand, he locked all together, by closing his hand. Then he deliberately said, ' I baptise thee in the name of the Father, and of the Son, and of the Holy Ghost;' and while he uttered these words, standing wide, he gently leaned him backward, and dipped him once.* As soon as he had raised him, a

---

* It is worthy of remark that Mr. Robinson gives a different account of the mode of immersing the body among primitive Christians, which

person in a boat, fastened there for the purpose, took hold of the man's hand, wiped his face with a napkin, and led him with a few steps to another attendant, who then gave his arm, walked with him to the house, and assisted him to dress. There were many in waiting, who, like the primitive susceptors, assisted during the whole service. The rest of the men followed the first, and were baptised in like manner. After them the women were baptised. A female friend took off at the water-side the hat and cloak. A deacon of the church led one to the administrator and another from him; and a woman at the water-side took every one as she came out of the river, and conducted her to the apartment in the house, where they dressed themselves. When all were baptised, the administrator coming out of the river, and standing at the side, gave a short exhortation on the honour and pleasure of obedience to the divine commands, and then with the usual benediction dismissed the assembly. About half an hour after, the men newly-baptised, having dressed themselves, went from their room into a large hall in the house, where they were presently joined by the women, who came from their apartments to the same place. Then they sent a messenger to the administrator, who was dressing in his apartment, to inform him they waited for him. He presently came, and first prayed a few minutes, and then closed the whole by a short discourse on the blessings of civil and religious liberty, the sufficiency of Scripture, the pleasure of a good conscience, the importance of a holy life, and the prospect of a blessed immortality. This they call a public baptism."

he describes as follows :—" The administrator whether in or out of the water, stood on the right side of the candidate, his face looking to his shoulder. The candidate stood erect, and the administrator while he pronounced the baptismal words, laid his right hand on the hind part of the head of the candidate, and bowed him gently forward till he was all under water. Baptism was taken for an act of divine worship, a stooping and paying a profound homage to God. The baptised person raised himself up and walked out of the water, and another candidate followed, the administrator standing all the time erect in his place. The method hath more than antiquity to recommend it. It is so decent and expeditious, that it is a wonder it is not universally practised."

A more private baptism takes place after a similar manner in baptisteries, which are in or near the places of worship; thus every convenience is afforded for the purpose. This, indeed, is now the most common way of administering the ordinance among the Baptists, either with the attendance of friends, or in the presence of the congregation.

In the recently discovered theological work of John Milton, he shows himself an advocate of the notions of this sect in regard to baptism, in these memorable words: "Under the Gospel, the first of the sacraments, commonly so called, is Baptism, wherein the bodies of believers who engage themselves to pureness of life are immersed in *running* water, to signify their regeneration by the Holy Spirit, and their union with Christ in death, burial, and resurrection." Dr. Sumner, the translator, has this note on the passage: "*In profluentem aquam*—By the admission of this word into the definition, it is evident that Milton attributed some importance to this circumstance; probably considering that the superior purity of *running* water was peculiarly typical of the thing signified. Hence it appears that the same epithet, employed in 'Paradise Lost,' in a passage very similar to the present, is not merely a poetical ornament:

'Them who shall believe,
Baptising in the *profluent* stream—the sign
Of washing them from guilt of sin to life,
Pure and in mind prepared,—if so befall,—
For death, like that which the Redeemer died.'",
Book xii. 441.

Tertullian concludes differently, arguing that *any* water which can be conveniently procured is sufficient for the spirit of the ordinance. Milton was decidedly in favour of the *perpetuity* of baptism; using, however, these remarkable words: "Indeed I should be disposed to consider baptism as necessary for proselytes, and not for those born in the church, had not the apostle taught that baptism is not merely an initiatory rite, but a figurative representation of our death, burial, and resurrection with

Christ." Milton examines the passages adduced in behalf of infant baptism, showing their irrelevancy in this long, and often not over-charitable controversy.

In the year 1639, the celebrated Roger Williams formed the first Baptist church in America at Providence, R. I. From that time, the sect has multiplied exceedingly until it has assumed a commanding position among the religious communities of the country. In 1843, the Baptists numbered in the United States, eight thousand three hundred and eighty-three churches, five thousand three hundred and ninety-eight ministers, and six hundred and eleven thousand five hundred and seventy-seven communicants. They have increased astonishingly within a few years, and number among their clergy many men of pre-eminent abilities.

The missionary labours of the Baptists have been zealous, unremitting and liberal. The annual expenditure of the board of missions is about eighty thousand dollars. They have establishments among the North American Indians, and in West Africa, in Asia and Europe. No sect has done more, in proportion to their means, than the Baptists, towards evangelising the heathens.

FREE-WILL BAPTISTS.

The first church gathered, of this order, was in New Durham, N. H., in the year 1780, principally by the instrumentality of Elder Benjamin Randall, who then resided in that town. Soon after, several branches were collected, which united with this church; and several preachers, of different persuasions, were brought to see the beauties of a *free salvation*, and united as fellow-labourers with Elder Randall.

They believe that, by the death of Christ, salvation was provided for all men; that, through faith in Christ, and sanctification of the Spirit,—though by nature entirely sinners,—all men may, if they improve every means of grace in their power, become new creatures in this life, and, after death, enjoy eternal happiness; that all who, having actually sinned, die in an unrenewed state, will suffer eternal misery.

Respecting the divine attributes of the Father, Son, and Holy Spirit, they in substance agree with other Trinitarian Christians. They hold the holy Scriptures to be their only rule of religious faith and practice, to the exclusion of all written creeds, covenants, rules of discipline, or articles of organization. They consider that elders and deacons are the officers of the church designed in the Scriptures, and maintain that piety, and a call to the work, are the essential qualifications of a minister, without regard to literary attainments.

SABBATARIANS.

The Sabbatarians are a body of Christians, who keep the seventh day as the Sabbath. They are to be found principally, if not wholly, among the Baptists. The common reasons why Christians observe the first day of the week as the Sabbath, are, that on this day Christ rose from the dead; that the apostles assembled, preached, and administered the Lord's Supper; and that it has been kept by the church for several ages, if not from the time when Christianity was originally promulgated. The Sabbatarians, however, think these reasons unsatisfactory, and assert that the change of the Sabbath from the seventh to the first day of the week, was effected by Constantine, upon his conversion to the Christian religion.

The three following propositions contain a summary of their principles as to this article of the Sabbath, by which they stand distinguished:—First, That God hath required the observation of the seventh, or last day of the week, to be observed by mankind universally for the weekly Sabbath. Secondly,—That this command of God is perpetually binding on man till time shall be no more. Thirdly, That this sacred rest of the seventh-day Sabbath is not by divine authority, changed from the seventh and last to the first day of the week, or that the Scripture doth no where require the observation of any other day of the week for the weekly Sabbath, but the seventh day only.

There were several congregations of Sabbatarians at one time in the United States, particularly in Rhode Island and New Jersey. They differ only from the other Baptist sects in this peculiar notion respecting the Sabbath. They are sometimes called Seventh-Day Baptists; but, from the inconvenience of observing as the Sabbath a day different from that set apart by the great body of Christians, their numbers have gradually diminished, until they can hardly be regarded now as an important sect.

SIX-PRINCIPLE BAPTISTS.

By this name are called those, who consider that the imposition of hands subsequent to baptism, and generally on the admission of candidates into the church, is an indispensable pre-requisite for church membership and communion. They support their peculiar principle chiefly from Heb. 6: 1, 2—"Therefore, leaving the principles of the doctrine of Christ, let us go on unto perfection; not laying again the foundation of repentance from dead works, and of faith toward God, of the doctrine of baptisms, and of laying on of hands, and of resurrection of the dead, and of eternal judgment."

As these two verses contain six distinct propositions, one of which is the laying on of hands, these brethren have, from thence, acquired the name of "Six-Principle Baptists," to distinguish them from others, whom they sometimes call "Five-Principle Baptists." They have fourteen churches in Massachusetts and Rhode Island.

MENNONITES.

The Mennonites were a society of Baptists in Holland, so called from Mennon Simonis, of Friesland, who lived in the sixteenth century. Some of them came to the United States and settled in Pennsylvania, where a considerable body of them still reside.

The fundamental maxim of this denomination is, that

practical piety is the essence of religion, and that the surest mark of the true church is the sanctity of its members. They advocate perfect toleration in religion, and exclude none—unite in pleading for toleration in religion, and debar none from their assemblies who lead pious lives, and own the Scriptures for the word of God. They teach that infants are not the proper subjects of baptism; that ministers of the gospel ought to receive no salary; and that it is not lawful to swear, or wage war, upon any occasion. They also maintain that the terms *person* and *Trinity* are not to be used in speaking of the Father, Son, and Holy Ghost.

The Mennonites meet privately, and every one in the assembly has the liberty to speak, to expound the Scriptures, to pray, and sing.

The Mennonites in Pennsylvania do not baptize by immersion, though they administer the ordinance to none but adult persons. Their common method is this: The person who is to be baptized, kneels; the minister holds his hands over him, into which the deacon pours water, and through which it runs on the crown of the kneeling person's head; after which follow imposition of hands and prayer.

Mr. Van Beuning, the Dutch ambassador, speaking of these "Harmless Christians," as they choose to call themselves, says: "The Mennonites are good people, and the most commodious to a state of any in the world; partly, because they do not aspire to places of dignity; partly, because they edify the community by the simplicity of their manners, and application to arts and industry; and partly, because we need fear no rebellion from a sect who make it an article of their faith never to bear arms."

DUNKERS.

Conrad Peysel, a German Baptist, was the founder o the Dunkers about the year 1724. Weary of the world, he retired to an agreeable solitude, within fifty miles of Philadelphia, that he might give himself up to contemplation. Curiosity brought several of his countrymen to visit his retreat, and by degrees, his pious, simple and peaceable manners induced others to settle near him. They formed a little colony of German Baptists, which they call *Euphrata or Euphrates*, in allusion to the Hebrews, who used to sing psalms on the border of that river.

This little city forms a triangle, the outsides of which are bordered with mulberry and apple trees, planted with great regularity. In the middle is a very large orchard, and between the orchard and these ranges of trees are houses built of wood, three stories high, where every Dunker is left to enjoy the pleasures of his meditations without disturbance. Their number in 1777 did not exceed five hundred, and since that period they have not multiplied greatly. They do not foolishly renounce marriage, but when married they detach themselves from the rest of the community and retire into another part of the country.

The Dunkers lament the fall of Adam, but deny the imputation of his sin to posterity. They use *trine* immersion (dipping three times) in baptism, and employ the ceremony of the imposition of hands when the baptised are received into the church. They dress like Dominican friars, shaving neither head nor beard; have different apartments for the sexes, and live chiefly on roots and vegetables, except at their love-feast, when they eat mutton. It is said no bed is allowed except in case of sickness, having in their separate cells a bench to lie upon, and a block of wood for their pillow! They deny the eternity of future punishment—believe that the dead have the gospel preached to them by our Saviour, and that the souls of the just are employed to preach the gospel to those who have had no revelation in this life.

But their chief tenet is, that future happiness is only to be obtained by penance and outward mortification, so as that Jesus Christ by his meritorious sufferings became the Redeemer of mankind in general, so each individual of the human race by a life of abstinence and restraint may work out his own salvation. Nay, it is said they admit of works of supererogation.

They use the same form of government and the same discipline as other Baptists do, except that every person is allowed to speak in the congregation, and their best speaker is usually ordained to be a minister. They have also deacons, and deaconesses from among their ancient widows, who may all use their gifts, and exhort at stated times.

FREE COMMUNION BAPTISTS.

This denomination of Christians dissent from the regular Baptists, who hold that immersion is a pre-requisite to the privilege of a church relation. The Free Communion Baptists permit Christians of all denominations, in regular church standing, to partake with them at the Lord's table.

The Rev. Robert Hall, of England, one of the most learned and eloquent Baptist ministers of the age, was an unflinching opposer of the practice of " close communion :" which he denounced as " unchristian and unnatural." In a tract written in defence of his views on this subject, he remarks : " It is too much to expect an enlightened public will be eager to enroll themselves among the members of a sect which displays much of the intolerance of Popery, without any portion of its splendour, and prescribes, as the pledge of conversion, the renunciation of the whole Christian world."

In reference to the mode of baptism, Mr. Hall says : " I would not myself baptise in any other way than by immersion, because I look upon immersion as the ancient mode; that it best represents the meaning of the original term employed, and the substantial import of this institution ; and because I should think it right to guard against the spirit of innovation, which, in positive rites, is always dangerous and progressive ; *but I should not think myself authorised to baptise any one who has been sprinkled in adult age.*"

This class of Baptists are found chiefly in the western and northern parts of the state of New York. They number between forty and fifty churches and ministers.

CHAPTER XI.

QUAKERS, OR FRIENDS—GEORGE FOX AND WILLIAM PENN—HICKSITES—THE SHAKERS.

QUAKERS, OR FRIENDS.

This sect had its origin in England about the middle of the seventeenth century, and spread by the emigration of its members, who were exposed to many restrictions and persecutions, over various parts of Europe and North America. The founder of the sect was George Fox, who, being equally dissatisfied with the tenets of the established church and those of the Puritans, succeeded in attaching to himself various persons who agreed with him in the view which he took of the internal operations of religion on men's hearts, conceiving it to supersede all the observances of different denominations, and not to be evidenced in any degree by them.

The Quakers, therefore, reject both the sacraments; nor do they appoint any order of ministers, but consider the instruction and edification of their congregations to be the province of whatsoever person of either sex conceives himself to be impelled thereto at the time by an internal suggestion of the Spirit. Upon doctrinal points, however, they profess to maintain opinions coincident with those generally received by the orthodox. Their internal affairs are managed by yearly, quarterly, and monthly meetings. A similar arrangement takes place among the females of the society, who are allowed a considerable share in the management of the affairs of their own sex.

This society is distinguished in its intercourse with the world by great seriousness of deportment, uniform soberness in dress, and generally a scrupulous avoidance of everything which can encourage vanity and frivolity. They are all sensitively averse from all matters of ceremony, which they conceive to have their origin in flattery and deception. Their refusal to take judicial oaths used frequently in former times to subject them to very severe penalties.

Up to the accession of James II. their history is an unvaried series of persecutions; either such as they endured in common with other dissenters, or such as were peculiar to themselves in consequence of their refusal to pay tithes and to take oaths. Under James, the severity of the penal law was relaxed; but William III. was the first prince who enacted laws for the especial relief of the Quakers. From this time, their affirmation, as well in England as the United States, is received in lieu of oath in judicial proceedings; and an alteration in the method of levying tithes in the former country has been provided, by which their scruples are satisfied.

George Fox, the founder of this sect, was born in 1624, at Drayton, in Leicestershire, and was the son of a weaver, a pious and virtuous man, who gave him a religious education. Being apprenticed to a grazier, he was employed in keeping sheep—an occupation, the silence and solitude of which were well calculated to nurse his naturally enthusiastic feelings. When he was about nineteen, he believed himself to have received a divine command to forsake all, renounce society, and dedicate his existence to the service of religion. For five years, he accordingly led a wandering life, fasting, praying, and living secluded; but it was not till about 1648 that he began to preach his doctrines. Manchester was the place where he first promulgated them. Thenceforth he pursued his career with untirable zeal and activity, in spite of frequent imprisonment and brutal usage.

It was at Derby that his followers were first denominated *Quakers*, either from their tremulous mode of speaking, or from their calling on their hearers to " tremble at the name of the Lord." The labours of Fox were crowned with considerable success; and, in 1669, he extended the sphere of them to America, where he spent two years. He also twice visited the continent. He died in 1690. His writings were collected in three volumes folio.

The religion and worship, which Fox recommended, were simple and without ceremonies. He put forth few articles of faith, and insisted mostly on morality, mutual charity, and the love of God. To wait in profound silence for the influence of the Spirit, was one of the chief points he inculcated. The tenor of his doctrine, when he found himself concerned to instruct others, was to wean men from systems, ceremonies, and the outside of religion, in every form, and to lead them to an acquaintance with themselves by a solicitous attention to what passed in their own minds; to direct them to a principle in their own hearts, which, if duly attended to, would introduce rectitude of mind, simplicity of manners, a life and conversation adorned with every Christian virtue. Drawing his doctrine from the pure source of religious truth, the New Testament, and the conviction of his own mind, abstracted from the comments of men—he asserted the freedom of man in the liberty of the gospel, against the tyranny of custom, and against the combined powers of severe persecution, the greatest contempt and keenest ridicule. Unshaken and undismayed, he persevered in disseminating principles and practices conducive to the present and everlasting well-being of mankind, with great honesty, simplicity, and success.

The influence and extent of this sect were soon much enlarged by the example and efforts of William Penn, the most distinguished, perhaps, of its adherents. This remarkable man was born in London in 1644. About the year 1661, while a gentleman commoner at Christ Church, Oxford, he listened, in company with some other students, to the preaching of one Thomas Loe, a Quaker of eminence, and became a convert to his views. In consequence of adhering to these views, he was soon afterwards expelled from college. He had several violent altercations with his father, because of his refusing to appear uncovered before him and the king. In 1668, William Penn first appeared as a preacher and an author among the Quakers. In consequence of some controversial dispute he was sent to the Tower, where he remained confined for seven months.

In 1677, he went with George Fox and Robert Barclay, to the continent, on a religious excursion. Soon after his return to England, Charles II. granted him, in consideration of the services of his father, and for a debt due to him from the crown, a province of North America, then called New Netherlands, but now making the state of Pennsylvania. In consequence of this acquisition, he invited, under the royal patent, settlers from all parts of the kingdom, and drew up in twenty-four articles, the fundamental constitution of his new province, in which he held out a greater degree of religious liberty than was at that time enjoyed in the Christian world. A colony of people, chiefly of his persuasion, soon flocked to share his fortunes; the lands of the country were cleared and improved, and a town was built, which, on the principle of brotherly love, received the name of *Philadelphia.*

In 1682, Penn visited the province, and confirmed that good understanding which he had recommended with the natives; and after two years' residence, and with the satisfaction of witnessing and promoting the prosperity of the colonists, he returned to England. In 1669, he revisited America with his family, and returned to England in 1710. He died, 30th July, 1718; leaving behind him a character for humanity, sagacity and benevolence, such as few legislators have achieved. The city which he founded still numbers the members of his sect among the most numerous, respectable and philanthropic of her citizens.

As an author, William Penn was remarkably prolific; and his writings indicate much ability. The following title of one of the most noted of his tracts will convey an idea of some of the peculiar religious opinions, which he adopted:—" The Sandy Foundation Shaken, or those so generally believed and applauded Doctrines, of one God subsisting in Three distinct and separate Persons; the impossibility of God's pardoning sin without a plenary satisfaction; the qualification of impure persons by an imputative righteousness, refuted from the authority of Scripture testimonies and right reason."

It appears that Penn, having in this work reprobated the leading doctrines of Calvinism, a violent outcry was raised against him. He therefore vindicated himself in a pamphlet, called " Innocency with her Open Face," in which he says : " As for my being a Socinian, I must confess I have read of one Socinus, of (what they call) a noble family in Sene, Italy, who about the year 1574, being a young man, voluntarily did abandon the glories, pleasures, and honours of the Great Duke of Tuscany's court at Florence, that noted place for all worldly delicacies, and became a perpetual exile for his conscience, whose parts, wisdom, gravity, and just behaviour, made him the most famous with the Polonian and Transylvanian churches; but I was never baptised into his name, and therefore deny that reproachful epithet; and if in any thing I acknowledge the verity of his doctrine, it is for the truth's sake, of which, in many things he had a clearer prospect than most of his contemporaries : but not therefore a Socinian any more than a son of the English church, while esteemed a Quaker, because I justify many of her principles since the Reformation against the Romish church." But we will add another paragraph, where Penn's principles are epitomised : " And to shut up my apology for religious matters, that all may see the simplicity, Scripture doctrine, and phrase of my faith, in the most important matters of eternal life, I shall here subjoin a short confession :—

" I sincerely own, and unfeignedly believe, (by virtue of the sound knowledge and experience received from the gift of that holy unction and divine grace inspired from on high) in one holy, just, merciful, almighty, and eternal God, who is the father of all things; that appeared to the holy patriarchs and prophets of old, at sundry times and in divers manners; and in one Lord Jesus Christ, the everlast ing Wisdom, divine Power, true Light, only Saviour, and Preserver of all; the same one holy, just, merciful, almighty, and eternal God, who in the fulness of time took and was manifest in the flesh, at which time he preached (and his disciples after him) the everlasting gospel of repentance, and promise of remission of sins, and eternal life to all that heard and obeyed; who said, he that is with you (in the flesh) shall be in you (by the spirit); and though he left them (as to the flesh), yet not comfortless, for he would come to them again (in the spirit); for a little while, and they should not see him (as to the flesh); again, a little while and they should see him (in the spirit); for the Lord (Jesus Christ) is that spirit, a manifestation whereof is given to every one, to profit withal; in which Holy Spirit I believe, as the same almighty and eternal God, who as in those times, he ended all shadows, and became the infallible guide to them that walked therein, by which they were adopted heirs and co-heirs of glory; so am I a living witness, that the same holy, just, merciful, almighty and eternal God, is now, as then (after this tedious night of idolatry, superstition, and human inventions, that hath overspread the world) gloriously manifested to discover and save from all iniquity, and to conduct unto the holy land of pure and endless peace; in a word, to tabernacle in men. And, I also firmly believe, that without repenting and forsaking of past sins, and walking in obedience to the heavenly voice, which would guide into all truth, and establish there, remission and eternal life can never be obtained; but unto them that fear his name and keep his commandments, they, and only they, shall have right to the tree of life; for whose name's sake, I have been made willing to relinquish and forsake all the vain fashions, enticing pleasures, alluring honours and glittering glories of this transitory world, and readily accept the portion of a fool from this deriding generation, and become a man of sorrow, and a perpetual reproach to my familiars; yea, and with the greatest cheerfulness, obsignate and confirm (with no less zeal, than the loss of whatsoever this doating world accounts dear) this faithful confession; having my eye fixed upon a more enduring substance and lasting inheritance, and being most infallibly assured, that when time shall be no more, I shall, (if faithful hereunto) possess the mansions of eternal life, and be received into his everlasting habitation of rest and glory."

This is an explicit declaration of the principles of Quakerism, taken from the works of William Penn. As the Quakers have been sometimes charged with Socinianism, the following passages from a summary of their doctrines and discipline, published in London in 1809, and sanctioned by the orthodox society of Friends in the United States, may be regarded as authoritative on this subject:

" They agree, with other professors of the christian name, in the belief of one eternal God, the Creator and Preserver of the universe, and in Jesus Christ, his Son, the Messiah, and Mediator of the new covenant.

" When we speak of the gracious display of the love of God to mankind, in the miraculous conception, birth, life, miracles, death, resurrection, and ascension, of our Saviour, we prefer the use of such terms as we find in Scripture; and, contented with that knowledge which Divine Wisdom hath seen meet to reveal, we attempt not to explain those mysteries which remain under the veil; *nevertheless, we acknowledge and assert the divinity of Christ*, who is the wisdom and power of God unto salvation."

The Quakers hold that water baptism and the Lord's Supper were only commanded for a time. Their moral doctrines are chiefly comprehended in the following precepts:

I. That it is not lawful to give to men such flattering titles as, Your Honour, Esquire, your Lordship, &c. nor to use those flattering words commonly called compliments.

II. That it is not lawful for Christians to kneel or prostrate themselves to any man, or to bow the body, or to uncover the head to them.

III. That it is not lawful for a Christian to use such superfluities in apparel, as are of no use, save for ornament and vanity.

IV. That it is not lawful to use games, sports, or plays, among Christians, under the notion of recreations, which do not agree with Christian gravity and sobriety; for laughing, sporting, gaming, mocking, jesting, vain talking, &c., are not Christian liberty nor harmless mirth.

V. That it is not lawful for Christians to swear at all, under the gospel, not only vainly, and in their common discourse, which was also forbidden under the law, but even not in judgment before the magistrate.

VI. That it is not lawful for Christians to resist evil, or to war, or to fight, in any case.

The Quakers do not plead for entirely silent meetings, but only for a retired waiting for the divine aid, which alone qualifies to pray or preach.

Among the passages in the New Testament, to which the Friends appeal, as confirmatory of their views, are the following:—Heb. 12 : 24. 1 Cor. 1 : 24. John 1 : 1. 2 Pet. 1 : 21. 1 Tim. 3 : 15. Matt. 16 : 27. John 1 : 9—16, 33. 1 John 2 : 20, 27. Heb. 10 : 25. Rom. 8 : 26. Jer. 23 : 30—32. Matt. 10. : 8. Joel 2 : 28, 29. Acts 2 : 16, 17. Eph. 4 : 5. John 3 : 30. 2 Pet. 1 : 4. Rev. 3 : 20. Matt. 5 : 48. Eph. 4 : 13. Col. 4 : 12. Matt. 5 : 34, 39, 44, &c.; 26 : 52, 53. Luke 22 : 51. John 18 : 11. Eph. 2 : 8. John 7 : 17. Isa. 28 : 6. John 10 : 7, 11.

To effect the salutary purposes of discipline, meetings were appointed, at an early period among the Friends, which from the times of their being held, were called *quarterly meetings*. It was afterward found expedient to divide the districts of those meetings, and to meet more frequently; from whence arose *monthly meetings*, subordinate to those held quarterly. At length, in 1669, a *yearly meeting* was established, to superintend, assist, and provide rules for the whole; previously to which, *general meetings* had been occasionally held.

This system of discipline is still continued. The yearly meeting has the general superintendence of the society in the country in which it is established; and, therefore, as the accounts which it receives discover the state of inferior meetings, as particular exigencies require, or as the meeting is impressed with a sense of duty, it gives forth its advice, makes such regulations as appear to be requisite, or excites to the observance of those already made, and sometimes appoints committees to visit those quarterly meetings which appear to be in need of immediate advice. Appeals from the judgment of quarterly meetings are here finally determined; and a brotherly correspondence, by epistles, is maintained with other yearly meetings.

It may here be repeated, that as the Friends believe that women may be rightly called to the work of the ministry, they also think that to them belongs a share in the support of their Christian discipline, and that some parts of it, wherein their own sex is concerned, devolve on them with peculiar propriety; accordingly, they have monthly, quarterly, and yearly meetings of their own sex, held at the same time and in the same place with those of the men, but separately, and without the power of making rules; and it may be remarked, that during the persecutions, which, in the last century, occasioned the imprisonment of so many of the men, the care of the poor often fell on the women, and was by them satisfactorily administered.

The sentiments of the Friends respecting government, oaths, war, and the maintenance of a Gospel ministry, are four of the great tenets of the society. In the United States, they have been distinguished for their humane efforts in behalf of the persecuted Indians, as well as for their opposition to the continuance of negro slavery. They are always found arrayed on the side of human freedom, although principled against war and its kindred abuses. They are an intelligent, unobtrusive and thrifty people, and give the best proof of the elevation and sincerity of their doctrines in the correctness and daily beauty of their lives.

The American Friends are divided in sentiment upon certain theological points, and now virtually compose two sects, the Orthodox Friends and the Hicksites. The latter derive their name from Elias Hicks, who died in the

State of New York, at the age of seventy-six, in 1830. Some idea of his sentiments in regard to the Saviour may be formed from the following extract from one of his published sermons:

"He that laid down his life, and suffered his body to be crucified by the Jews, without the gates of Jerusalem, is Christ, the only Son of the most high God. But that the *outward person which suffered* was properly the Son of God, we utterly deny. Flesh and blood cannot enter into heaven. By the analogy of reason, spirit cannot beget a material body, because the thing begotten must be of the same nature with its father. Spirit cannot beget any thing but spirit: it cannot beget flesh and blood. '*A body hast thou prepared me,*' said the Son: *then the Son was not the body*, though the body was the Son's."

The Hicksites compose about one half of the whole body of American Friends.

In England and Ireland the Quakers number about fifty thousand; and in America, about two hundred thousand, and are divided into four hundred and fifty congregations.

SHAKERS.

In the account which the Shakers give of themselves, they mention the Quakers in the time of Oliver Cromwell and the French prophets of a later date, as being the first who had a peculiar testimony from the Lord to deliver to the Christian world. But they complain that the former degenerated, losing that desire of love and power with which they first set out, and the latter being of short continuance, "their extraordinary communications" have long ago ceased. This Testimony was revived in the persons of "James Wardley, a tailor by trade, and Jane his wife, who wrought at the same occupation." And the work under them began at Bolton and Manchester, in Lancashire, about the year 1747. They had belonged to the society of Quakers, but receiving the spirit of the French prophets, and a further degree of light and power by which they were separated from that community, they continued for several years disconnected from every denomination During this time their testimony according to what they saw by vision and revelation from God was, " That the Second Appearing of Christ was at hand, and that the Church was rising in her full and transcendant glory, which would effect the final downfall of Antichrist!"

From the shaking of their bodies in religious exercises, they were called Shakers, and some gave them the name of Shaking Quakers. This name, though used in derision, they acknowledge to be proper, because they are both the subjects and instruments of the work of God in this latter day.

" Thus the Lord promised, that he would shake the earth with terror:" Lowth's translation of Isaiah ii. 19, 21. " That, in that day, there should be a great shaking in the land of Israel:" Ezek. xxxviii. 19, 20. " That he would shake the heavens and the earth !" Isaiah xiii. 13; Joel iii. 16; Hag. ii. 6, 7, 21. " That he would shake all nations, and that the desire of all nations should come." And according to the apostle, " That yet once more, he would shake not the earth only, but also heaven :" Heb. xii. 26. Signifying the removing of things that are shaken, as of things that are made, that those things which cannot be shaken may remain. All which, particularly alluded to the latter day, and now, in reality, began to be fulfilled; of which the name itself was a striking evidence, and much more the nature and operations of the work.

This work went on under Wardley, till the year 1770, " when the present Testimony of Salutation and Eternal Life was fully opened according to the special gift and revelation of God through Anne Lee." She was born about the year 1736; her father, John Lee, lived in Toad Lane, Manchester, and was a blacksmith; with him she lived till she embarked for America. She herself was a cutter of hatter's fur, and had five brothers and two sisters. She was married to Abraham Standley, a blacksmith, and had four children, who died in their infancy.

In 1758, this singular woman joined the society under Wardley, and became a distinguished leader amongst them.

"When, therefore, Anne, who by her perfect obedience, had attained to all that was made manifest in the leading characters of the society, still, however, found in herself the seed or remains of human depravity, and a lack of the divine nature, which is eternal life abiding in the soul, she did not rest satisfied in that state, but laboured in continual watchings and fastings, and in tears and incessant cries to God, day and night, for deliverance. And under the most severe tribulation, and violent temptations, as great as she was able to resist and endure, such was, frequently, her extreme agony of soul, that she would clinch her hands together, till the blood would flow through the pores of her skin!

"By such deep mortification and suffering, her flesh wasted away, and she became like a skeleton, wholly incapable of helping herself, and was fed and nourished like an infant, although, naturally, free from bodily infirmities, and a person of strong and sound constitution, and invincible fortitude of mind.

"And from the light and power of God, which attended her ministry, and the certain power of salvation transmitted to those who received her testimony, she was received and acknowledged as the *first Mother*, or spiritual parent in the line of the female, and the second heir in the covenant of life, according to the present display of the gospel. Hence among believers, she hath been distinguished by no other name or title than that of *Mother*, from that period to the present day. To such as addressed her with the customary titles used by the world, she would reply,—'I am *Anne* the *Word*;' signifying that in her dwelt the *Word*."

In 1774, Anne Lee, with some of her followers, having been thought mad, and sorely persecuted, settled their temporal affairs in England, and set sail from Liverpool for New York. James Wardley and his wife remaining behind, were removed into an alms-house, and there died

The others, we are told, "being without lead or protection, lost their power, and fell into the common course and practice of the world!" Anne Lee and the brethren reached New York, after working a sort of miracle, for the ship sprang a leak on the voyage, and it is more than hinted, that had it not been for their exertions at the pump, the vessel would have gone down to the bottom of the ocean. They fixed their residence at Niskyuna, now Watervliet, near the city of Albany. In this retired spot, they greatly multiplied, but Anne was not without bitter reproaches and manifold persecutions. She and the elders would delight in missionary journeys—being out for two or three years, and returning with wonderful accounts of their success.

"The decease of Elder William served as a particular means of preparing the minds of believers for a still heavier trial, in being deprived of the visible presence and protection of Anne—the thought of which seemed almost insupportable to many. But having finished the work which was given her to do, she was taken out of their sight in the ordinary way of all living, at Watervliet, on the 8th day of the ninth month, 1784.

"Thus in the early dawn of the American Revolution, when the rights of conscience began to be established, the morning star of Christ's second coming, disappeared from the view of the world, to be succeeded by the increasing brightness of the Sun of righteousness and all the promised glory of the latter day.

"And thus the full revelation of Christ, in its first degree, was completed; which was according to that remarkable prophecy of Christopher Love, who was beheaded under Cromwell:—'Out of thee, O England! shall *a bright star* arise, whose light and voice shall make the heavens to quake, and knock under with submission to the blessed Jesus.'"

The most remarkable tenet of the Shakers is the abolition of marriage, or, indeed, the total separation of the sexes. The essence of their argument is, that the Resurrection spoken of in the New Testament means nothing more than conversion; our Saviour declares that in the Resurrection they neither marry nor are given in marriage, therefore on conversion, or the resurrection of the individual, marriage ceases. To speak more plainly, the single must continue single and the married must separate. Every passage in the Gospel and in the epistles is interpreted according to this hypothesis.

"Whatever degree of indulgence," say they, " was extended to some among the gentile nations, who professed faith in Christ, because they were not able to bear the whole truth; yet the truth did not conceal the pointed distinction which Christ made between his own true followers, and the children of this world.

"'But I would have you without carefulness,' saith the apostle; 'He that is unmarried careth for the things that belong to the Lord, how he may please the Lord:' (His noblest and principal affections are there.) But he that is married careth for the things that are of the world, how he may please his wife.' The wife is put in the place of the Lord, as the first object of his affections.

"The unmarried woman careth for the things of the Lord, (upon whom she places her affections,) that she may be holy both in body and spirit: but she that is married careth for the things of the world, how she may please her husband, instead of the Lord.

"The same pointed distinction is made by Christ; not only when he says of his disciples, 'they are not of the world, even as I am not of the world,' but when in answering the Sadducees, who denied and knew not that he was the resurrection, he says, 'The children of this world marry, and are given in marriage; but they which shall be accounted worthy to obtain that world, and the resurrection from the dead, neither marry nor are given in marriage.' Neither can they die any more (spiritually), for they are equal unto the angels, and are the children of God, being the children of the resurrection."

An idea of the notions of the Shakers in regard to their founder may be formed from the following passages: "In the fulness of time, according to the unchangeable purpose of God, that same Spirit and word of power, which created man at the beginning—which spake by the prophets—which dwelt in the man Jesus—which was given to the apostles and true witnesses, as the Holy Spirit and word of promise, which groaned in them waiting for the day of redemption—and which was spoken of in the language of prophecy as a woman travailing with child, and pained to be delivered, was revealed in a woman.

"And that woman, in whom was manifested the Spirit and Word of power, who was anointed and chosen of God, to reveal the mystery of iniquity, to stand as the first in order, to accomplish the purpose of God, in the restoration of that which was lost by the transgression of the first woman, and to finish the work of man's final redemption, was Anne Lee.

"As the chosen vessel, appointed by divine Wisdom, she, by her faithful obedience to that same anointing, became the temple of the Holy Ghost, and the second heir with Jesus, her Lord and head, in the covenant and promise of eternal life. And by her sufferings and travail for a lost world, and her union and subjection to Christ Jesus, her Lord and Head, she became the first-born of many sisters, and the true Mother of all living in the new creation.

"Thus the perfection of the translation of God in this latter day, excels particularly, in that which respects the most glorious part in the creation of man, namely, the woman. And herein is the most condescending goodness and mercy of God displayed, not only in redeeming that most amiable part of creation from the curse, and all the sorrows of the fall, but also in condescending to the lowest estate of the loss of mankind."

The four leading peculiarities of the Shakers are: first, community of property; secondly, the celibacy of the entire body, in both sexes; thirdly, the non-existence of any priesthood; and, fourthly, the use of the dance in their religious worship. All these they defend on Scriptural authority, and quote very largely from the writings of the Old and New Testaments in confirmation of their views.

The following are their rules for the admission of members:

"1. All persons who unite with the society must do it voluntarily and of their own free will.

"2. No one is permitted to do so without a full and clear understanding of all its obligations.

"3. No considerations of property are ever made use of to induce persons to join or to leave the society; because it is a principle of the sect, that no act of devotion or service that does not flow from the free and voluntary emotions of the heart, can be acceptable to God as an act of true religion.

"4. No believing husband or wife is allowed, by the principles of this society, to separate from an unbelieving partner, except by mutual agreement, unless the conduct of the unbeliever be such as to warrant a separation by the laws of God and man. Nor can any husband or wife, who has otherwise abandoned his or her partner, be received into communion with the society.

"5. Any person becoming a member must rectify all his wrongs, and, as fast and as far as it is in his power, discharge all just and legal claims, whether of creditors or filial heirs. Nor can any person, not conforming to this rule, long remain in union with the society. But the society is not responsible for the debts of any individual, except by agreement; because such responsibility would involve a principle ruinous to the institution.

"6. No difference is to be made in the distribution of parental estate among the heirs, whether they belong to the society or not; but an equal partition must be made, as far as may be practicable and consistent with reason and justice.

"7. If an unbelieving wife separate from a believing husband by agreement, the husband must give her a just and reasonable share of the property; and if they have children who have arrived at years of understanding sufficient to judge for themselves, and who choose to go with their mother, they are not to be disinherited on that account. Though the character of this institution has been much censured on this ground, yet we boldly assert that the rule above stated has never, to our knowledge, been violated by this society.

"8. Industry, temperance, and frugality, are prominent features of this institution. No member who is able to labour can be permitted to live idly upon the labours of others. All are required to be employed in some manual occupation, according to their several abilities, when not engaged in other necessary duties."

As all persons enter this society voluntarily, so they may voluntarily withdraw; but, while they remain members, they are required to obey the regulations of the society.

The leading authority of the society is vested in a ministry, generally consisting of four persons, including both sexes. These, together with the elders and trustees, constitute the general government of the society in all its branches.

No creed is framed to limit the progress of improvement. It is the faith of the society that the operations of Divine light are unlimited. All are at liberty to improve their talents and exercise their gifts, the younger being subject to the elder.

In the beginning of the year 1780, the society consisted of but about ten or twelve persons, all of whom came from England. From this time there was a gradual and extensive increase in their numbers until the year 1787, when they began to collect at New-Lebanon. Here the Church was established, as a common centre of union for all who belonged to the society in various parts of the country. This still remains as the mother-church, being the first that was established; all the societies in various parts of the country are considered branches of this; and here are now twenty separate communities, numbering about 4000 members.

In Ohio there are two societies, one at Union Village, in the county of Warren, 30 miles northeast from Cincinnati, which contains nearly 600 members; and one at Beaver Creek, in the county of Montgomery, six miles southeast from Dayton, which contains 100 members. In Kentucky there are also two societies, one at Pleasant Hill, in Mercer county, 21 miles southwest of Lexington, containing nearly 500 members; the other at South Union, Jasper Springs, in Logan county, 15 miles northeast from Russellville, which contains nearly 400 members. In Indiana there is one society, at West Union, Knox county, 16 miles above Vincennes, which contains more than 200 members.

"The Shakers," says one of their visitors, "are, in their religious notions, a compound of almost all the other sects. They are a kind of religious eclectics, with this commendable trait, that they are enemies to every sort of coercion in matters of religion. They have chosen what appeared to them to be good out of every denomination. The Shaker unites with the *Quakers* in an entire submission to the spirit, and in the rejection of baptism and the Lord's Supper—with the *Calvinists* and *Methodists* in laying great stress on conversion—with the *Arminians* in rejecting election and reprobation, as well as the imputation of Adam's guilt to his posterity—with the *Unitarians* in exploding a Trinity of three persons in one God, together with the satisfaction of Christ—with the *Roman Catholics* in contending for the continuation of miracles in the church—with the *Sandemanians* in practising a sort of community of goods, and having no persons regularly educated for the ministry—with *the followers of Joanna Southcott*, in believing that a woman is the instrument to bring on the glory of the latter day—with the *Moravians* and *Methodists* in encouraging missionary undertakings—with the *Swedenborgians* in denying the resurrection of the body, and asserting that the day of judgment is past—with the *Jumpers* in dancing and shouting during divine worship; and lastly, with the *Universalists* in renouncing the eternity of hell torments. To all this, they have added a tenet hitherto unthought of by any body of Christians. The Catholics indeed led the way in enjoining the celibacy of the clergy, and in the institution of monachism.

It was left to the Shakers to enjoin celibacy as one of their religious exactions."

As far as the history of the Shakers can establish the fact, it has certainly shown that, where property is held in community, and not individually, the disposition to bestow it in works of charity and benevolence to others is greatly increased. And that the property itself is better managed for accumulation and preservation, no one can doubt who has watched the progressive advancement which this society has made in the augmentation, as well as improvement, of its possessions, and in the neatness, order, and perfection by which everything they do or make is characterized: this is so much the case, that over all the United States, the seeds, plants, fruits, grain, cattle, and manufactures furnished by any settlement of Shakers, bear a premium in the market above the ordinary price of similar articles from other establishments. There being no idleness among them, all are productive. There being no intemperance among them, none are destructive. There being no misers among them, nothing is hoarded, or made to perish for want of use; so that while production and improvement are at their maximum, and waste and destruction at their minimum, the society must go on increasing the extent and value of its temporal possessions, and thus increase its means of doing good, first within, and then beyond its own circle.

The most remarkable religious ceremony among the Shakers is that of dancing. The following account, from Buckingham's Travels in America, appears to be a wholly unprejudiced one:

"The males were first arranged in pairs, following each other like troops in a line of march; and when their number was completed, the females followed after, two and two, in the same manner. In this way they formed a complete circle round the open space of the room. In the centre of the whole was a small band of about half a dozen males and half a dozen females, who were there stationed to sing the tunes and mark the time; and these began to sing with a loud voice and in quick time, like the allegro of a sonata, or the vivace of a canzonet, the following verse:

> 'Perpetual blessings do demand,
> Perpetual praise on every hand;
> Then leap for joy, with dance and song,
> To praise the Lord forever.'

"The motion of the double line of worshippers, as they filed off before us, was something between a march and a dance. Their bodies were inclined forward like those of persons in the act of running; they kept the most perfect time with their feet, and beat the air with their hands to the same measure. Some of the more robust and enthusiastic literally 'leaped' so high as to shake the room by the weight with which they fell to their feet on the floor; and others, though taking the matter more moderately, bore evident signs of the effects of the exercise and heat united on their persons. The first dance lasted about five minutes, and was performed to the air of 'Scots wha' ha'e wi' Wallace bled,' sung with great rapidity. The second dance was of still quicker measure, and to the much less respectable old English tune of 'Nancy Dawson,' and to this lively and merry tune the whole body, now formed into three abreast instead of two, literally scampered round the room in a quick gallopade, every individual of both the choir and the dancers singing with all their might these words:

> 'Press on, press on, ye chosen band,
> The angels go before ye;
> We're marching through Emanuel's land,
> Where saints shall sing in glory.'

"This exercise was continued for at least double the time of the former, and by it the worshippers were wrought up to such a pitch of fervour, that they were evidently on the point of some violent outbreak or paroxysm. Accordingly, the whole assembly soon got into the 'most admired disorder,' each dancing to his own tune and his own measure, and the females became perfectly ungovernable

About half a dozen of these whirled themselves round in what opera-dancers call a *pirouette*, performing at least fifty revolutions each, their arms extended horizontally, their clothes being blown out like an air-balloon all round their persons, their heads sometimes falling on one side, and sometimes hanging forward on the bosom, till they would at length faint away in hysterical convulsions, and be caught in the arms of the surrounding dancers.

"This, too, like the singing and dancing which preceded it, was accompanied by clapping of hands to mark the time, while the same verse was constantly repeated, and at every repetition with increased rapidity. Altogether the scene was one of the most extraordinary I had ever witnessed, and, except among the howling dervishes of Bagdad and the whirling dervishes of Damascus, I remember nothing in the remotest degree resembling it."

The Shakers vindicate this singular ceremony by quotations from the Bible. "The exercise of dancing, in the worship of God," say they, " was brought to light not as an exercise of human invention, instituted by human authority, but as a manifestation of the will of God, through the special operations of his Divine power. No reader of the Scriptures can doubt but that dancing was acceptable to God as an exercise of religious worship in times past, and will be in time to come, according to the prediction of the prophet:

"'Again I will build thee, and thou shalt be built, O virgin of Israel! thou shalt again be adorned with thy tabrets, and shalt go forth in the dances of them that make merry. Then shall the virgin rejoice in the dance, both young men and old together. Turn again, O virgin of Israel! turn again to these thy cities.'*

"God requires the faithful improvement of every created talent. 'O clap your hands, all ye people; shout unto God with the voice of triumph. Sing unto the Lord a new song; sing his praise in the congregation of the

---

* Jeremiah, c. 31, v. 4, 13, 21.

saints. Let the children of Zion be joyful in their King let them praise his name in the dance.'*

"These expressions of the inspired Psalmist are worthy of serious consideration. Do they not evidently imply that the Divine Spirit which dictated them requires the devotion of all our faculties in the service of God? How, then, can any people professing religion expect to find acceptance with God by the service of the tongue only?

"Since we are blessed with hands and feet, those active and useful members of the body on which we mostly depend in our own service, shall we not acknowledge our obligations to God who gave them by exercising them in our devotions to him? There is too powerful a connexion between the body and mind, and too strong an influence of the mind upon the body, to admit of much activity of mind in the service of God without the co-operating exercises of the body. But where the heart is sincerely and fervently engaged in the service of God, it has a tendency to produce an active influence on the body."

"From every inquiry I could make," says Mr. Buckingham, "of those longest resident in the neighbourhood of the Shakers, I could learn no authenticated case of evil practices among them. On the contrary, every one appeared ready to bear testimony to their honesty, punctuality, industry, sobriety, and chastity."

* Psa. xlvii., 1, and cxlix, 1, 2, 2.

CHAPTER XII.

UNIVERSALISTS—SWEDENBORGIANS, OR NEW CHURCH PEOPLE.

UNIVERSALISTS.

Universalists claim that the final salvation of all men was taught by Jesus Christ and his apostles. It was also taught by several of the most eminent Christian fathers; such as Clemens Alexandrinus, Origen, &c. In the third and fourth centuries, this doctrine prevailed extensively, and for aught which appears to the contrary, was then accounted orthodox. It was at length condemned, however, by the fifth general council, A. D. 553; after which, we find few traces of it through the dark ages, so called.

It revived at the period of the reformation, and since that time has found many able and fearless advocates;— in Switzerland, Petitpierre and Lavater; in Germany, Seigvolk, Everhard, Steinbart, and Semler; in Scotland, Purves, Douglass, and T. S. Smith; in England, Coppin, Jeremy White, Dr. H. More, Dr. T. Burnet, Whiston, Hartley, Bishop Newton, Stonehouse, Barbauld, Lindsey, Priestley, Belsham, Carpenter, Relly, Vidler, Scarlett, and many others.

At the present day, Universalism prevails more extensively than elsewhere in England, Germany, and the United States. In England, the Unitarian divines, generally, believe in the final salvation of all men. In Germany, nearly every theologian holds the same doctrine. Speaking of Professor Tholuck, Professor Sears says: "The most painful disclosures remain yet to be made. This distinguished and excellent man, in common with the *great majority of Evangelical divines* of Germany, though he professes to have serious doubts, and is cautious in avowing the sentiment, believes that all men and fallen spirits will finally be saved." Mr. Dwight says: "The doctrine of the eternity of future punishments is almost universally rejected. I have seen but one person in Germany who believed it, and but one other whose mind was wavering on this subject." Universalism may, therefore, be considered the prevailing religion in Germany.

In the United States, Universalism was little known until about the middle of the eighteenth century; and afterwards it found but few advocates during several years. Dr. George de Benneville, of Germantown, Penn., Rev. Richard Clarke, of Charleston, S. C., and Jonathan Mayhew, D. D., of Boston, were, perhaps, the only individuals who publicly preached the doctrine before the arrival of Rev. John Murray, in 1770. Mr. Murray laboured almost alone until 1780, when Rev. Elhanan Winchester, a popular Baptist preacher, embraced Universalism, though on different principles. About ten years afterwards, Rev. Hosea Ballou adopted the same doctrine, but on principles different from those advocated by Mr. Murray or Mr. Winchester. To the efforts of these three men is to be attributed much of the success which attended the denomination in its infancy. Although they differed widely from one another in their views of punishment, yet they labored together in harmony and love, for the advancement of the cause which was dear to all their hearts.

The following is the " Profession of Belief," adopted by the General Convention of Universalists in the United States, at the session holden in 1803.

" 1. We believe that the Holy Scriptures, of the Old and New Testaments, contain a revelation of the character of God, and of the duty, interest, and final destination of mankind.

" 2. We believe that there is one God, whose nature is love; revealed in one Lord Jesus Christ, by one Holy Spirit of Grace, who will finally restore the whole family of mankind to holiness and happiness.

" 3. We believe that holiness and true happiness are inseparably connected, and that believers ought to be careful to maintain order, and practise good works; for these things are good and profitable unto men."

The Universalists quote the following texts of Scripture,

among others, in support of their sentiments :—Gen. 22 18. Ps. 22 : 27 ; 86 : 9. Isa. 25 : 6, 7, 8 ; 45 : 23, 24. Jer. 31 : 33, 34. Lam. 3 : 31—33. John 12 : 32. Acts 3 : 21. Rom. 5 : 18, 21 ; 8 : 38, 39 ; 11 : 25—36. 1 Cor. 15: 22—28, and 51—57. 2 Cor. 5 : 18, 19. Gal. 3 : 8. Eph. 1 : 9, 10. Phil. 2 : 9—11. Col. 1 : 19, 20. 1 Tim. 2: 1—6. Heb. 8 : 10, 11. Rev. 5 : 13 ; 21 : 3, 4.

Some of the Universalists believe that all punishment for sin is endured in the present state of existence, while others believe it extends into the future life. All agree, however, that it will finally terminate, and be succeeded by a state of perfect and endless holiness and happiness.

There certainly seems to be an evident propriety in calling all who believe in the final holiness and happiness of all mankind, *Universalists*. There appears no good reason why those who believe in a limited punishment in a future state, should have a less or a greater claim to be called Universalists, than those who entertain a hope that all sin and misery end when the functions of life cease in the mortal body. As they both agree in the belief that God is the Saviour of all men, if this belief entitle one to the name of Universalist, of course it gives the other the same title.

A portion of the Universalists, however, call themselves Restorationists. One party believe that a full and perfect retribution for sin takes place in this world, that our conduct here cannot affect our future condition, and that the moment man exists after death, he will be as pure and as happy as the angels. From these views the Restorationists dissent. They maintain that a just retribution does not take place in time; that the conscience of the sinner becomes callous, and does not increase in the severity of its reprovings with the increase of guilt ; that men are invited to act with reference to a future life; that, if all are made perfectly happy at the commencement of the next state of existence, they are not rewarded according to their deeds ; that if death introduces them into heaven, they are saved by death and not by Christ ; and if they are made happy by being raised from the dead, they are saved by physical, and not by moral means, and made happy without their agency or consent; that such a sentiment weakens the motives to virtue, and gives force to the temptatious of vice; that it is unreasonable in itself, and opposed to many passages of Scripture. (See Acts 24: 25; 17: 30, 31. Heb. 9: 27, 28. Matt. 11: 23, 24. 2 Pet. 2: 9. 2 Cor. 5; 8—11. John 5: 28, 29. Matt. 10: 28. Luke 12: 4, 5; 16: 19—31. 1 Pet. 3, 18—20.)

Among the distinguished writers, who have maintained the doctrines of the Restorationists, may be mentioned the names of Jeremy White, of Trinity College, Dr. Burnet, Dr. Cheyne, Chevalier Ramsay, Dr. Hartley, Bishop Newton, Mr. Stonehouse, Mr. Petitpierre, Dr. Cogan, Mr. Lindsey, Dr. Priestley, Dr. Jebb, Mr. Relly, Mr. Kenrick, Mr. Belsham, Dr. Southworth, Smith and many others. And among the Christian fathers of the first four centuries, it is said that Clemens Alexandrinus, Origen Didymus of Alexandria, Gregory Nyssen, and several others, advocated the doctrine of the restoration of all fallen intelligences.

The Universalists contend that the words rendered *everlasting*, *eternal*, and *forever*, which are, in a few instances, in the Scriptures, applied to the misery of the wicked, do not prove that misery to be endless, because these terms are loose in their signification, and are frequently used in a limited sense; that the original terms, being often used in the plural number, clearly demonstrate that the period, though indefinite, is limited in its very nature.

They maintain that the meaning of the term must always be sought in the subject to which it is applied, and that there is nothing in the nature of punishment which will justify an endless sense. They believe that the doctrine of the restoration is the most consonant to the perfections of the Deity, the most worthy of the character of Christ, and the only doctrine which will accord with pious and devout feelings, or harmonize with the Scriptures. They teach their followers that ardent love to God, ac tive benevolence to man, and personal meekness and purity, are the natural results of these views.

The attention of this denomination in various parts of the country has lately been turned to the education of their ministry; and conventions and associations have adopted resolves requiring candidates to pass examination in certain branches of literature. The same motives have governed many in their effort to establish literary and theological institutions. The desire to have the ministry respectable for literary acquirements, is universal among the members; and they may be regarded as one of the most flourishing and enterprising religious sects of the United States.

SWEDENBORGIANS, OR NEW CHURCH PEOPLE.

This sect derive their interpretation of the meaning of the old and new testament, from the writings of Emanuel Swedenborg, who believed himself to have had his spiritual sight opened, and whose history presents many extra ordinary facts in confirmation of his declaration on this head. Swedenborg, like Luther, objected to having his followers called after his name, and among themselves, accordingly, the term Swedenborgian is not much used.

The following letter, containing some account of himself and family, was written by Swedenborg in 1769, in Latin, to the Rev. Thomas Hartley, M.A., Rector of Winwick, in Northamptonshire, England. We give only the translation:

"I was born at Stockholm, in the year of our Lord 1689,* Jan. 29. My father's name was Jesper Swedberg, who was bishop of Westrogothia, and of celebrated character in his time. He was also a member of the Society for the Propagation of the Gospel, formed on the model of that in England, and appointed president of the Swedish churches in Pennsylvania and London, by King Charles XII. In the year 1710, I began my travels—first

* It has since been ascertained that this should be 1688.

into England, and afterwards into Holland, France, and Germany, and returned home in 1714. In the year 1716, and afterwards, I frequently conversed with Charles XII. King of Sweden, who was pleased to bestow on me a large share of his favour, and in that year appointed me to the office of assessor in the Metallic College, in which office I continued from that time till the year 1747, when I quitted the office, but still retain the salary annexed to it as an appointment for life. The reason of my withdrawing from the business of that employment was, that I might be more at liberty to apply myself to that new function to which the Lord had called me. About this time a place of higher dignity in the state was offered me, which I declined to accept, lest it should prove a snare to me. In 1719, I was ennobled by Queen Ulrica Eleonora, and named Swedenborg; from which time I have taken my seat with the nobles of the equestrian order, in the triennial assemblies of the States. I am a fellow, by invitation, of the Royal Academy of Sciences, at Stockholm, but have never desired to be of any other community, as I belong to the society of angels, in which things spiritual and heavenly are the only subjects of discourse and entertainment; whereas in our literary societies the attention is wholly taken up with things relating to the body and this world. In the year 1734, I published the Regnum Minerale, at Leipsic, in three volumes, folio; and in 1738 I took a journey into Italy, and staid a year at Venice and Rome.

"With respect to my family connection: I had four sisters; one of them was married to Erick Benzelius, afterward promoted to the Archbishopric of Upsal; and thus I became related to the two succeeding archbishops of that see, both named Benzelius, and younger brothers of the former. Another of my sisters was married to Lars Benzelstierna, who was promoted to a provincial government; but these are both dead; however, two bishops, who are related to me, are still living; one of them is named Filenius, bishop of Ostrogothia, who now officiates as president of the ecclesiastical order in the genera, assembly at Stockholm, in the room of the archbishop, who is infirm; he married the daughter of my sister; the other who is named Benzelstierna, bishop of Westermannia and Dalecarlia, is the son of my second sister; not to mention others of my family who are dignified. I live, besides, on terms of familiarity and friendship with all the bishops of my country, which are ten in number, and also with the sixteen senators, and the rest of the grandees; who know that I am in fellowship with angels. The King and Queen themselves, as also the princes their sons, show me all kind countenance; and I was once invited to eat with the king and queen at their table, (an honour granted only to the peers of the realm,) and likewise since with the hereditary prince. All in my own country wish for my return home; so far am I from the least danger of persecution there, as you seem to apprehend, and are also so kindly solicitous to provide against; and should anything of that kind befal me elsewhere, it will give me no concern.

"Whatever of worldly honour and advantage may appear to be in the things before mentioned, I hold them as matters of low estimation, when compared to the honour of that sacred office to which the Lord himself hath called me, who was graciously pleased to manifest himself to me, his unworthy servant, in a personal appearance* in the year 1743; to open in me a sight of the spiritual world, and enable me to converse with spirits and angels; and this privilege has been continued to me to this day. From that time I began to print and publish various unknown

---

* The following passage from Swedenborg's "Apocalypse Revealed," explains what he may be supposed to mean here by "a personal appearance" of the Lord:—"He, (the Lord) appears in the heavens—when he manifests himself—as an angel; *for he fills some angel with his divinity* in accommodation to the reception of those to whom he gives to see him. His presence itself, such as he is himself or in his own essence, *cannot be supported by any angel, much less by any man;* wherefore he appears above the heavens as a sun, at a distance from the angels, as the sun of this world is from men; there he dwells in his Divinity from eternity, and at the same time in his Divine Humanity, which are a one like soul and body."

Arcana, that have been either seen by me, or revealed to me, concerning heaven and hell; the state of men after death; the true worship of God; the spiritual sense of the Scriptures, and many other important truths tending to salvation and true wisdom, and that mankind might receive benefit from these communications, was the only motive which has induced me at different times to leave my home to visit other countries. As to this world's wealth, I have sufficient, and more I neither seek nor wish for.

"Your letter has drawn the mention of these things from me, in case, as you say, they may be a means to prevent or remove any false judgment or wrong prejudices with regard to my personal circumstances. Farewell; and I heartily wish you prosperity both in things spiritual and temporal, of which I make no doubt, if so be you go on to pray to our Lord, and to set him always before you. EMAN. SWEDENBORG.
LONDON, 1769."

Many extraordinary and well-authenticated instances are on record, tending to prove that Swedenborg's claims to spiritual communion are not to be lightly set aside. The following letter from the celebrated philosopher, Kant, was lately brought forward by Dr. Tafel of Germany, with other documents, to prove the intercourse of Swedenborg. It is dated 10th August 1758, and addressed to a lady of quality, Charlotte de Knoblock, afterwards widow of Lieutenant General Klingsporn. Kant highly esteemed this lady, who was remarkable for her thirst after knowledge. It appears that she had asked his opinion concerning Swedenborg and his writings. The letter is as follows:

"I would not have deprived myself so long of the honour and pleasure of obeying the request of a lady, who is the ornament of her sex, in communicating the desired information, if I had not deemed it necessary previously to inform myself thoroughly concerning the subject of your request. Permit me, gracious lady, to justify my proceedings in this matter, inasmuch as it might appear that an erroneous opinion has induced me to credit the various relations concerning it without careful examination. I am not aware that any body has ever perceived in me an inclination to the marvellous, or a weakness approaching to credulity. So much is certain, that notwithstanding all the narrations of apparitions, and visions concerning the spiritual world, of which a great number of the most probable are known to me, I have always considered it to be most in agreement with the rule of sound reason to incline to the negative side; not as if I had imagined such a case to be impossible, although we know but very little concerning the nature of a spirit, but because the instances are not in general sufficiently proved. There arise, moreover, from the incomprehensibility and inutility of this sort of phenomena, too many difficulties; and there are, on the other hand, so many proofs of deception, that I have never considered it necessary to suffer fear or dread to come upon me, either in the cemeteries of the dead, or in the darkness of night. This is the position in which my mind stood for a long time, until the accounts of Swedenborg came to my notice.

"These accounts I received from a Danish officer, who was formerly my friend, and attended my lectures; and who, at the table of the Austrian ambassador, Dietrichstein, at Copenhagen, together with several other guests, read a letter which the ambassador had lately received from Baron de Lutzow, the Mecklenburg ambassador at Stockholm; in which he says, that he, in company with the Dutch ambassador, was present at the Queen of Sweden's residence, at the extraordinary transaction respecting M. de Swedenborg, which your ladyship will undoubtedly have heard. The authenticity thus given to the account surprised me. For it can hardly be believed, that one ambassador should communicate a piece of information to another for public use, which related to the Queen of the court where he resided, and which he himself, together with a splendid company, had the opportunity of witnessing, if it were not true. Now in order not to reject blindfold the prejudice against apparitions and visions by a new prejudice, I found it desirable to inform myself as to the particulars of this surprising transaction. I accordingly wrote to the officer I have mentioned at Copenhagen, and made various inquiries respecting it. He answered that he had again had an interview concerning it with Count Dietrichstein; that the affair had really taken place in the manner described; and that professor Schlegel also had declared to him, that it could by no means be doubted. He advised me, as he was then going to the army, under general St. Germain, to write to Swedenborg himself, in order to ascertain the particular circumstances of the extraordinary case. I then wrote to this singular man, and the letter was delivered to him, at Stockholm, by an English merchant. I was informed that Swedenborg politely received the letter, and promised to answer it. But the answer was omitted In the mean time I made the acquaintance of an English gentleman who spent the last summer at this place, whom, relying on the friendship we had formed, I commissioned, as he was going to Stockholm, to make particular inquiries respecting the miraculous gift which M. de Swedenborg is said to possess. In his first letter, he states, that the most respectable people in Stockholm declare, that the singular transaction alluded to had happened in the manner you have heard described. He had not then had an interview with Swedenborg, but hoped soon to embrace the opportunity; although he found it difficult to persuade himself that all could be true which the most reasonable persons of the city asserted, respecting his communication with the spiritual world. But his succeeding letters were of a different purport. He had not only spoken with Swedenborg, but had also visited him at his house; and he is now in the greatest astonishment respecting such a remarkable case. Swedenborg is a reasonable, polite, and open-hearted man: he also is a man of learning; and my friend has promised to send me some of his writings in a short time. He told this gentleman, without reserve, that God had accorded to him the remarkable gift of communicating with departed souls at pleasure. In proof of this he appealed to certain known facts. As he was reminded of my letter, he said that he was aware he had received it, and that he would already have answered it, had he not intended to make the whole of this singular affair public to the eyes of the world. He should proceed to London in the month of May this year, where he would publish a book, in which the answer to my letter, as to every point, might be met with.

"In order, gracious lady, to give you two proofs, of which the present existing public is a witness, and the person who related them to me had the opportunity of investigating them at the very place where they occurred, I will narrate to you the two following occurrences.

"Madame Harteville, the widow of a Dutch envoy at Stockholm, was, some time after the death of her husband, asked by Croon, the goldsmith, for the payment of a set of silver plate which her husband had ordered to be made by him. The widow was indeed convinced that her deceased husband was too orderly and particular in his affairs, not to have settled and paid the account; however, she could find no receipt to testify the payment. In her trouble, and as the value was considerable, she intreated M. de Swedenborg to pay her a visit. After some apologies, she besought him, if he possessed the gift of being able to speak with departed souls, as every body said he did, to have the kindness to inquire of her departed husband, respecting the demand of payment for the set of silver plate. Swedenborg was very affable, and promised to serve her in this affair. Three days afterwards, the same lady had company, when M. de Swedenborg came, and told her in his cool manner, that he had spoken with her husband. The debt had been paid seven months before his death, and the receipt had been put in a bureau which was in an upper apartment. The lady replied that this bureau had been cleared out, and that the receipt could not be found amongst any of the papers. Swedenborg returned, that her husband had told him, that if a drawer on the left side of the bureau was pulled out, a board would be observed, which must be pushed away, and then a secret drawer would be discovered, in which he used to keep his secret Dutch correspondence, in which, also, he had placed the receipt. At this indication, the lady, accompanied by all her friends, went to the upper apartment. They opened the bureau, and proceeded according to Swedenborg's instruction. They found the drawer of which the lady had not known, and in it the papers and receipts were met with, to the very great astonishment of all present.

"But the following occurrence appears to me to have the greatest weight of proof, and to set the assertion respecting Swedenborg's extraordinary gift, out of all possibility of doubt. In the year 1756, when M. de Swedenborg, towards the end of September, on Saturday, at four o'clock P. M., arrived at Gothenburg from England, Mr. William Castel invited him to his house, together with a party of fifteen persons. About six o'clock M. de Swedenborg went out, and after a short interval, returned to the company quite pale and alarmed. He said that a dangerous fire had broken out in Stockholm, at the Sundermalm, (Gothenburg is about fifty miles* from Stockholm), and that it was spreading very fast. He was restless, and went out often. He said that the house of one of his friends, whom he named, was already in ashes, and that his own was in danger. At eight o'clock, after he had been out again, he joyfully exclaimed, 'Thank God! the fire is extinguished, the third door from my house.' This news occasioned great commotion through the whole city, and particularly amongst the company in which he was. It was announced to the governor the same evening. On Sunday morning, Swedenborg was sent for by the governor, who questioned him concerning the disaster. Swedenborg described the fire precisely, how it began, in what manner it ceased, and how long it continued. On the same day the news was spread through the city, and as the governor had thought it worthy of attention, the consternation was considerably increased; because many were in trouble on account of their friends and property, which might have been involved in the disaster. On the Monday evening a messenger arrived at Gothenburg, who was despatched during the time of the fire. In the letters

---

* German miles; near three hundred English.

brought by him, the fire was described precisely in the manner stated by Swedenborg. On the Tuesday morning the royal courier arrived at the governor's with the melancholy intelligence of the fire, of the loss it had occasioned, and of the houses it had damaged and ruined, not in the least differing from that which Swedenborg had given immediately after it had ceased, for the fire was extinguished at eight o'clock.

"What can be brought forward against the authenticity of this occurrence? My friend, who wrote this to me, has not only examined the circumstances of this extraordinary case at Stockholm, but also about two months ago, at Gothenburg, where he is acquainted with the most respectable houses, and where he could obtain the most authentic and complete information; as the greatest part of the inhabitants, who are still alive, were witnesses to the memorable occurrence. I am, with profound reverence, &c. EMANUEL KANT.

"Kœnigsburg, Aug. 10, 1758."

The editors of the Intellectual Repository, who have copied the above letter in that work, make the following remarks:

"Swedenborg's omitting to answer, by letter, Professor Kant's inquiries of him relating to the above affair, may appear extraordinary. But it is to be observed, that he never, himself, laid any stress upon these miraculous proofs of the truth of his pretensions. If asked respecting them by those who had heard them from others, he would say that the reports are true; but he abstained from writing any accounts of them; and never does he appeal to them, or so much as mention them in his works. How strong an evidence is this of his elevation of mind; and of his perfect conviction of the truth of the views he was made an instrument of unfolding, with his own divine appointment to that purpose, as standing in need of no such evidence for their support! Could it be possible for any of the merely fanatical pretenders to divine communications to appeal to such testimonies of supernatural endowment, now continually would they do so,—how eagerly would they seek to silence objectors by referring to queens, counts, ambassadors, governors, and university professors, that had been witnesses of their power! But it is precisely on account of the silencing nature of such evidence, that Swedenborg declines to make use of it. It is a principle in his theology, that nothing which externally compels assent can impart internal reception of genuine truth, which is the only kind of reception that can do the subject of it any real good: it is to the praise, then, of his consistency, that he never adverts to the external demonstrations, which under peculiar circumstances he had occasionally been induced to give, of the reality of his communications with the spiritual world."

The principal tenets of Swedenborg, in the formation of which he assumes to have been preternaturally illuminated by means of his spiritual researches, are these: He teaches that there is one God, the Lord Jesus Christ, in whom there is a divine Trinity, which is not a Trinity of persons, but is analagous to that which exists in man, the image and likeness of God. In man is a soul or essential principle of life, a form or body, natural in this world and spiritual in the spiritual world, in which the soul exists, and by which it manifests itself in operation: these three, soul, form and operation, are as the Father, Son and Holy Spirit. And as some affection is within all thought, and causes it and forms it, and as all action is the effect of volition, or affection operating by and through thought, so the Father is the divine love, the Son the divine wisdom, and the Holy Spirit the divine operation. So, too, as every effect must be produced by some cause, and for some end, end, cause and effect exist in all things, as a Trinity. This Trinity Swedenborg does not consider as arbitrary and figurative, but as most real, grounded in the divine nature, and existing from the divine nature in all things.

With regard to regeneration, Swedenborg teaches, that, as the Lord glorified his humanity by resisting and overcoming the infernal influences which assailed it, so man, by following the Lord in his regeneration, through his divine grace, may gradually become regenerate; that is, receptive of good affection and wisdom from the Lord through the heavens; and in proportion as his sins are resisted and put away, he becomes thus receptive more and more perpetually.

Swedenborg teaches that the Lord foredooms none to hell, condemns none, and punishes none; that his divine grace is constantly with all, aiding those on earth who strive to co-operate with him, sustaining and leading forward angels in heaven, and endeavouring to preserve the devils from the evils which they love and seek; but that he always perfectly regards and preserves the free will of every one, giving to every one the utmost aid that will leave him at liberty to turn himself to heaven or to hell, and to no one more.

Salvation, according to Swedenborg, is not salvation from punishment, but salvation from sinfulness. Those who co-operate with the Lord, and confirm in themselves a principle of good, in the other life become angels, and associate with angels; and their association constitutes heaven. Those who resist the divine grace, and confirm in themselves a principle of self-love, which is the root of all evil, become devils; and their association constitutes hell.

Both in heaven and in hell there are many societies, each influenced by some principle of good or of evil, like seeking like, both in general and in particular. None go into the other life entirely good or evil: while here, the good and evil are permitted to endure the conflicts of opposing influences, within them, that the good may thereby be made better, and the evil good; but after death, when no further radical change can take place, the ruling principle of every one is made manifest, and the whole character conformed to it.

This final change is accomplished by degrees; and while it is going on, deceased men are neither angels nor devils, but are spoken of by Swedenborg as not in heaven nor hell, but, "in the world of spirits;" and, in the writings of Swedenborg, spirits are thus distinguished from angels and devils.

With regard to the resurrection, Swedenborg teaches that it is not a resurrection of the natural body, but of the spiritual body from the natural; and that this occurs generally about the third day after apparent death, when the flesh becomes rigid, and all vital warmth and motion cease. According to him, the spiritual body forms the natural body, and, while within it, uses it as an instrument—agreeably to the words of St. Paul: "*There is a natural body, and there is a spiritual body.*" Thus the natural eye sees only because the spiritual eye sees natural things through it, the sense strictly residing in the spiritual organ; and so of the other senses. Hence, when the spiritual body rises, it finds itself in perfect possession of the senses and organs, and the man is still perfectly a man. So the spiritual world forms the natural world, and all things which exist naturally in this natural world are spiritually in the spiritual world. There, spiritual things affect the spiritual organs and senses of men, as natural things affect their natural organs and senses here. Hence, says Swedenborg, many who die do not know, upon their awaking, that they are in another world.

Those who, in this life, have their spiritual senses opened, as Swedenborg says was the case with himself, see plainly spiritual persons and things, as did the prophets in their visions. From this circumstance, say the Swedenborgians, connected with their belief in the active and constant influence of disembodied spirits upon men in the body, has arisen the common notion of their believing in a perpetual intercourse between the living and the dead. Spiritual things have not, however, a similar permanence and independent existence with natural things. Swedenborg rather represents them as appearances, changing with the state of those about whom they are—existing from their relation to them, and exactly reflecting and manifesting their affections and thoughts.

From the principle that natural things correspond to spiritual things, and represent them, comes the doctrine of CORRESPONDENCES, according to which Swedenborg explains the spiritual sense of the Word; that is, the sense in which the Bible is read by those in the spiritual world. He teaches that the spiritual sense is within the literal, as the spiritual body is within the natural, or as the soul within the body; that it is in every word and letter of the literal sense, which every where exists from it, and on account of it, and derives from it all its power and use.

With regard to differences of opinion in the Christian church, Swedenborg's doctrine is summed up in these words: " There are three essentials of the church; an acknowledgment of the Lord's (Christ's) divinity; an acknowledgment of the holiness of the Word; and the life, which is charity. Conformable to his life—that is, to his charity—is every man's *real faith*. From the Word he hath the knowledge of what his life ought to be; and from the Lord he hath reformation and salvation. If these three had been held as essentials of the church, intellectual dissensions would not have divided it, but only have varied it, *as the light varieth colours in beautiful objects, and various jewels constitute the beauty of a kingly crown.*"

Swedenborg considers the New Jerusalem, foretold in the Apocalypse, to be a church now about to be established, the true Scriptural doctrines of which have been unfolded in his writings, and in which will be known the true nature of God and of man, of the Word, of heaven and of hell— concerning all which subjects error and ignorance prevail, and in which church this knowledge will bear its proper fruits,—love to the Lord and to one's neighbour, and purity of life.

With regard to the state of the soul in the next world, Swedenborg says: " Every one carries with him into the other world such a quality of life as he had procured to himself in this; thus each one carries with him his own hell. The quality of every one's life may be known from his ruling love, for it is this which makes his life. It is this, from which all a man's subordinate loves derive their quality. If one's ruling love be of the Lord and the neighbour, and he has lived in performance of uses from this love or from the love of use, then the quality of his life is good; and when he is removed to the spiritual world he enters some angelic society which is in a similar state of love with himself. But if his ruling love be of self and the world, and whenever he has performed any uses he has done it not from any love of use but from the love of self, then the quality of his life is evil; and when he passes into the other world, he enters some infernal society, whose quality of life is in general similar to his own."

Milton seems not to have differed much from Swedenborg on this subject, when he said:

> "The mind is its own place, and, in itself,
> Can make a heaven of hell, a hell of heaven."

In his treatise concerning Heaven and Hell, and the wonderful things therein, as heard and seen by him, Swedenborg says:—"As often as I conversed with angels face to face, it was in their habitations, which are like to our houses on earth, but far more beautiful and magnificent, having rooms, chambers, and apartments in great variety, as also spacious courts belonging to them, together with the gardens, parterres of flowers, fields, &c. where the angels are formed into societies. They dwell in contiguous habitations, disposed after the manner of our cities, in streets, walks, and squares. I have had the privilege to walk through them, to examine all around about me, and to enter their houses, and this when I was fully awake, having my inward eyes opened."

The number of Swedenborgians in the United States is estimated at six or eight thousand. There are prosperous societies in Maine, Massachusetts, Rhode Island, New York, Pennsylvania, Maryland, Virginia, Ohio, Illinois, South Carolina and Missouri; and there are periodical publications advocating their doctrines, published at Boston, New York, and Cincinnati.

The writings of Swedenborg seem to be daily attracting more and more attention in this country. The most important of them, ably translated from the original Latin, have been published in Boston; and an interesting " Life of Swedenborg, with some account of his Writings," compiled by B. F. Barrett, minister of the New Jerusalem Church, has recently appeared in New York. This work has been made the text for an able article in the Southern Quarterly Review for October, 1843, in which the writer places in their proper light, the claims of the great Swede.

"There has been," he says, "a singular timidity evinced, even by bold thinkers, in respect to the very perusal of his works. They have been read by stealth, away from company—free from the curiosity of the prying eye. Persons have been afraid, as if they were engaged in some necromantic orgies, to breathe a word to their friends of their peculiar and forbidden occupation. They have come to their teacher, as Nicodemus came to the Saviour, in the night time, and have listened to his instructions with equal incredulity and equal wonder.

"The ridicule levelled at the celebrated Swede by Dr. Southey, more than a quarter of a century ago, in his 'Espriella's Letters,' has led many to turn with indifference and contempt from his works—works full of light and consolation—lest they, too, if detected in their perusal, should come in for a share of the sarcasm of some lively and witty satirist. The style in which these compositions are clothed—in some degree eccentric and unique—but deriving its singularity rather from the elevated character of the subjects treated of, than from any want of tact and skill in the writer, has deterred others who have commenced the examination of them, from proceeding much beyond the threshold.—Prescriptive authority—educational biases—pride of opinion—of opinion imbibed in other schools—long entertained, and mistaken for truth—these have stood in the way of others.

"Then the pretensions of Swedenborg, scarcely less lofty than those of a prophet, though preferred with a modesty and even a humility, which, taken in connection with the solemn and startling developments he has made, and the unblemished purity of his life and manners, forbid the slightest suspicion of imposture—these pretensions, we say, have led others to affirm, that his mind may have been shattered and warped from its healthful tone—a charge, we know, once preferred against a greater than Swedenborg.

"But to those who are inspired with a larger share of courage—who can recognize intellectual superiority, in some cases, where there is more than a slight divergence from old and beaten paths—who have been willing to say to worldly considerations, 'Get ye behind me,' and to authority, 'Thou art not my master in matters of this nature;'—to those who have been animated more by a love of truth, than alarmed by fears of reproach and contumely;—to those, who, like the wisest of sages, could send up, from the inmost depths of their being, the earnest entreaty, 'Give me understanding'—to such—and there are not a few of them—the works of the author under consideration have proved a rare treasure."

The doctrines of the sect which bears his name, are founded on the Bible and the following books, written by Swedenborg, in Latin, between the years 1747 and 1771: Arcana Cœlestia; De Cœlo et Inferno; De Telluribus; De Ultimo Judicio; De Equo Albo; De Nova Hierosolyma et ejus Doctrina Cœlesti; De Domino; De Scriptura Sacra; De Vita; De Fide; De Divino Amore et Divina Providentia; De Amore Conjugiali; De Commercio Animæ et Corporis; Summaria Expositio Sensus Prophetici; Apocalypsis Explicata; Apocalypsis Revelata; De Vera Theologia Christiana. Of the Bible, they consider canonical only the Pentateuch, the book of Joshua, the book of Judges, the books of Samuel and of Kings, the Psalms the Prophets, the Gospels, and the Apocalypse.

CHAPTER XIII.

BEREANS—CHRISTIAN CONNECTION—SANDEMANIANS—DALEITES—COME-OUTERS.

DISCIPLES OF CHRIST, OR CAMPBELLITES.

This society is of comparatively recent origin. About the commencement of the present century, the Bible alone, without any human addition in the form of creeds or confessions of faith, began to be preached by many distinguished ministers of different denominations, both in Europe and America. With various success, and with many of the opinions of the various sects imperceptibly carried with them from the denominations to which they once belonged, did they plead for the union of Christians of every name, on the broad basis of the apostle's teaching. But it was not until the year 1823, that a restoration of the *original gospel* and *order of things,* began to be advocated in a periodical, edited by Alexander Campbell, of Bethany, Virginia, entitled "The Christian Baptist."

He and his father, Thomas Campbell, renounced the Presbyterian system, and were immersed, in the year 1812. They, and the Congregations which they had formed, united with the Redstone Baptist Association, protesting against all human creeds as bonds of union, and professing subjection to the Bible alone. This union took place in the year 1813. But in pressing upon the attention of that society and the public the all-sufficiency of the *sacred* Scriptures for every thing necessary to the perfection of Christian character,—whether in the private or social relations of life, in the church or in the world,—they began to be opposed by a strong creed party in that association. After some ten years' debating and contending for the Bible alone, and the Apostle's doctrine, Alexander Campbell, and the church to which he belonged, united with the Mahoning association, in the Western Reserve of

Ohio; that association being more favorable to his views of reform.

In his debates on the subject and action of baptism with Mr. Walker, a seceding minister, in the year 1820, and with Mr. M'Calla, a Presbyterian minister, in the year 1823, his views of reformation began to be developed, and were very generally received by the Baptist society, as far as these works were read.

But in his "Christian Baptist," which began July 4, 1823, his views of the need of reformation were more fully exposed; and as these gained ground by the pleading of various ministers of the Baptist denomination, a party in opposition began to exert itself, and to oppose the spread of what they regarded as heterodox opinions. But not till after great numbers began to act upon these principles, was there any attempt towards separation. Not until after the Mahoning association appointed Mr. Walter Scott, an evangelist, in the year 1827, and when great numbers began to be immersed into Christ, under his labours, and new churches began to be erected by him and other labourers in the field, did the Baptist associations begin to declare non-fellowship with the brethren of the reformation. Thus by constraint, not of choice, were the Campbellites obliged to form societies out of those communities that split, upon the ground of adherence to the apostles' doctrine. The distinguishing characteristics of their views and practices are the following:—

They regard all the sects and parties of the Christian world as having, in greater or less degrees, departed from the simplicity of faith and manners of the first Christians, and as forming what the apostle Paul calls " the apostacy." This defection they attribute to the great varieties of speculation and metaphysical dogmatism of the countless creeds, formularies, liturgies, and books of discipline, adopted and inculcated as bonds of union and platforms of communion in all the parties which have sprung from the Lutheran reformation. The effect of these synodical covenants, conventional articles of belief, and rules of ecclesiastical polity, has been the introduction of a new nomenclature,—a human vocabulary of religious words, phrases and technicalities, which has displaced the style of the living oracles, and affixed to the sacred diction ideas wholly unknown to the apostles of Christ.

To remedy and obviate these aberrations, they propose to ascertain from the holy Scriptures, according to the commonly-received and well-established rules of interpretation, the ideas attached to the leading terms and sentences found in the holy Scriptures, and then to use the words of the Holy Spirit in the apostolic acceptation of them.

By thus expressing the ideas communicated by the Holy Spirit, in the terms and phrases learned from the apostles, and by avoiding the artificial and technical language of scholastic theology, they propose to restore a pure speech to the household of faith; and by accustoming the family of God to use the language and dialect of the heavenly Father, they expect to promote the sanctification of one another through the truth, and to terminate those discords and debates which have always originated from the words which man's wisdom teaches, and from a reverential regard and esteem for the style of the great masters of polemic divinity; believing that speaking the same things in the same style, is the only certain way to thinking the same things.

They make a very marked difference between faith and opinion; between the testimony of God and the reasonings of men; the words of the Spirit and human inferences. Faith in the testimony of God, and obedience to the commandments of Jesus, are their bond of union, and not an agreement in any abstract views or opinions upon what is written or spoken by divine authority. Hence, all the speculations, questions, debates of words, and abstract reasonings, found in human creeds, have no place in their religious fellowship. Regarding Calvinism and Arminianism, Trinitarianism and Unitarianism, and all the opposing theories of religious sectaries, as *extremes* begotten by each other, they cautiously avoid them, as equidistant from the simplicity and practical tendency of the promises and precepts of the doctrine and facts, of the exhortations and precedents, of the Christian institution.

They look for unity of spirit and the bonds of peace in the practical acknowledgment of one faith, one Lord, one immersion, one hope, one body, one Spirit, one God and Father of all; not in unity of opinions, nor in unity of forms, ceremonies, or modes of worship.

The holy Scriptures of both Testaments they regard as containing revelations from God, and as all necessary to make the man of God perfect, and accomplished for every good word and work; the New Testament, or the living oracles of Jesus Christ, they understand as containing the Christian religion; the testimonies of Matthew, Mark, Luke and John, they view as illustrating and proving the great proposition on which our religion rests, viz., *that Jesus of Nazareth is the Messiah, the only-begotten and well-beloved Son of God, and only Saviour of the world;* the Acts of the Apostles as a divinely authorised narrative of the beginning and progress of the reign or kingdom of Jesus Christ, recording the full development of *the gospel* by the Holy Spirit sent down from heaven, and the procedure of the apostles in setting up the church of Christ on earth; the Epistles as carrying out and applying the doctrine of the apostles to the practice of individuals and congregations, and as developing the tendencies of the gospel in the behaviour of its professors; and all as forming a complete standard of Christian faith and morals, adapted to the interval between the ascension of Christ and his return with the kingdom which he has received from God; the apocalypse, or revelation of Jesus Christ to John, in Patmos, as a figurative and prospective view of all the fortunes of Christianity, from its date to the return of the Saviour.

Every one who sincerely believes the testimony which God gave of Jesus of Nazareth, saying, " *This is my son, the beloved, in whom I delight,*" or, in other words, believes what the evangelists and apostles have testified concerning him, from his conception to his coronation in heaven as Lord of all, and who is willing to obey him in ev erything, they regard him as a proper subject for immersion, and no one else. They consider immersion in the name of the Father, Son, and Holy Spirit, after a public, sincere, and intelligent confession of the faith in Jesus, as necessary to admission to the privileges of the kingdom of the Messiah, and as a solemn pledge, on the part of heaven, of the actual remission of all past sins, and of adoption into the family of God.

The Holy Spirit is promised only to those who believe and obey the Saviour. No one is taught to expect the reception of that heavenly Monitor and Comforter, as a resident in his heart, till he obeys the gospel.

Thus, while they proclaim faith and repentance, or faith and a change of heart, as preparatory to immersion, remission, and the Holy Spirit, they say to all penitents, or all those who believe and repent of their sins, as Peter said to the first audience addressed after the Holy Spirit was bestowed, after the glorification of Jesus, "Be immersed, every one of you, in the name of the Lord Jesus, for the remission of sins, and you shall receive the gift of the Holy Spirit." They teach sinners that God commands *all men*, every where, to reform, and to turn to God; that the Holy Spirit strives with them, so to do, by the apostles and prophets; that God beseeches them to be reconciled, through Jesus Christ; and that it is the duty of all men to believe the gospel, and turn to God.

The immersed believers are congregated into societies, according to their propinquity to each other, and taught to meet every first day of the week, in honour and commemoration of the resurrection of Jesus, and to break the loaf, which commemorates the death of the Son of God, to read and hear the living oracles, to teach and admonish one another, to unite in all prayer and praise, to contribute to the necessities of saints and to perfect holiness in the fear of the Lord.

Every congregation chooses its own overseers and deacons, who preside over and administer the affairs of the congregations; and every church, either from itself or in co-operation with others, sends out, as opportunity offers, one or more evangelists, or proclaimers of the word, to preach the word, and to immerse those who believe, to gather congregations, and to extend the knowledge of salvation where it is necessary, as far as their means extend. But, every church regards these evangelists as its servants, and, therefore, they have no control over any congregation; each congregation being subject to its own choice or presidents or elders, whom they have appointed. Perseverance in all the disciples is essential to admission into the heavenly kingdom.

Such are the prominent outlines of the faith and practice of those who wish to be known as the disciples of Christ; but no society among them would agree to make the preceding items either a confession of faith or a standard of practice; but, for the information of those who wish an acquaintance with them, they are willing to give, at any time, a reason for their faith, hope, and practice.

BEREANS.

The Bereans are a sect of Protestant dissenters from the church of Scotland, who take their title from, and profess to follow the example of, the ancient Bereans, in building their system of faith and practice upon the Scriptures alone, without regard to any human authority whatever. The Bereans first assembled, as a separate society of Christians, in the city of Edinburgh, in the autumn of 1773. Mr. Barclay, a Scotch clergyman, was the founder of this sect.

The Bereans agree with the great majority of Christians respecting the doctrine of the Trinity, which they hold as a fundamental article; and they also agree, in a great measure, with the professed principles of our Orthodox churches, respecting predestination and election, though they allege that these doctrines are not consistently taught. But they differ from the majority of all sects of Christians in various other important particulars such as,—

1. Respecting our knowledge of the Deity. Upon this

subject, they say the majority of professed Christians stumble at the very threshold of revelation; and, by admitting the doctrine of natural religion, natural conscience, natural notices, &c., not founded upon revelation, or derived from it by tradition, they give up the cause of Christianity at once to the infidels, who may justly argue, as Mr. Paine, in fact, does, in his " Age of Reason," that there is no occasion for any revelation or word of God, if man can discover his nature and perfections from his works alone. But this, the Bereans argue, is beyond the natural powers of human reason; and, therefore, our knowledge of God is from revelation alone; and, without revelation, man would never have entertained an idea of his existence.

2. With regard to faith in Christ, and assurance of salvation through his merits, they differ from almost all other sects whatsoever. These they reckon inseparable, or rather the same, because (they say) " God hath expressly declared, He that believeth shall be saved; and, therefore, it is not only absurd, but impious, and, in a manner, calling God a liar, for a man to say, ' I believe the gospel, but have doubts, nevertheless, of my own salvation.' " With regard to the various distinctions and definitions that have been given of different kinds of faith, they argue that there is nothing incomprehensible or obscure in the meaning of this word, as used in Scripture; but that, as faith, when applied to human testimony, signifies neither more nor less than the mere simple belief of that testimony as true, upon the authority of the testifier, so, when applied to the testimony of God, it signifies precisely " the belief of his testimony, and resting upon his veracity alone, without any kind of collateral support from concurrence of any other evidence or testimony whatever." And they insist that, as this faith is the gift of God alone, so the person to whom it is given is as conscious of possessing it, as the being to whom God gives life is of being alive; and, therefore, he entertains no doubts, either of his faith, or his consequent salvation through the merits of Christ, who died and rose again for that purpose. In a word, they argue that the gospel would not be what it is

held forth to be,—glad tidings of great joy,—if it did not bring full personal assurance of eternal salvation to the believer; which assurance, they insist, is the present infallible privilege and portion of every individual believer of the gospel.

3. Consistently with the above definition of faith, they say that the sin against the Holy Ghost, which has alarmed and puzzled so many in all ages, is nothing else but unbelief; and that the expression, " it shall not be forgiven, neither in this world nor that which is to come," means only that a person dying in infidelity would not be forgiven, neither under the former dispensation by Moses, (the then present dispensation, kingdom, or government, of God,) nor under the gospel dispensation, which, in respect of the Mosaic, was a kind of future world, or kingdom to come.

4. The Bereans interpret a great part of the Old Testament prophecies, and, in particular, the whole of the Psalms, excepting such as are merely historical or laudatory, to be typical or prophetical of Jesus Christ, his sufferings, atonement, mediation, and kingdom; and they esteem it a gross perversion of these psalms and prophecies, to apply them to the experiences of private Christians. In proof of this, they not only urge the words of the apostle, that no prophecy is of any private interpretation, but they insist that the whole of the quotations from the ancient prophecies in the New Testament, and particularly those from the Psalms, are expressly applied to Christ. In this opinion, many other classes of Protestants agree with them.

5. Of the absolute, all-superintending sovereignty of the Almighty, the Bereans entertain the highest idea, as well as of the uninterrupted exertion thereof over all his works, in heaven, earth, and hell, however unsearchable by his creatures. A God without election, they argue, or choice in all his works, is a God without existence, a mere idol, a nonentity. And to deny God's election, purpose, and express will, in all his works, is to make him inferior to ourselves.

The Bereans consider infant baptism as a divine ordinance, instituted in the room of circumcision, and think it absurd to suppose that infants, who, all agree, are admissible to the kingdom of God in heaven, should, nevertheless, be incapable of being admitted into his visible church on earth.

They commemorate the Lord's supper generally once a month; but, as the words of the institution fix no particular period, they sometimes celebrate it oftener, and sometimes at more distant periods, as it may suit their general convenience. They meet every Lord's day, for the purpose of preaching, praying, and exhorting to love and good works.

They do not think that they have any power to deliver a backsliding brother to Satan; that text, and other similar passages, such as, "Whatsoever ye shall bind on earth shall be bound in heaven," &c., they consider as restricted to the apostles, and to the inspired testimony alone, and not to be extended to any church on earth, or any number of churches, or of Christians, whether decided by a majority of votes, or by unanimous voices. Neither do they think themselves authorized, as a Christian church, to inquire into each other's political opinions, any more than to examine into each other's notions of philosophy.

They both recommend and practise, as a Christian duty, submission to lawful authority; but they do not think that a man, by becoming a Christian, or joining their society, is under any obligation, by the rules of the gospel, to renounce his right of private judgment upon matters of public or private importance. Upon all such subjects, they allow each other to think and act as each may see it his duty; and they require nothing more of the members, than a uniform and steady profession of the apostolic faith, and a suitable walk and conversation. (See Acts 17: 11. Rom. 10: 9.)

The Berean doctrines have found converts in various parts of Europe and America.

CHRISTIAN CONNECTION.

This denomination, among themselves, are generally called simply *Christians*. This they do merely to denote their character as the followers of Christ; but when applied to them collectively, it necessarily becomes the name of a denomination. They are sometimes called *Christians*; but this pronunciation of the word they universally reject as improper.

The Christians began to associate and form a distinct people about the beginning of the nineteenth century, so that they may be said to have existed but about forty years. They seem to have sprung up almost simultaneously in different parts of the United States, without any interchange of sentiments, concert of action, or even knowledge of one another's views or movements, till after a public stand had been taken in several parts of the country.

The first branch arose in Virginia and North Carolina, and consisted of seceders from the Methodists. At first, there were about one thousand communicants.

The northern branch of this denomination sprung up in New England. It commenced by the formation of several new churches, under the administration of a few ministers who had separated themselves from the Baptists, who were soon joined by several other ministers, and nearly whole churches from the same denomination.

The western branch arose in Kentucky, and was composed of seceders from the Presbyterians. Some of their ministers were men of strong and well-cultivated minds, who urged forward the reform they had undertaken, till they have spread over most of the Western States.

In all these different sections, their leading purpose, at first, appears to have been, not so much to establish any peculiar or distinctive doctrine, as to assert for individuals and churches more liberty and independence in relation to matters of faith and practice; to shake off the authority of human creeds, and the shackles of prescribed modes and forms; to make the Bible their only guide, claiming for every man the right to judge for himself what is its doctrine, and what are its requirements; and in practice to follow more strictly the simplicity of the apostles and primitive christians.

This class of believers recognize no individual as a leader or founder, and no man claims this high eminence, although several persons were instrumental in giving rise and progress to the society. They point all to Christ as the Leader and Founder, and professedly labour to bring all to the first principles of original, apostolic christianity.

Seceding, as the first ministers did, from different denominations, they necessarily brought with them some of the peculiarities of faith and usage in which they had been educated. But the two prominent sentiments that led them out, kept them together, by rendering them tolerant toward each other, and gradually brought them to be very similar both in faith and practice. These two sentiments were, that the Scriptures *only* should be consulted as a rule of faith and duty, and that all christians should enjoy universal toleration. Hence scarcely any churches have written creeds, although nearly all record their principles of action. Very few are Trinitarians, though nearly all believe in the pre-existence and proper Sonship of Christ. Perhaps not any believe in or practise sprinkling, but almost all practise immersion; from which circumstance many, though very improperly, call them Christian Baptists.

Perfect uniformity does not exist among all the members of this community, although the approximation to it is far greater than many have supposed it ever could be without a written creed. But there are several important points in which they generally agree fully; and these are regarded as sufficient to secure Christian character, Christian fellowship, and concert of action. The following are very generally regarded by them as Scripture doctrines:—

That there is one living and true God, the Father Almighty, who is unoriginated, independent, and eternal, the Creator and Supporter of all worlds; and that this God is one spiritual intelligence, one infinite mind, ever the same, never varying.

That this God is the moral governor of the world, the absolute source of all the blessings of nature, providence and grace, in whose infinite wisdom, goodness, mercy, benevolence, and love, have originated all his moral dispensations to man.

That all men sin and come short of the glory of God, consequently fall under the curse of the law.

That Christ is the Son of God, the promised Messiah and Saviour of the world, the Mediator between God and man, by whom God has revealed his will to mankind; by whose sufferings, death, and resurrection, a way has been provided by which sinners may obtain salvation, may lay hold on eternal life; and that he is appointed of God to raise the dead and judge the world at the last day.

That the holy Spirit is the power and energy of God, that holy influence by whose agency, in the use of means, the wicked are regenerated, converted, and recovered to a virtuous and holy life, sanctified and made meet for the inheritance of the saints in light; and that by the same spirit, the saints, in the use of means, are comforted, strengthened, and led in the path of duty. The free forgiveness of sins, flowing from the rich mercy of God, through the labours, and sufferings, and blood of our Lord Jesus Christ. The necessity of repentance towards God, and faith towards our Lord Jesus Christ. The absolute necessity of holiness of heart and rectitude of life to enjoy the favour and approbation of God. The doctrine of a future state of immortality. The doctrine of a righteous retribution, in which God will render to every man according to the deeds done in the body. The baptism of believers by immersion. And the open communion at the Lord's table of Christians of every denomination, having a good standing in their respective churches.

The principles upon which their churches were at first constituted, and upon which they still stand, are the following :—The Scriptures are taken to be the only rule of faith and practice, each individual being at liberty to determine, for himself, in relation to these matters, what they enjoin. No member is subject to the loss of church-fellowship on account of his sincere and conscientious belief, so long as he manifestly lives a pious and devout life No member is subject to discipline and church censure but for disorderly and immoral conduct. The name Christian to be adopted to the exclusion of all sectarian names, as the most appropriate designation of the body and its members. The only condition or test of admission as a member of a church, is a personal profession of the Christian religion, accompanied with satisfactory evidence of sincerity nd piety, and a determination to live according to the divine rule or the gospel of Christ. Each church is considered an independent body, possessing exclusive authority to regulate and govern its own affairs.

For the purpose of promoting the general interest and prosperity of the Connection by mutual efforts and joint counsels, associations were formed, denominated Conferences. Minister and churches represented by delegates, formed themselves in each state, into one or more conferences, called State Conferences, and delegates from these conferences formed the United States General Christian Conference. This General Conference has been given up. The Local or State Conferences are still continued, possessing, however, no authority or control over the independence of the churches. In twenty of the United States, there are now (1833) thirty-two Conferences, one in Upper Canada, and one in the province of New Brunswick. The number of their ministers is estimated at about 700; of churches 1000; of communicants from 75,000 to 100,000; and from 250 to 300,000 who entertain their views and attend upon their ministry.

Several periodicals have been published under the patronage of the Connection.

Very few of their ministers are thoroughly educated men; but they are generally well acquainted with the bible, and many of them good, powerful preachers. All the important means by which pure Christianity may be advanced, are fast gaining favour both in the ministry and the churches.

Within the last few years, there has been a very rapid

increase in their numbers; and the prospects of the connection are regarded as most promising.

SANDEMANIANS.

So called from Mr. Robert Sandeman, a Scotchman, who published his sentiments in 1757. He afterwards came to America, and established societies at Boston, and other places in New England, and in Nova Scotia.

This sect arose in Scotland about the year 1728, where it is distinguished at the present day by the name of *Glassites*, after its founder, Mr. John Glass, a minister of the established church.

The Sandemanians consider that faith is neither more nor less than a simple assent to the divine testimony concerning Jesus Christ, delivered for the offences of men, and raised again for their justification, as recorded in the New Testament. They also maintain that the word *faith*, or belief, is constantly used by the apostles to signify what is denoted by it in common discourse, viz., a persuasion of the truth of any proposition; and that there is no difference between believing any common testimony and believing the apostolic testimony, except that which results from the testimony itself, and the divine authority on which it rests.

They differ from other Christians in their weekly administration of the Lord's supper; their love-feasts, of which every member is not only allowed, but required, to partake, and which consist of their dining together at each other's houses in the interval between the morning and afternoon service; their kiss of charity, used on this occasion, at the admission of a new member, and at other times, when they deem it necessary and proper; their weekly collection, before the Lord's supper, for the support of the poor, and defraying other expenses; mutual exhortation; abstinence from blood and things strangled; washing each other's feet, when, as a deed of mercy, it might be an expression of love, the precept concerning which, as well as other precepts, they understand literally;

community of goods, so far as that every one is to con‑ sider all that he has in his possession and power liable to the calls of the poor and the church; and the unlawfulness of laying up treasures upon earth, by setting them apart for any distant, future, or uncertain use. They allow of public and private diversions, so far as they are not connected with circumstances really sinful; but, apprehending a lot to be sacred, disapprove of lotteries, playing at cards, dice, &c.

They maintain a plurality of elders, pastors, or bishops, in each church, and the necessity of the presence of two elders in every act of discipline, and at the administration of the Lord's supper.

In the choice of these elders, want of learning and engagement in trade are no sufficient objections, if qualified according to the instructions given to Timothy and Titus; but second marriages disqualify for the office; and they are ordained by prayer and fasting, imposition of hands, and giving the right hand of fellowship.

In their discipline they are strict and severe, and think themselves obliged to separate from communion and worship all such religious societies as appear to them not to profess the simple truth for their only ground of hope, and who do not walk in obedience to it. (See John 13: 14, 15; 16: 13. Acts 6: 7. Rom. 3: 27: 4: 4, 5; 16: 16. 1 Cor. 16: 20. 2 Cor. 4: 13. 1 Pet. 1: 22.)

DALEITES,

The followers of David Dale, a very industrious manufacturer, a most benevolent Christian, and the humble pastor of an Independent congregation at Glasgow. At first, he formed a connection with the *Glassites*, in many of whose opinions he concurred, but was disgusted by their narrow and worldly spirit: he therefore separated from them, chiefly on the ground of preferring practical to speculative religion, and Christian charity to severity of church discipline. As he grew rich by industry, he devo‑ ted all his property to doing good, and ranks high among the philanthropists of his age. He was founder of the celebrated institution of New Lanark, now under Mr. Robert Owen, his son-in-law. The Daleites now form the second class of Independents in Scotland.

COME-OUTERS.

This is a term which has been applied to a considerable number of persons in various parts of the Northern States, principally in New England, who have recently *come out* of the various religious denominations with which they were connected;—hence the name. They have not themselves assumed any distinctive name, not regarding themselves as a sect, as they have not formed, and do not contemplate forming, any religious organization. They have no creed, believing that every one should be left free to hold such *opinions* on religious subjects as he pleases, without being held accountable for the same to any human authority.

Hence, as might be expected, they hold a diversity of opinions on many points of belief upon which agreement is considered essential by the generality of professing Christians. Amongst other subjects upon which they differ is that of the authority of the Scriptures of the Old and the New Testaments, some among them holding the prevailing belief of their divine inspiration, whilst others regard them as mere human compositions, and subject them to the same rules of criticism as they do any other book, attaching to them no authority any further than they find evidence of their truth. They believe the commonly-received opinion of the plenary inspiration of the writers of those books to be unfounded, not claimed by the writers themselves, and therefore *unscriptural*, as well as unreasonable.

Whilst, then, they believe the authors of the Gospels to have been fallible men, liable to err both in relation to matters of fact and opinion, they believe they find in their writings abundant evidence of their honesty. Therefore they consider their testimony satisfactory as regards the main facts there stated of the life of Jesus Christ, at least so far, that there can be no difficulty in deducing therefrom the great principles of the religion which he taught. They *all* believe him to have been a divinely-inspired teacher, and his religion, therefore, to be a revelation of eternal truth. They regard him as the only authorized expositor of his own religion, and believe that to apply in practice its principles as promulgated by him, and as exemplified in his life, is all that is essential to constitute a Christian, according to his testimony, (Matt. 7: 24,)—*" Whosoever heareth these sayings of mine, and doeth them, I will liken him unto a wise man which built his house upon a rock,"* &c. Hence they believe, that to make it essential to Christianity to assent to all the opinions expressed by certain men, good men though they were, who wrote either before or after his time, involves a denial of the words of Christ. They believe that, according to his teachings, true religion consists in purity of heart, holiness of life, and not in opinions; that *Christianity, as it existed in the mind of Christ, is a life rather than a belief.*

This class of persons *agree* in the opinion that *he only is a Christian who has the spirit of Christ;* that all such as these are members of his church, and that it is composed of none others; therefore that membership in the Christian church is not, and cannot, in the nature of things, be determined by any human authority. Hence they deem all attempts to render the church identical with any outward organizations as utterly futile, not warranted by Christ himself, and incompatible with its spiritual character. Having no organized society, they have no stations of authority or superiority, which they believe to be inconsistent with the Christian idea, (Matt. 23: 8,)—" But be not ye called Rabbi: for one is your Master, even Christ; and all ye are brethren." (Matt. 20: 25, 26,)—" Ye know that the princes of the Gentiles exercise dominion over them, and they that are great exercise authority upon them. *But it shall not be so among you.*"

As might be inferred from the foregoing, they discard

all outward ordinances as having no place in a spiritual religion, the design of which is to purify the heart, and the extent of whose influence is to be estimated by its legitimate effects in producing a life of practical righteousness, and not by any mere arbitrary sign, which cannot be regarded as a certain indication of the degree of spiritual life, and must consequently be inefficient and unnecessary.

Their views of worship correspond, as they believe, with the spiritual nature of the religion they profess. They believe that true Christian worship is independent of time and place; that it has no connection with forms, and ceremonies, and external arrangements, any further than these are the exponents of a divine life; that it spontaneously arises from the pure in heart at all times and in all places: in short, they regard the terms *Christian worship* and *Christian obedience* as synonymous, believing that he gives the highest and only conclusive evidence of worshipping the Creator, who exhibits in his life the most perfect obedience to his will. These views they consider in perfect harmony with the teachings of Jesus, particularly in his memorable conversation with the woman of Samaria.

They also agree in the belief that the religion of Christ asserts the equality of all men before God; that it confers upon no man, or class of men, a monopoly of Heaven's favours; neither does it give to a portion of his children any means of knowing his will not common to the race. They believe the laws of the soul are so plain that they may be easily comprehended by all who sincerely seek to know them, without the intervention of any human teacher or expounder. Hence they regard no teaching as authoritative but that of the Spirit of God, and reject all priesthoods but the universal priesthood which Christianity establishes. They believe that every one whose soul is imbued with a knowledge of the truth, is qualified to be its minister, and it becomes his duty and his pleasure, by his every word and action, to preach it to the world. It follows, then, that, as Christ prepares and appoints his own ministers, and as they receive their commissions only from him, they are accountable to him alone for their exercise, and not to any human authority whatsoever. They therefore reject all human ordinations, appointments, or control, or any designation by man of an order of men to preach the gospel, as invasions of his rightful prerogative.

Amongst the prevailing sins, against which they feel bound to bear testimony, are slavery and war; and it is alleged as the main reason why many of them have disconnected themselves from the professedly Christian denominations to which they belonged, that those bodies gave their sanction to those anti-Christian practices. They believe slaveholding to be sinful under all circumstances, and that, therefore, it should be immediately abandoned. They believe, not only that national wars are forbidden by Christianity, but that the taking of human life for any purpose, by governments or individuals, is incompatible with its spirit. A large proportion of them, also, consider all resort to punishment, as a penalty for crime, equally inconsistent with the law of love. Hence they deem it their duty to withhold their voluntary sanction or support from human governments, and all institutions which claim the right to exercise powers which they thus regard as unlawful.

In various places, these persons hold meetings on the first day of the week, which are conducted consistently with their views of Christian freedom and equality. It is understood that the object of thus meeting together, is to promote their spiritual welfare. For this purpose, they encourage a free interchange of sentiment on religious subjects, without any restraint or formality. They have no prescribed exercises, but every one is left free to utter his thoughts as he may feel inclined; and even those who differ from them in opinion are not only at liberty, but are invited, to give expression to their thoughts. They believe this to be the only mode of holding religious meetings consistent with the genius of their religion, and for an example of like gatherings they refer to those of the primitive Christians.

CHAPTER XIV.

HUTCHINSONIANS—MILLENARIANS—MILLERITES—FOLLOWERS OF JOANNA SOUTHCOTT—WHIPPERS—WILKINSONIANS—MYSTICS—MORMONITES

HUTCHINSONIANS.

HUTCHINSONIANS, the followers of John Hutchinson, born in Yorkshire, 1674, and who in the early part of life served the Duke of Somerset in the capacity of a steward. The Hebrew Scriptures, he says, comprise a perfect system of natural philosophy, theology, and religion. In opposition to Dr. Woodward's Natural History of the Earth, Mr. Hutchinson, in 1724, published the first part of his curious book, called Moses Principia. Its second part was presented to the public in 1727, which contains, as he apprehends, the principles of the Scripture philosophy, which are a plenum and the air. So high an opinion did he entertain of the Hebrew language, that he thought the Almighty must have employed it to communicate every species of knowledge, and that accordingly every species of knowledge is to be found in the Old Testament. Of his mode of philosophising, the following specimen is brought forward to the reader's attention : " The air (he supposes) exists in three conditions, fire, light, and spirit : the two latter are the finer and grosser parts of the air in motion ; from the earth to the sun, the air is finer and finer till it becomes pure light near the confines of the sun, and fire in the orb of the sun, or solar focus. From the earth towards the circumference of this system, in which he includes the fixed stars, the air becomes grosser and grosser till it becomes stagnant, in which condition it is at the utmost verge of this system, from whence (in his opinion) the expression of outer darkness, and blackness of darkness used in the New Testament, seems to be taken."

The followers of Mr Hutchinson are numerous, and number among others the Rev. Mr. Romaine, Lord Duncan Forbes, of Culloden, and the late Dr. Horne, Bishop of Norwich, who published an abstract of Mr. Hutchinson's writings. See also the preface to Bishop Horne's Life, second edition, by William Jones. They have never formed themselves into any distinct church or society.

MILLENARIANS.

The Millenarians are those who believe that Christ will reign personally on earth for a thousand years; and their name, taken from the Latin, *mille*, a thousand, has a direct allusion to the duration of this spiritual empire. The doctrine of the millennium, or a future paradisaical state of the earth, is not of christian, but of Jewish origin. The tradition is attributed to Elijah, which fixes the duration of the world in its present imperfect condition to six thousand years, and announces the approach of a sabbath of a thousand years of universal peace and plenty, to be ushered in by the glorious advent of the Messiah! This idea may be traced in the epistle of Barnabas, and in the opinions of Papias, who knew of no written testimony in its behalf. It was adopted by the author of the Revelations, by Justin Martyr, by Irenæus, and by a long succession of the fathers. As the theory is animating and consolatory, and when divested of cabalistic numbers and allegorical decorations, probable even in the eye of philosophy, it will, no doubt, always retain a number of adherents.

But as the Millennium has for these few years past attracted the attention of the public, we shall enter into a short detail respecting it:—

Mr. Joseph Mede, Dr. Gill, Bishop Newton, and Mr. Winchester, contend for the personal reign of Christ on earth. To use that prelate's own words, in his Dissertations on the Prophecies:—" When these great events shall come to pass, of which we collect from the prophecies, this is to be the proper order:—the Protestant witnesses shall be greatly exalted, and the 1260 years of their prophesying in sackcloth, and of the tyranny of the beast, shall end together; the conversion and restoration of the Jews succeed; then follows the ruin of the Othman Empire; and then the total destruction of Rome and Antichrist. When these great events, I say, shall come to pass, then shall the kingdom of Christ commence, or the reign of the saints upon earth. So Daniel expressly informs us, that the kingdom of Christ and the saints will be raised upon the ruins of the kingdom of Antichrist, vii. 26, 27 :— 'But the judgment shall sit, and they shall take away his dominion, to consume and destroy *it* unto the end : and the kingdom and dominion, and the greatness of the kingdom under the whole heaven, shall be given to the saints of the Most High, whose kingdom *is* an everlasting kingdom, and all dominions shall serve and obey him.' So, likewise, St. John saith, that, upon the final destruction of the beast and the false prophet, Rev. xx., Satan is bound for a thousand years; and I saw thrones and they sat on them, and judgment was given unto them; and I *saw* the souls of them that were beheaded for the witness of Jesus Christ and for the word of God; which had not worshipped the beast, neither his image; neither had received *his* mark upon their foreheads or in his hands; and they lived and reigned with Christ a thousand years. But the rest of the dead lived not again till the thousand years were finished. This *is* the first resurrection. It is, I conceive, to these great events, the fall of Antichrist, the re-establishment of the Jews, and the beginning of the glorious Millennium, that the three different dates, in Daniel, of 1,260 years, 1,290 years, and 1,335 years, are to be referred. And as Daniel saith, xii. 12 :—' Blessed *is* he that waiteth and cometh to the thousand three hundred five and thirty days.' So St. John saith, Rev. xx. 6 :—' Blessed and holy *is* he that hath part in the first resurrection.' Blessed and happy indeed will be this period: and it is very observable, that the martyrs and confessors of Jesus, in Papist as well as Pagan times, will be raised to partake of this felicity Then shall all those gracious promises in the old Testament be fulfilled—of the amplitude and extent, of the peace and prosperity, of the glory and happiness of the church in the latter days. Then, in the full sense of the words, Rev. xi. 15 :—Shall ' the kingdoms of this world become *the kingdoms* of our Lord, and of his Christ ; and he shall reign for ever and ever.' According to tradition,* these thousand years of the reign of Christ and the saints, will be the seventh Millenary of the world: for as God created the world in six days, and rested on the seventh; so the world, it is argued, will continue six thousand years, and the seventh thousand years will be the great Sabbatism, or holy rest to the people of God. ' One day (2 Peter iii, 8) *is* with the Lord as a thousand years, and a thousand years as one day.' According to tradition, too, these thousand years of the reign of Christ and the saints, are the great day of judgment, in the morning or beginning whereof, shall be the coming of Christ in flaming fire, and the particular judgment of Antichrist and the first resurrection ; and in the evening or conclusion whereof, shall be the *General Resurrection* of the dead, small and great; and they shall be judged, every man according to their works."†

This is a just representation of the Millennium, according to the common opinion entertained of it, that Christ will reign personally on earth during the period of one thousand years! But Dr. Whitby, in a Dissertation on the subject ; Dr. Priestley in his Institutes of Religion ; and the author of the Illustration of Prophecy, contend against the literal interpretation of the Millenium, both as to its nature and duration. On such a topic, however, we can-

---

* See Burnet's Theory.

† Mr. Winchester, in his Lectures on the Prophecies, freely indulges his imagination on this curious subject. He suggests, that the large rivers in America are all on the eastern side, that the Jews may waft themselves the more easily down to the Atlantic, and then across that vast ocean to the Holy Land; that Christ will appear at the equinoxes (either March or September), when the days and nights are equal all over the globe; and finally, that the body of Christ will be luminous, and being suspended in the air over the equator for twenty-four hours, will be seen with circumstances of peculiar glory, from pole to pole, by all the inhabitants of the world!

not suggest our opinions with too great a degree of modesty.

Dr. Priestley, entertaining an exalted idea of the advantages to which our nature may be destined, treats the limitation of the duration of the world to seven thousand years as a Rabbinical fable; and intimates that the thousand years may be interpreted prophetically: then every day would signify a year, and the Millennium would last for three hundred and sixty-five thousand years! Again he supposes that there will be no resurrection of any individuals till the general resurrection; and that the Millennium implies only the revival of religion.

MILLERITES.

The following letter from the Rev. WILLIAM MILLER to the Rev. JOSHUA V. HIMES, contains a synopsis of Mr. Miller's views on the subject of the second advent of Christ:

Rev. J. V. Himes:

"My dear brother:—You have requested a synopsis of my views of the Christian faith. The following sketch will give you some idea of the religious opinions I have formed, by a careful study of the word of God:—

"I believe all men, coming to years of discretion, do and will disobey God; and this is, in some measure, owing to corrupted nature by the sin of our parent. I believe God will not condemn us for any pollution in our father; but the soul that sinneth shall die. All pollution of which we may be partakers from the sins of our ancestors, in which we could have no agency, can and will be washed away in the blood and sacrifice of Jesus Christ, without our agency. But all sins committed by us as rational, intelligent agents, can only be cleansed by the blood of Jesus Christ, through our repentance and faith. I believe in the salvation of all men who receive the grace of God by repentance and faith in the mediation of Jesus Christ. I believe in the condemnation of all men who reject the gospel and mediation of Christ, and thereby lose the effi cacy of the blood and righteousness of our Redeemer, as proffered to us in the gospel. I believe in practical godliness, as commanded us in the Scriptures, (which are our only rule of faith and practice,) and that they only will be entitled to heaven and future blessedness, who obey and keep the commandments of God, as given us in the bible, which is the word of God. I believe in God, the Father of our Lord Jesus Christ, who is a Spirit, omnipresent, omniscient, having all power, Creator, Preserver, and self-existent. As being holy, just, and beneficent, I believe in Jesus Christ, the Son of God, having a body in fashion and form like man, divine in his nature, human in his person, god-like in his character and power. He is a Saviour for sinners, a Priest to God, a Mediator between God and man, and King in Zion. He will be all to his people, God with us forever. The spirit of the Most High is in him, the power of the Most High is given him, the people of the Most High are purchased by him, the glory of the Most High shall be with him, and the kingdom of the Most High is his on earth.

"I believe the Bible is the revealed will of God to man, and all therein is necessary to be understood by Christians in the several ages and circumstances to which they may refer;—for instance, what may be understood to-day, might not have been necessary to have been understood a thousand years ago; for its object is to reveal things new and old, that the man of God may be thoroughly furnished for, and perfected in, every good word and work, for the age in which he lives. I believe it is revealed in the best possible manner for all people, in every age and under every circumstance, to understand, and that it is to be understood as literal as it can be and make good sense; and that in every case where the language is figurative, we must let the Bible explain its own figures. We are in no case allowed to speculate on the Scriptures, and suppose things which are not clearly expressed, nor reject things which are plainly taught. I believe all of the prophecies are revealed to try our faith, and to give us hope, without which we could have no reasonable hope. I believe that the Scriptures do reveal unto us, in plain language, that Jesus Christ will appear again on this earth; that he will come in the glory of God, in the clouds of heaven, with all his saints and angels; that he will raise the dead bodies of all his saints who have slept, change the bodies of all that are alive on the earth that are his, and both these living and raised saints will be caught up to meet the Lord in the air. There the saints will be judged and presented to the father, without spot or wrinkle. Then the gospel kingdom will be given up to God the Father. Then will the Father give the bride to the Son Jesus Christ; and when the marriage takes place, the church will become the 'New Jerusalem,' the 'beloved city.' And while this is being done in the air, the earth will be cleansed by fire, the elements will melt with fervent heat, the works of men will be destroyed, the bodies of the wicked will be burned to ashes, the devil and all evil spririts, with the souls and spirits of those who have rejected the gospel, will be banished from the earth, shut up in the pit or place prepared for the devil and his angels, and will not be permitted to visit the earth again until a thousand years. This is the first resurrection, and first judgment. Then Christ and his people will come down from the heavens, or middle air, and live with his saints on the new earth in a new heaven, or dispensation, forever, even for ever and ever. This will be the restitution of the right owners to the earth.

"Then will the promise of God to his Son be accomplished—'I will give him the heathen for his inheritance, and the utmost parts of the earth for his possession.' Then 'the whole earth shall be full of his glory.' And then will the holy people take possession of their joint heirship with Christ, and his promise be verified, 'The meek shall inherit the earth,' and the kingdom of God will have come, and 'his will be done in earth as in heaven.' After a thousand years shall have passed away, the saints will all be gathered and encamped in the beloved city. The sea, death and hell, will give up their dead, which will rise up on the breadths of the earth, out of the city, a great company like the sand of the sea-shore. The devil will be let loose, to go out and deceive this wicked host. He will tell them of a battle against the saints, the beloved city; he will gather them in the battle around the camp of the saints. But there is no battle; the devil has deceived them. The saints will judge them; the justice of God will drive them from the earth into the lake of fire and brimstone, where they will be tormented day and night, forever and ever. 'This is the second death.' After the second resurrection, second judgment, the righteous will then possess the earth forever.

"I understand that the judgment day will be a thousand years long. The righteous are raised and judged in the commencement of that day, the wicked in the end of that day. I believe that the saints will be raised and judged about the year 1843, according to Moses' Prophecy, Lev. ch. 26; Ezek. ch. 39; Daniel, ch. 2, 7, 8—12; Hos. 5: 1—3; Rev., the whole book; and many other prophets have spoken of these things. Time will soon tell if I am right, and soon he that is righteous will be righteous still, and he that is filthy will be filthy still. I do most solemnly entreat mankind to make their peace with God, be ready for these things. 'The end of all things is at hand.' I do ask my brethren in the gospel ministry to consider well what they say before they oppose these things. Say not in your hearts, 'My lord delayeth his coming.' Let all do as they would wish they had if it does come, and none will say they have not done right if it does not come. I believe it will come; but if it should not come, then I will wait and look until it does come. Yet I must pray, 'Come Lord Jesus, come quickly.'

"This is a synopsis of my views. I give it as a matter of faith. I know of no scripture to contradict any view given in the above sketch. Men's theories may oppose. The ancients believed in a temporal and personal reign of Christ on earth. The moderns believe in a temporal, spiritual reign, as a millennium. Both views are wrong; both are too gross and carnal. I believe in a glorious, immortal, and personal reign of Jesus Christ, with all his people, on the purified earth forever. I believe the millennium is between the two resurrections and two judgments, the righteous and the wicked, the just and the unjust. I hope the dear friends of Christ will lay by all prejudice, and look at and examine these three views by the only rule and standard, the BIBLE.

"WILLIAM MILLER."

The followers of Mr. Miller have much decreased within the last year, and appear to be daily decreasing in number.

FOLLOWERS OF JOANNA SOUTHCOTT.

"The mission of this prophetess," says one of her followers, "commenced in the year 1792, and the number of people who have joined with her from that period to the present time, as believing her to be divinely inspired, is considerable. It is asserted that she is the instrument under the direction of Christ, to announce the establishment of his kingdom on earth, as a fulfillment of the promises in the Scriptures, and of that prayer which he himself gave to his followers; and more particularly of the promise made to the woman in the fall, through which the human race is to be redeemed from all the effects of it in the end. We are taught by the communication of the Spirit of Truth to her, that the seven days of the Creation were types of the two periods in which the reign of Satan and of Christ are to be proved and contrasted; Satan was conditionally to have his reign tried for six thousand years, shadowed by the six days in which the Lord worked, as his spirit has striven with man while under the powers of darkness; but Satan's reign is to be shortened, for the sake of the elect, as declared in the gospel; and Satan is to have a further trial at the expiration of the thousand years, for a time equal to the number of days shortened.

"At the close of the seven thousand years the Day of Judgment is to take place, and then the whole human race will collectively bring forward the testimony of the evil they have suffered under the reign of Satan, and of the good they have enjoyed under the spiritual reign of Christ. These two testimonies will be evidence before the whole creation of God, that the pride of Satan was the cause of his rebellion in heaven, and that he was the root of evil upon earth; and, consequently, when those two great proofs have been brought forward, that part of the human race that has fallen under his power to be tormented by being in the society of Satan and his angels, will revolt from him in that great day, will mourn that they have been deluded, will repent, and the Saviour of all will hold out his hand to them in mercy; and will then prepare a new earth for them to work righteousness, and prepare them ultimately to join his saints, who have fought the good fight in this world, while under the reign of Satan.

"The mission of Joanna is to be accomplished by a perfect obedience to the spirit that directs her, and so to be made to claim the promise of 'bruising the head of the serpent;' and which promise was made to the woman on her casting the blame upon Satan, whom she unwittingly obeyed, and thus man became dead to the knowledge of the good; and so he blamed his Creator for giving him the woman, who was pronounced his helpmate for good. To fulfil the attribute of justice, Christ took upon himself that blame, and assumed his humanity to suffer on the cross for it, that he might justly bring the cross upon Satan, and rid him from the earth, and then complete the creation of man, so as to be after his own image. It is declared that the 'seed of the woman' are those who in faith shall join with her in claiming the promise made in the fall; and they are to subscribe with their hands unto the Lord, that they do thus join with her, praying for the destruction of the powers of darkness, and for the establishment of the kingdom of Christ. Those who thus come forward in this spiritual war, are to have the seal of the Lord's protection, and if they remain faithful soldiers, death and hell shall not have power over them; and these are to make up the sealed number of one hundred and forty-four thousand to stand with the Lamb on Mount

Sion! The fall of Satan's kingdom will be a second deluge over the earth; so that from his having brought the human race under his power, a great part of them will fall with him; for the Lord will pluck out of his kingdom all that offend and do wickedly. The voice which announces the coming of the Messiah is accompanied with judgments, and the nations must be shaken and brought low before they will lay these things to heart. When all these things are accomplished, then the desire of nations will come in glory, so that 'every eye shall see him,' and he will give his kingdom to his saints!

"It is represented that in the Bible is recorded every event by which the Deity will work the ultimate happiness of the human race; but that the great plan is, for the most part, represented by types and shadows, and otherwise so wrapped up in mysteries as to be inscrutable to human wisdom. As the Lord pronounced that man should become dead to knowledge, if he ate the forbidden fruit, so the Lord must prove his words true. He, therefore, selected a peculiar people, as depositaries of the records of that knowledge; and he appeared among them, and they proved themselves dead to every knowledge of him by crucifying him. He will in like manner put 'the wild olive' to the same test; and the result will be, that he will be now crucified in the spirit!

"The mission of Joanna began in 1792, at which time she had prophecies given her, showing how the whole was to be accomplished. Among other things, the Lord said he should visit the surrounding nations with various calamities for fifteen years, as a warning to this land; and that then he should bring about events here which should more clearly manifest the truth of her mission, by judgment and otherwise; so that this should be the happy nation to be the first redeemed from its troubles, and the instrument for awakening the rest of the world to a sense of what is coming upon all, and for destroying the beast, and those who worship his image!"

Such is the account of the opinions of Joanna Southcott. But Joanna Southcott, in her last production, dated March 10, 1814, made this declaration respecting herself:

"I am now answered, that impostors will arise, saying, that they are the Women, and they might succeed in deceiving, if the Lord had not worked a way to prevent them by the *three signs* I am now ordered to put in print. Therefore, to prevent all imposition that may be attempted, I here give notice, not to receive any person who may come in the name of Joanna Southcott, unless they can prove, that they stand on the will of the late James Cousins, and can produce the probate of his will; (he died Nov. 17, 1812). I am, likewise, ordered to print the register of my age—'Joanna, daughter of William and Hannah Southcott, baptised the 6th day of June 1750, as appears by the Register of baptisms of Ottery, St. Mary's Parish, Devon. I was born in April, but do not know the day of the month.' Another sign I am ordered to mention: There have been many impostors who have gone about in London, from whose scandalous conduct, and calling themselves Joanna Southcott, much mischief has been caused to my friends, and being misrepresented in various ways, I was inclined to have my likeness taken, in order to expose these false misrepresentations, when I should be no more. I was answered—'It was the will of the Lord that it should be done!' Mr. Sharp took my likeness and engraved it. In it I had the Bible placed before me, as opened by me promiscuously at the two last chapters of Isaiah."

Joanna died of a protracted illness, Dec. 27th, 1814. It was given out that she was to be the mother of a *Second Shiloh*. Presents were accordingly made her for the *Babe*, especially a superb cradle, with a Hebrew inscription in poetry! But she expired, and no child appeared on the occasion. A stone placed over her remains has this mystic incription:

> While through all thy wondrous days
> Heaven and earth enraptured gaze,
> While vain sages think they know
> Secrets thou alone canst show,
> Time alone will tell what hour
> Thou'lt appear in greater power!

This article shall be closed with a specimen of **Joanna Southcott's** poetry, with which her numerous pamphlets abound:

> "And now the knowledge it is in her hand,
> By such writings as we cannot command,
> And sealed from us, what shortly will appear,
> And what all nations are to hope and fear;
> And all our Bibles we see open wide,
> And now in Adam we see how we died,
> And so in Christ we now are made alive!
> For in the woman we died all at first,
> And in the woman now we're brought to Christ;
> That as in Adam—Man is pronounced dead,
> So now in Christ we see our living head!"

The death of this infatuated woman did not annihilate the sect. Her followers yet exist in various parts of England.

WHIPPERS.

This denomination sprang up in Italy, in the thirteenth century, and was thence propagated through almost all the countries of Europe. The society that embraced this new discipline, ran in multitudes, composed of persons of both sexes, and all ranks and ages, through the public streets, with whips in their hands, lashing their naked bodies with the most astonishing severity, with a view to obtain the divine mercy for themselves and others, by their voluntary mortification and penance. This sect made their appearance anew in the fourteenth century, and taught, among other things, that flagellation was of equal virtue with baptism and other sacraments; that the forgiveness of all sins was to be obtained by it from God, without the merit of Jesus Christ; that the old law of Christ was soon to be abolished, and that a new law, enjoining the baptism of blood, to be administered by whipping, was to be substituted in its place.

A new denomination of Whippers arose in the fifteenth century, who rejected the sacraments and every branch of external worship, and placed their only hopes of salvation in *faith* and *flagellation*.

WILKINSONIANS.

The followers of Jemima Wilkinson, who was born in Cumberland, R. I. In 1776, she asserted that she was taken sick, and actually died, and that her soul went to heaven. Soon after, her body was reanimated with the spirit and power of Christ, upon which she set up as a public teacher, and declared she had an immediate revelation for all she delivered, and was arrived to a state of absolute perfection. It is also said she pretended to foretell future events, to discern the secrets of the heart, and to have the power of healing diseases; and if any person who had made application to her was not healed, she attributed it to his want of faith. She asserted that those who refused to believe these exalted things concerning her, will be in the state of the unbelieving Jews, who rejected the counsel of God against themselves; and she told her hearers that was the eleventh hour, and the last call of mercy that ever should be granted them; for she heard an inquiry in heaven, saying, " Who will go and preach to a dying world ?" or words to that import; and she said she answered, " Here am I—send me;" and that she left the realms of light and glory, and the company of the heavenly host, who are continually praising and worshipping God, in order to descend upon earth, and pass through many sufferings and trials for the happiness of mankind. She assumed the title of the *universal friend of mankind*.

Jemima made some converts in Rhode Island and New York, and died in 1819. She is said to have been a very beautiful, but artful woman.

MYSTICS.

This denomination derived their name from their maintaining, that the scriptures have a *mystic* and *hidden sense*, which must be sought after, in order to understand their true import. They derived their origin from Dionysius, the Areopagite, who was converted to Christianity, in the first century, by the preaching of St. Paul at Athens. To support this idea, they attributed to this great man various treatises, which are generally ascribed to writers who lived at a later period, particularly to a famous Grecian Mystic, who, it is said, wrote under the protection of the venerable name of Dionysius, the Areopagite.

This denomination appeared in the third century; and increased in the fourth. In the fifth century, they gained ground in the eastern provinces. In the year eight hundred and twenty-four, the supposed works of Dionysius kindled the flame of Mysticism in the western provinces. In the twelfth century, they took the lead in their method of expounding the scriptures. In the thirteenth century, they were the most formidable antagonists of the schoolmen; and towards the close of the fourteenth century, they resided, and propagated their sentiments, in almost every part of Europe. In the fifteenth and sixteenth centuries, many persons of distinguished merit embraced their tenets. In the seventeenth century, the radical principle of Mysticism was adopted by the Behemists, Bourignonists, and Quietists.

The ancient Mystics were distinguished by their professing pure, sublime, and perfect devotion, with an entire disinterested love of God, and by their aspiring to a state of passive contemplation.

The first suggestions of these sentiments have been supposed to proceed from the known doctrine of the Platonic school, which was adopted by Origen and his disciples, that the divine nature was diffused through all human souls, or, in other words, that the faculty of reason, from which proceeds the health and vigour of the mind, was an emanation from God into the human soul, and comprehended in it the principles and elements of all truth, human and divine.

They denied that men could, by labour or study, excite this celestial flame in their breasts. Therefore, they disapproved highly of the attempts of those, who, by definitions, abstract theorems, and profound speculations, endeavoured to form distinct notions of truth, and to discover its hidden nature. On the contrary, they maintained, that silence, tranquillity, repose, and solitude, accompanied with such acts of mortification as might tend to attenuate and exhaust the body, were the means, by which the hidden and internal word was excited to produce its latent virtues, and to instruct men in the knowledge of divine things. For thus they reasoned:

They, who behold, with a noble contempt, all human affairs, who turn away their eyes from terrestrial vanities, and shut all the avenues of the outward senses against the contagious influence of an outward world, must necessarily return to God, when the spirit is thus disengaged from the impediments which prevent this happy union: And in this blessed frame, they not only enjoy inexpressible raptures from their communion with the Supreme Being, but also are invested with the inestimable privilege of contemplating truth undisguised, in its native purity, while others behold it in a vitiated and delusive form.

The apostle tells us, that *The Spirit makes intercession for us,* &c. Now, if the Spirit prays in us, we must resign ourselves to its motions, and be swayed and guided by its impulses, by remaining in a state of mere inaction.

As the late Rev. William Law, who was born in 1687, makes a distinguished figure among the modern Mystics, a brief account of the outlines of his system, may, perhaps, be entertaining to some readers.

He supposed, that the material world was the very region, which originally belonged to the fallen angels. At length, the light and spirit of God entered into the chaos, and turned the angels' ruined kingdom into a paradise on earth. God then created man, and placed him there. He was made in the image of the Triune God, a living mirror of the divine nature, formed to enjoy communion with Father, Son, and Holy Ghost, and live on earth, as the angels do in heaven. He was endowed with immortality; so that the elements of this outward world could not have any power of acting on his body. But, by his fall, he changed the light, life, and spirit of God, for the light, life, and spirit of the world. He died, the very day of his transgression, to all the influences and operations of the spirit of God upon him, as we die to the influences of this world, when the soul leaves the body: And all the influences and operations of the elements of this life were open in him, as they are in any animal, at its birth into this world. He became an earthly creature, subject to the dominion of this outward world; and stood only in the highest mark of animals.

But the goodness of God would not leave man in this condition. Redemption from it was immediately granted; and the bruiser of the serpent brought the life, light, and spirit of heaven, once more into the human nature. All men, in consequence of the redemption of Christ, have in them the first spark, or seed, of the divine life, as a treasure hidden in the centre of our souls, to bring forth, by degrees, a new birth of that life, which was lost in paradise. No son of Adam can be lost, only by turning away from the Saviour within him. The only religion, which can save us, must be that, which can raise the light, life, and spirit of God, in our souls. Nothing can enter into the vegetable kingdom, till it has the vegetable life in it; or be a member of the animal kingdom, till it has the animal life. Thus all nature joins with the gospel in affirming, that no man can enter into the kingdom of heaven, till the heavenly life is born in him. Nothing can be our righteousness or recovery, but the divine nature of Jesus Christ derived to our souls.

The arguments, which are brought in defence of this system, cannot easily be abridged in such a manner, as to render them intelligible. Those who are fond of mystical writings, are referred to the works of this ingenious author.

MORMONITES, OR LATTER-DAY SAINTS

The Book of Mormon, which may be said to be at the foundation of Mormonism, was first published in the year

1830. Since that period, its believers and advocates have zealously propagated its doctrines. Through every state in the Union, and in Canada, they have disseminated its principles. They have crossed the ocean, and, in England, if their own accounts may be credited, have made thousands of converts; and recently some of their missionaries have even been sent to Palestine.

The Book of Mormon purports to be the record, or history, of a certain people, who inhabited America previous to its discovery by Columbus. This people, according to it, were the descendants of one Lehi, who crossed the ocean, from the eastern continent, to this. Their history and records, containing prophecies and revelations, were engraven, by the command of God, on small plates, and deposited in the hill Comora, which appears to be situated in Western New York. Thus was preserved an account of this race, (together with their religious creed,) up to the period when the descendants of Laman, Lemuel and Sam, who were the three eldest sons of Lehi, arose and destroyed the descendants of Nephi, who was the youngest son. From this period, the descendants of the eldest sons 'dwindled in unbelief,' and 'became a dark, loathsome and filthy people.' The last mentioned are our present Indians.

The plates above mentioned remained in their depository until about the year 1825, when, as the Mormons say, they were found by Joseph Smith, Jr., who was directed in the discovery by the Angel of the Lord. On these plates were certain hieroglyphics, said to be of the Egyptian character, which Smith, by the direction of God, being instructed by inspiration as to their meaning, proceeded to translate. The following is Smith's own account of the mode in which these plates came into his possession. It is contained in a letter dated March 1, 1842:

" On the evening of the 21st of September, A.D. 1823, while I was praying unto God, and endeavouring to exercise faith in the precious promises of Scripture, on a sudden a light like that of day, only of a far purer and more glorious appearance and brightness, burst into the room;

indeed, the first sight was as though the house was filled with consuming fire; the appearance produced a shock that affected the whole body. In a moment, a personage stood before me surrounded with a glory yet greater than that with which I was already surrounded. This messenger proclaimed himself to be an angel of God, sent to bring the joyful tidings, that the covenant which God made with ancient Israel was at hand to be fulfilled; that the preparatory work for the second coming of the Messiah was speedily to commence; that the time was at hand for the gospel in all its fulness, to be preached, in power, unto all nations, that a people might be prepared for the millennial reign.

" I was also informed concerning the aboriginal inhabitants of this country, and shown who they were, and from whence they came; a brief sketch of their origin, progress, civilization, laws, governments, of their righteousness and iniquity, and the blessings of God being finally withdrawn from them as a people, was made known unto me. I was also told where there were deposited some plates, on which was engraven an abridgment of the records of the ancient prophets that had existed on this continent. The angel appeared to me three times the same night, and unfolded the same things. After having received many visits from the angels of God, unfolding the majesty and glory of the events that should transpire in the last days, on the morning of the 22d September, A.D. 1827, the angel of the Lord delivered the records into my hands.

" These records were engraven on plates which had the appearance of Gold; each plate was six inches wide and eight inches long, and not quite so thick as common tin. They were filled with engravings, in Egyptian characters, and bound together in a volume, as the leaves of a book, with three rings running through the whole. The volume was something near six inches in thickness, a part of which was sealed. The characters on the unsealed part were small, and beautifully engraved. The whole book exhibited many marks of antiquity in its construcion, and much skill in the art of engraving. With the record was found a curious instrument, which the ancients called 'Urim and Thummim,' which consisted of two transparent stones set in the rim of a bow fastened to a breast-plate.

"Through the medium of the Urim and Thummim I translated the record, by the gift and power of God.

"In this important and interesting book the history of ancient America is unfolded, from its first settlement by a colony that came from the tower of Babel, at the confusion of languages, to the beginning of the fifth century of the Christian era. We are informed by these records that America in ancient times, has been inhabited by two distinct races of people. The first were called Jaredites, and came directly from the tower of Babel. The second race came directly from the city of Jerusalem, about six hundred years before Christ. They were principally Israelites, of the descendants of Joseph. The Jaredites were destroyed about the time that the Israelites came from Jerusalem, who succeeded them in the inheritance of the country. The principal nation of the second race fell in battle towards the close of the fourth century. The remnant are the Indians that now inhabit this country. This book also tells us that our Saviour made his appearance upon this continent after his resurrection, that he planted the gospel here in all its fulness, and richness, and power, and blessing; that they had apostles, prophets, pastors, teachers, and evangelists; the same order, the same priesthood, the same ordinances, gifts, powers, and blessings, as were enjoyed on the eastern continent; that the people were cut off in consequence of their transgressions; that the last of their prophets who existed among them was commanded to write an abridgment of their prophecies, history, &c., and to hide it up in the earth, and that it should come forth, and be united with the Bible, for the accomplishment of the purposes of God in the last days. For a more particular account, I would refer to the Book of Mormon, which can be purchased at Nauvoo, or from any of our travelling elders.

"As soon as the news of this discovery was made known, false reports, misrepresentation, and slander, flew, as on the wings of the wind, in every direction; the house was frequently beset by mobs and evil-designing persons; several times I was shot at, and very narrowly escaped, and every device was made use of to get the plates from me; but the power and blessing of God attended me, and several began to believe my testimony.

"On the 6th of April, 1830, the 'Church of Jesus Christ of Latter-Day Saints' was first organized in the town of Manchester, Ontario county, State of New York. Some few were called and ordained by the spirit of revelation and prophecy, and began to preach as the spirit gave them utterance; and though weak, yet were they strengthened by the power of God, and many were brought to repentance, were immersed in the water, and were filled by the Holy Ghost by the laying on of hands. They saw visions and prophesied; devils were cast out, and the sick healed by the laying on of hands. From that time, the work rolled forth with astonishing rapidity, and churches were soon formed in the States of New York, Pennsylvania, Ohio, Indiana, Illinois, and Missouri. In the last-named state, a considerable settlement was formed in Jackson county; numbers joined the church, and we were increasing rapidly; we made large purchases of land, our farms teemed with plenty, and peace and happiness were enjoyed in our domestic circle and throughout our neighbourhood; but we could not associate with our neighbours, who were many of them of the basest of men."

After giving an account of their removal from Jackson to Clay, and from Clay to Caldwell and Davies counties, Missouri, with a relation of their persecutions and consequent distresses, the prophet proceeds:—

"We arrived in the State of Illinois in 1839, where we found a hospitable people and a friendly home; a people who were willing to be governed by the principles of law and humanity. We have commenced to build a city, called 'Nauvoo," in Hancock county. We number from six to eight thousand here, besides vast numbers in the country around, and in almost every county of the state. We have a city charter granted us, and a charter for a legion, the troops of which now number fifteen hundred. We have also a charter for a university, for an agricultural and manufacturing society, have our own laws and administrators, and possess all the privileges that other free and enlightened citizens enjoy.

" Persecution has not stopped the progress of truth, but has only added fuel to the flame; it has spread with increasing rapidity. Proud of the cause which they have espoused, and conscious of their innocence, and of the truth of their system, amidst calumny and reproach have the elders of this church gone forth, and planted the gospel in almost every state in the Union; it has penetrated our cities, it has spread over our villages, and has caused thousands of our intelligent, noble and patriotic citizens to obey its divine mandates, and be governed by its sacred truths. It has also spread into England, Ireland, Scotland and Wales. In the year 1839, where a few of our missionaries were sent, over five thousand joined the standard of truth. There are numbers now joining in every land.

" Our missionaries are going forth to different nations; and in Germany, Palestine, New Holland, the East Indies, and other places, the standard of truth has been erected. No unhallowed hand can stop the work from progressing. Persecutions may rage, mobs may combine, armies may assemble, calumny may defame, but the truth of God will go forth boldly, nobly, and independent, till it has penetrated every continent, visited every clime, swept every country, and sounded in every ear, till the purposes of God shall be accomplished, and the great Jehovah shall say, 'The work is done!'

" We believe in God, the eternal Father, and in his son Jesus Christ, and in the Holy Ghost.

" We believe that men will be punished for their own sins, and not for Adam's transgressions.

" We believe that, through the atonement of Christ, all mankind may be saved by obedience to the laws and ordinances of the Gospel.

"We believe that these ordinances are, 1. faith in the Lord Jesus Christ; 2. repentance; 3. baptism, by immersion, for the remission of sins; 4. laying on of hands for the gift of the Holy Ghost.

"We believe that a man must be called of God by 'prophecy, and by laying on of hands,' by those who are in authority to preach the gospel, and administer in the ordinances thereof.

"We believe in the same organization that existed in the primitive church, viz. apostles, prophets, pastors, teachers, evangelists, &c.

"We believe in the gift of tongues, prophecy, revelation, visions, healing, interpretation of tongues, &c.

"We believe the bible to be the word of God, as far as it is translated correctly; we also believe the Book of Mormon to be the word of God.

"We believe all that God has revealed, all that he does now reveal, and we believe that he will yet reveal many great and important things pertaining to the kingdom of God.

"We believe in the literal gathering of Israel, and in the restoration of the ten tribes; that Zion will be built upon this continent; that Christ will reign personally upon the earth; and that the earth will be renewed and receive its paradisaic glory.

"We claim the privilege of worshipping Almighty God according to the dictates of our conscience, and allow all men the same privilege, let them worship how, where, or what they may.

"We believe in being subject to kings, presidents, rulers, and magistrates, in obeying, honouring and sustaining the law.

"We believe in being honest, true, chaste, benevolent, virtuous, and in doing good to *all* men. Indeed, we may say that we follow the admonition of Paul,—we 'believe all things, we hope all things;'—we have endured many things, and hope to be able to endure all things. If there is any thing virtuous, lovely, or of good report, or praiseworthy, we seek after these things."

Nauvoo, the Holy City of the Mormons and present capital of their empire, is situated in the north-western part of Illinois, on the east bank of the Mississippi, in latitude N. 40° 35', and longitude W. 14° 23'. It is bounded on the north, south, and west, by the river, which there forms a large curve, and is nearly two miles wide. Eastward of the city is a beautiful undulating prairie. It is distant ten miles from Fort Madison, in Iowa, is fifty-five miles above Quincy, Illinois, and more than two hundred above St. Louis.

Before the Mormons gathered there, the place was named *Commerce*, and was but a small and obscure village of some twenty houses. So rapidly, however, have they accumulated, that there are now, within three years of their first settlement, upwards of seven thousand inhabitants in the city, and three thousand more, of the Saints, in its immediate vicinity.

The surface of the ground upon which Nauvoo is built is very uneven, though there are no great elevations. A few feet below the soil is a vast bed of limestone, from which excellent building material can be quarried, to almost any extent. A number of tumuli, or ancient mounds, are found within the limits of the city, proving it to have been a place of some importance with the extinct inhabitants of this continent.

The chief edifices of Nauvoo are the Temple, and a hotel, called the Nauvoo House, neither of which is yet finished. The latter is of brick, upon a stone foundation, and presents a front, on two streets, of one hundred and twenty feet each, by forty feet deep, and is to be three stories high, exclusive of the basement.

The Mormon Temple is a splendid structure of stone, quarried within the bounds of the city. Its breadth is eighty feet, and its length one hundred and twenty, besides an outer court of thirty feet, making the length of the whole structure one hundred and fifty feet.

In the basement of the Temple is the baptismal font, constructed in imitation of the famous brazen sea of Solomon. It is upborne by twelve oxen, handsomely carved, and overlaid with gold. Upon the surface of it, in panels, are represented various scenes, handsomely painted. This font is used for baptism of various kinds, viz., baptism for admission into the Church—baptism for the healing of the sick—baptism for the remission of sins—and lastly, which is the most singular of all, baptism for the *dead.* By this latter rite, living persons, selected as the representatives of persons deceased, are baptized for them, and thus the dead are released from the penalty of their sins! This baptism has been performed, it is said, for General Washington, among many others.

It has often been asserted, in the Eastern States, that the Mormon settlement in Illinois had a community of goods; but this is not the case. Individual property is held, and society organized, as in other American cities Not far from the city, however, is a community farm, which is cultivated in common by the poorer classes; but in the city itself each family has an acre allotted to it.

The neighbourhood of Nauvoo is pretty thickly populated, and chiefly, though not exclusively, by Mormons.

The population of the "Holy City" itself is rather of a motley kind. The general gathering of the "Saints" has, of course, brought together men of all classes and characters. The great majority of them are uneducated and unpolished persons, who are undoubtedly sincere believers in the Prophet and his doctrines. A great proportion of them consist of emigrants from the English manufacturing districts, who were easily persuaded by Smith's missionaries to exchange their wretchedness at home for ease and plenty in the Promised Land. These men are devotedly attached to the Prophet's will, and obey his dictates as they would those of a messenger of God himself

NOTE.—The Mormons, after persecution from mobs, have removed to Utah (West). Nauvoo is now held by Cabet and his followers (Socialists).

CHAPTER XV.

ARMENIANS — NESTORIANS — PELAGIANS — PAULIANS — ORIGENISTS — QUIETISTS — MANICHEISTS — MOLINISTS — GNOSTICS.

ARMENIANS.

THE Armenians are a division of eastern Christians, so called from Armenia, a country which they anciently inhabited. The chief point of separation between them on the one side, and the Greeks and the Papists on the other, is, that while the latter believe in two natures and one person of Christ, the former believe that the humanity and divinity of Christ were so united as to form but *one nature;* and hence they are called *Monophysites,* signifying *single nature.*

Another point on which they are charged with heresy by the Papists is, that they adhere to the notion that the spirit proceeds from the father only; and in this the Greeks join them, though the Papists say that he proceeds from the father and the son. In other respects, the Greeks and Armenians have nearly the same religious opinions, though they differ somewhat in their forms and modes of worship. For instance, the Greeks make the sign of the cross with three fingers, in token of their belief in the doctrine of the Trinity, while the Armenians use two fingers.

The Armenians hold to seven sacraments, like the Latins, although baptism, confirmation, and extreme unction are all performed at the same time; and the forms of prayer for confirmation and extreme unction are perfectly intermingled, which leads one to suppose that, in fact, the latter sacrament does not exist among them, except in name, and that this they have borrowed from the Papists.

Infants are baptized both by triple immersion and pouring water three times upon the head; the former being done, as their books assert, in reference to Christ's having been three days in the grave, and probably suggested by the phrase, *buried with him in baptism.*

The latter ceremony they derive from the tradition, that when Christ was baptized he stood in the midst of Jordan, and John poured water from his hand three times upon his head. In all their pictures of this scene, such is the representation of the mode of our Saviour's baptism. Converted Jews, or Mahometans, though adults, are baptised in the same manner.

The Armenians acknowledge sprinkling as a lawful mode of baptism, for they receive from other churches those that have merely been sprinkled, without baptising them. They believe firmly in transubstantiation, and worship the consecrated elements as God. Unleavened bread is used in the sacrament, and the broken pieces of bread are dipped in undiluted wine, and thus given to the people. The latter, however, do not handle it, but receive it into their mouths from the hands of the priest. They suppose it has in itself a sanctifying and saving power. The Greeks, in this sacrament, use leavened bread, and wine mixed with water.

The Armenians discard the Popish doctrine of purgatory, but yet, most inconsistently, they pray for the dead. They hold to confession of sins to the priests, who impose penances and grant absolution, though without money, and they give no indulgences. They pray through the mediation of the virgin Mary, and other saints. The belief that Mary was always a virgin is a point of very high importance with them; and they consider the thought of her having given birth to children after the birth of Christ, as in the highest degree derogatory to her character, and impious.

They regard baptism and regeneration as the same thing, and have no conception of any spiritual change; and they know little of any other terms of salvation than penance, the Lord's supper, fasting, and good works in general. Their priests are permitted to marry once only; but their patriarchs and bishops must remain in a state of strict celibacy.

The Armenians are strict Trinitarians in their views, holding firmly to the supreme divinity of Christ, and the doctrine of atonement for sin; though their views on the latter subject, as well as in regard to faith and repentance, are somewhat obscure. They say that Christ died to atone for original sin, and that actual sin is to be washed away by penances,—which, in their view, is repentance. Penances are prescribed by the priests, and sometimes consist in an offering of money to the church, a pilgrimage, or more commonly in repeating certain prayers, or reading the whole book of Psalms a specified number of times. Faith in Christ seems to mean but little more than believing in the mystery of transubstantiation.

NESTORIANS.

This denomination, which arose in the fifth century, is so called from Nestorius, a patriarch of Constantinople, who was born in Germanica, a city of Syria, in the latter part of the fourth century. He was educated and baptised at Antioch, and, soon after his baptism, withdrew to a monastery in the vicinity of that city. His great reputation for eloquence, and the regularity of his life, induced the emperor Theodosius to select him for the see of Constantinople; and he was consecrated bishop of that church A. D. 429. He became a violent persecutor of heretics; but, because he favoured the doctrine of his friend Anastasius, that "the virgin Mary cannot with propriety be called the mother of God," he was anathematized by Cyril, bishop of Alexandria, who, in his turn, was anathematized by Nestorius. In the council of Ephesus, A. D. 431, (the third General Council of the church,) at which Cyril presided, and at which Nestorius was not present, he was judged and condemned without being heard, and deprived of his see. He then retired to his monastery in Antioch, and was afterwards banished to Petra, in Arabia, and thence to Oasis, in Egypt, where he died, about A. D. 435 or 439.

The decision of the council of Ephesus caused many

difficulties in the church; and the friends of Nestorius carried his doctrines through all the Oriental provinces, and established numerous congregations, professing an invincible opposition to the decrees of the Ephesian council. Nestorianism spread rapidly over the East, and was embraced by a large number of the oriental bishops. Barsumus, bishop of Nisibis, laboured with great zeal and activity to procure for the Nestorians a solid and permanent footing in Persia; and his success was so remarkable that his fame extended throughout the East. He established a school at Nisibis, which became very famous, and from which issued those Nestorian doctors who, in that and the following centuries, spread abroad their tenets through Egypt, Syria, Arabia, India, Tartary, and China.

The Nestorian church is Episcopal in its government, like all the Oriental churches. Its doctrines, also, are, in general, the same with those of those churches, and they receive and repeat, in their public worship, the Nicene creed. Their *distinguishing* doctrines appear to be, their believing that Mary was not the mother of Jesus Christ, *as God*, but only *as man*, and that there are, consequently, *two persons*, as well as *two natures*, in the Son of God This notion was looked upon in the earlier ages of the church as a most momentous error; but it has in latter times been considered more as an error of words than of doctrine; and that the error of Nestorius was in the words he employed to express his meaning, rather than in the doctrine itself. While the Nestorians believe that Christ had *two natures* and *two persons*, they say " that these natures and persons are so closely united that they have but one *aspect*." Now, the word *barsopa*, by which they express this *aspect*, is precisely of the same signification with the Greek word προσωπον which signifies *a person;* and hence it is evident that they attached to the word *aspect* the same idea that we attach to the word *person*, and that they understood by the word *person* precisely what we understand by the term *nature*.

The Nestorians, of all the Christian churches of the East, have been the most careful and successful in avoiding a multitude of superstitious opinions and practices, which have infected the Romish and many of the Eastern churches.

Dr. Asahel Grant, an American, has published an interesting work, in which he adduces strong evidence to prove that the Nestorians and the " Lost Tribes" are one people. The London Times of a recent date contains the following letter, relating to the massacre of a large body of the Nestorians, and the success of the Circassians :

"TEFLIS, September 10, 1843.

"The Kurds, who for a long period have entertained a ferocious hatred to this Christian republic, situated in the centre of the Mahometan states, committed, on their invasion, all kinds of atrocities. The villages were pillaged, women and young girls were violated, and, in fact, the massacres committed were worthy of a plundering tribe having in their power a detested enemy. In the districts adjoining Dzumalesk might be seen during several days the Christian villages on fire. Some of those villages were burned by the inhabitants themselves, who fled before the Pasha's hordes, destroying their property to prevent its falling into the hands of the Kurds. The result of this abominable outrage was, that the Nestorians, after much bloodshed, surrendered their territory to the Pasha of Mousul. This is a deplorable event, as the Nestorians of Dzumalesk formed a small state well worthy of liberty. They were brave, industrious, and peaceable. Dr. Grant, who has for a long time resided at Urmia, has left for Mousul, where he was about to take some steps in favour of those persecuted Christians."

PELAGIANS.

This denomination arose in the fifth century, and was so called from Pelagius, a monk, who looked upon the doctrines, which were commonly received, concerning the original corruption of human nature, and the necessity of divine grace to enlighten the understanding and purify the heart, as prejudicial to the progress of holiness and virtue, and tending to establish mankind in a presumptuous and fatal security. He maintained the following doctrines:

I. That the sins of our first parents were imputed to them only, and not to their posterity; and that we derive no corruption from their fall; but are born as pure and unspotted, as Adam came out of the forming hand of his Creator.

II. That mankind, therefore, are capable of repentance and amendment, and of arriving at the highest degrees of piety and virtue, by the use of their natural faculties and powers. That, indeed, external grace is necessary to excite their endeavours, but that they have no need of the internal succours of the Divine Spirit.

III. That Adam was, by nature, mortal; and, whether he had sinned or not, would certainly have died.

IV. That the grace of God is given in proportion to our merits.

V. That mankind may arrive at a state of perfection in this life.

VI. That the law qualified men for the kingdom of heaven, and was founded upon equal promises with the gospel.

PAULIANS.

The followers of Paul of Samosata were thus called. They appeared in the third century.

Their teacher asserted, that the Son and the Holy Ghost exist in God in the same manner, as the faculties of reason and activity do in man: That Christ was born of a mere man; but that the reason or wisdom of the Father descended into him, and by him wrought miracles upon earth, and instructed the nations: and finally, that, on account of this union of the Divine Word wih the man Jesus, Christ might, though improperly, be called God.

ORIGENISTS.

Origen was a presbyter of Alexandria, who flourished

in the third century. He was a man of vast and uncommon abilities, who interpreted the divine truths of religion according to the tenor of the Platonic philosophy. He alleged, that the source of many evils lies in adhering to the literal and external part of Scripture; and that the true meaning of the sacred writers was to be sought in a mysterious and hidden sense, arising from the nature of things themselves.

The principal tenets ascribed to Origen, together with a few of the reasons made use of, in their defence, are comprehended in the following summary:

I. That there is a pre-existent state of human souls.

For the nature of the soul is such as makes her capable of existing eternally, backward, as well as forward. For her spiritual essence, as such, makes it impossible that she should, either through age or violence, be dissolved: so that nothing is wanting to her existence, but his good pleasure, from whom all things proceed. And if, according to the Platonic scheme, we assign the production of all things to the exuberant fulness of life in the Deity, which, through the blessed necessity of his communicative nature, empties itself into all possibilities of being, as into so many capable receptacles, we must suppose her existence, in a sense, necessary, and, in a degree, co-eternal with God.

II. That souls were condemned to animate mortal bodies, in order to expiate faults they had committed in a pre-existent state.

For we may be assured, from the infinite goodness of their Creator, that they were at first joined to the purest matter,* and placed in those regions of the universe which were most suitable to the purity of essence they then possessed; for that the souls of men are an order of essentially incorporate spirits, their deep immersion into terrestrial matter, the modification of all their operations by it, and the heavenly body, promised in the Gospel, as

---

* Origen supposed that our souls, being incorporeal and invisible, always stand in need of bodies suitable to the nature of the places where they exist.

the highest perfection of our renewed nature, clearly evince. Therefore, if our souls existed before they appeared inhabitants of the earth, they were placed in a purer element, and enjoyed far greater degrees of happiness. And certainly, he, whose overflowing goodness brought them into existence, would not deprive them of their felicity, until, by their mutability, they rendered themselves less pure in the whole extent of their powers, and became disposed for the susception of such a degree of corporeal life, as was exactly answerable to their present disposition of spirit. Hence it was necessary, that they should become terrestrial men.

III. That the soul of Christ was united to the Word before the incarnation.*

For the scriptures teach us, that the soul of the Messiah was created before the beginning of the world. See Phil. ii. 5, 6, 7. This text must be understood of Christ's human soul, because it is unusual to propound the Deity as an example of humility, in scripture. Though the humanity of Christ was so God-like, he emptied himself of this fulness of life and glory, *to take upon him the form of a servant*. It was this Messiah, who conversed with the patriarchs under a human form: it was he, who appeared to Moses upon the Holy Mount: it was he, who spoke to the prophets under a visible appearance; and it is he, who will at last come in triumph upon the clouds, to restore the universe to its primitive splendour and felicity.

IV. That, at the resurrection, we shall be clothed with ethereal bodies.

For the elements of our terrestrial compositions are such, as almost fatally entangle us in vice, passion, and misery. The purer the vehicle the soul is united with, the more perfect is her life and operations. Besides, the Supreme Goodness, who made all things, assures us, he made all things best at first; and therefore, his recovery

---

* See this subject more fully illustrated in Dr. Watts's Glory of Christ.

of us to our lost happiness (which is the design of the Gospel) must restore us to our better bodies and happier habitations; which is evident from 1st Cor. xv. 49, 2d Cor. v. 1, and other texts of Scripture.

V. That, after long periods of time, the damned shall be released from their torments, and restored to a new state of probation.

For the Deity has such reserves in his gracious providence as will vindicate his sovereign goodness and wisdom from all disparagement. Expiatory pains are a part of his adorable plan. For this sharper kind of favour has a righteous place in such creatures as are by nature mutable. Though sin has extinguished or silenced the divine life, yet it has not destroyed the faculties of reason and understanding, consideration and memory, which will serve the life, which is most powerful. If, therefore, the vigorous attraction of the sensual nature be abated by a ceaseless pain, these powers may resume the seeds of a better life and nature.

As, in the material system, there is a gravitation of the less bodies towards the greater, there must, of necessity, be something analogous to this in the intellectual system: and since the spirits created by God are emanations and streams from his own abyss of being, and as self-existent power must needs subject all beings to itself, the Deity could not but impress upon her intimate natures and substances, a central tendency towards himself, an essential principle of reunion to their great original.

VI. That the earth, after its conflagration, shall become habitable again, and be the mansion of men and other animals, and *that* in eternal vicissitudes.

For it is thus expressed in Isaiah: *Behold, I make new heavens and a new earth*, &c.; and in Heb. i. 10–12 *Thou, Lord, in the beginning hast laid the foundations of the earth: As a vesture shalt thou change them, and they shall be changed,* &c. Where there is only a change, the substance is not destroyed; this change being only as that of a garment worn out and decaying. *The fashion of the world passes away* like a turning scene, to exhibit a fresh and new representation of things; and if only the present dress and appearance of things go off, the substance is supposed to remain entire.

QUIETISTS.

This name has been generally applied to a class of enthusiasts, who conceive the great object of religion to be the absorption of all human sentiments and passions into devout contemplation and love of God. This idea has found its admirers and encomiasts in all ages. A sect called by this name (in Greek Hesychastæ) existed among the religious of Mount Athos; and in the 17th century it was given in France to a peculiar class of devout persons with a tendency towards a higher spiritual devotion, which seems to have arisen, in a great measure, out of a natural opposition to the hierarchical coldness and positive immorality of the Roman Catholic religion at that time, especially under the influence of the Jesuits.

A Spanish priest, Molinos, published at Rome a work entitled *The Spiritual Guide* (1657), of which the ardent language attracted a multitude of partisans. Its leading feature was the description of the happiness of a soul reposing in perfect *quiet* on God, so as to become conscious of His presence only, and untroubled by external things. He even advanced so far as to maintain that the soul, in its highest state of perfection, is removed even beyond the contemplation of God himself, and is solely occupied in the passive reception of divine influences. The work of Molinos was afterwards condemned on the application of the Jesuits.

Akin to the ideas of Molinos seem to have been those of the French Quietists, of whom Madame de la Motte Guyon and Fenelon are the most celebrated names. The former was at one time treated as insane, on account of some strange delusions which led her to represent herself (unless she was calumniated) as the mystical woman of the Apocalypse; at another she was admitted to the intimacy of Madame de Maintenon, and high in court favour

Fenelon praised her in his treatise *Sur la Vie Interieure* (1691), in which many of the most dangerous tenets of Quietism were contained. The writings of the latter upon this subject were finally condemned by Innocent XII.; and the example of the Archbishop in submitting to the decision, and declaring himself satisfied and convinced by the opinion of the church, has been dwelt on by pious writers as a signal triumph of a truly religious mind.

The dissolute conduct of some hypocritical priests, under the pretence of inculcating the tenets and practice of Quietism, brought it eventually into disrepute more than the repeated condemnations of the head of the Roman Catholic church.

MANICHEISTS.

These were the followers of Manes, an Oriental heretic of the third century, who, having been ordained a Christian presbyter, attempted to effect a combination between the religion which he was appointed to preach and the current philosophical systems of the East. He pursued herein the same course as the Valentinians, Basilidians, and many others, whose leading ideas may be denominated Gnostic. He maintained a dualism of principles governing the world, and a succession of dualisms generated from them, like the Gnostic æons.

All things were effected by the combination or repulsion of the good and the bad; men had a double soul, good and evil; even their bodies were supposed to be formed, the upper half by God, the lower by the devil. The Old Testament was referred to the inspiration of the evil principle, the New to that of the good. In the latter, however, Manes proposed many alterations, and maintained also the authenticity of various apocryphal scriptures. A great part of his system related to cosmogony and psychology, in which fields of speculation he expatiated with the most arbitrary freedom. Like most other Oriental systems, the Manichean heresy was celebrated alike for the austerities which it enjoined, and for the scandalous excesses which were attrributed to its most zealous votaries. The charge of Manicheism, which in latter times becomes scarcely intelligible, was frequently brought against the early reforming sects, such as the Albigenses, Waldenses, Picards, &c.

Manes commanded his followers to mortify and macerate the body, which he looked upon as essentially corrupt; to deprive it of all those objects which could contribute either to its convenience or delight; to extirpate all those desires which lead to the pursuit of external objects; and to divest themselves of all the passions and instincts of nature.

MOLINISTS.

In Roman Catholic theology, Molinism is a system of opinions on the subjects of grace and predestination somewhat resembling that advocated by the Arminian party among Protestants. It derived its name from the Jesuit, Louis Molina, professor of theology in the university of Evora, in Portugal, who laid down a series of propositions on these debated questions in his work, entitled *Liberi arbitrii cum gratiæ donis, &c., concordia*, which appeared in 1588. He was attacked by the Dominicans on the charge of having advocated in it Pelagian or Semi-Pelagian sentiments, and accused before the Inquisition: he appealed to Rome, and the cause was debated for twenty years in the congregations, and left at last undecided by a decree of Paul V. in 1687.

Since that period Molinism has been taught as an opinion which believers are free to embrace in Roman Catholic schools, and generally supported by the Jesuit and attacked by the Jansenist party. It must not be confounded with *Molinosism:* a name which the doctrine of the Quietists has received from the work of a Spanish enthusiast (Molinos) on Mystical Life, condemned in 1687 by Innocent XI. The French Quietists professed to abjure and oppose the errors of Molinos.

GNOSTICS.

Gnosticism was a philosophical system of religion which prevailed in the East during the first four centuries of our era, and exercised great influence upon Christian theology, giving birth to numerous and widely-diffused heresies, and insinuating itself under a modified form even into the writings of the most orthodox fathers. The origin of the system is involved in considerable obscurity; in its leading principles it seems to point to the Oriental philosophy as its genuine parent; but it is objected to this solution that the fathers refer it, together with the errors similarly introduced by Platonism, to a Greek origin, and appeal to the cosmogonies of Hesiod and others, as the real exemplars, from which it is imitated. It is to be remarked, however, that the fathers were universally ignorant of the Oriental philosophy; from which we may conclude that their opinion upon such a point is not necessarily conclusive. A modern solution conceives Alexandria to have been the central point to which the speculations of the Greeks and the Orientals converged, and from whence they frequently re-issued, after having undergone the process of fusion into a common mass. It is certain that Alexandria was, during the time we have spoken of, a celebrated resort of Gnostic opinions, both within and without the Church.

The grand principle of this philosophy seems to have been an attempt to reconcile the difficulties attending upon the existence of evil in the world. Evil, it was supposed, being the contrary of good, must be contrary to, and therefore, the opponent of God; if the opponent of God, then independent of him and coeternal. From the many imperfections which are involved in all outward and sensible objects, it was held that matter must contain in itself the principle of all evil. The human soul on the contrary, which aspires after, and tends to a higher and more perfect development, was held to be the gift of the Supreme Deity, imparted to man for the sake of combatting against the material principle, and with the prospect of finally subduing it. From the Supreme God on the one hand, and matter on the other, succeeding philosophers produced various fanciful genealogies of superior intelligences, under the name of Æons—a Greek word, signifying properly, periods; thus representing these divinities themselves by a name expressive of the time and order of their generation, much as in our current language the terms reign, or government, are frequently put for the king or ministers governing. The Demiurgus who formed the world out of matter, appears to have been an Æon derived from the evil principle. He was also the God of the Old Testament, who was considered by the Gnostics to be an object of aversion to the One Supreme God, to counteract whose machinations the Æon Christ was sent into the world. This is the earlier and simpler system, which is attributed to Simon Magus; the number of the Æons was fancifully multiplied in latter times, and an extravagant theory of morals founded upon the system. The object of this principally was, as may be supposed, to depreciate the honour due to the body, as being a part of matter, and to elevate the thinking faculty, or at least, to remove it from all consideration of worldly things. The Gnostics imagined that by assiduous practice of certain mental and bodily austerities, they could obtain an intuition of the divine nature, and dwell in communion with it; and this part of their system is adopted to a considerable extent by Clemens Alexandrinus, whose opinions, as expressed in the *Pædagogus*, are very similar to those of a Pietist of more modern times.

The Gnostics split in process of time into various sects, distinguished rather by the different cosmogonies they invented, than by any variation in principle. Of these, the principal were founded by Carpocrates, Basilides, Tatian, and Valentinus. The system did not survive the 4th century. The Christians seem sometimes to have adopted the general designation of Gnostics.

CHAPTER XVI.

ST SIMONIANS—HUMANITARIANS—MOMIERS.

SAINT SIMONIANS.

CLAUDE Henri, Count de S. Simon, of the ancient family of that name, born in 1760, was engaged during the greater part of his life in a series of unsuccessful commercial enterprises, a traveller, and in the early portion of his life a soldier in America; but having dissipated a considerable fortune, and been unable to draw the attention of the public to a variety of schemes, political and social, which he was constantly publishing, he attempted suicide in 1820; he lived, however, a few years longer, and died in 1825, leaving his papers and projects to Olinde Rodriguez. St. Simon's views of society and the destiny of mankind are contained in a variety of works, and especially in a short treatise entitled the *Nouveau Christianisme*, published after his death by Rodriguez. This book does not contain any scheme for the foundation of a new religion, such as his disciples afterwards invented. It is a diatribe against both the Catholic and Protestant sects for their neglect of the main principle of Christianity, the elevation of the lower classes of society; and inveighs against "l'exploitation de l'homme par l'homme," the existing system of individual industry, under which capitalist and labourer have opposite interests and no common object.

The principle of association, and just division of the fruits of common labour between the members of society, he imagined to be the true remedy for its present evils. After his death these ideas were caught up by a number of disciples, and formed into something resembling a system. The new association, or St. Simonian *family*, was chiefly framed by Rodriguez, Bazar, Thierry, Chevalier, and other men of talent. After the revolution of July, 1830, it rose rapidly into notoriety, from the sympathy between the notions which it promulgated and those entertained by many of the republican party. In 1831 the society had about 3,000 members, a newspaper (the *Globe*), and large funds.

The views of the St. Simonian family were all directed to the abolition of rank and property in society, and the establishment of associations (such as the followers of Mr. Owen in this country have denominated co-operative), of which all the members should work in common and divide the fruits of their labour. But with these notions, common to many other social reformers, they united the doctrine, that the division of the goods of the community should be in due proportion to the merits or capacity of the recipient. Society was to be governed by a hierarchy, consisting of a supreme pontiff, apostles, disciples of the first, second, and third order.

It was not until about this period (1830) that they began to invest these opinions with the form and character of a religion; but shortly after having done so they went into great extravagances. There was a disunion among them as to the fittest person to preside in the society; and consequently Messrs. Bazar and Enfantin divided, for some time, the duties and dignity of the "Supreme Father," as he was termed. But on the 19th of November, 1831, Bazar and many others left the society, of which Enfantin remained the supreme father. Their doctrines and proceedings now became licentious and immoral to the last degree. On the 22d of January, 1832, the family was dispersed by the government. Enfantin and Rodriguez were tried on various charges, and imprisoned for a year. The former afterwards collected again a part of the society at Menilmontant; but it broke up for want of funds. Some former members of the St. Simonian association are now in places of rank and consideration: some of the most extravagant have gone to the East; but Enfantin, we believe, has no followers.

HUMANITARIANS.

This term has been applied to those who deny the divinity of Christ, and assert him to have been *mere man*. This, however, is more than the word exactly signifies, and the term Psilanthropist, or mere Humanitarian, has been suggested as conveying the idea more precisely.

One of the ablest of modern Humanitarians is the Rev. Theodore Parker, minister of a Unitarian church in Roxbury, Mass. The following extracts from one of his discourses will convey some idea of his views:

"Alas, what men call Christianity, and adore as the best thing they see, has been degraded; so that if men should be all that the pulpit commonly demands of them, they would by no means be Christians. To such a pass have matters reached, that if Paul should come upon the earth now, as of old, it is quite doubtful that he could be admitted to the Christian church; for though Felix thought much knowledge had made the Apostle mad, yet Paul ventured no opinion on points respecting the nature of God, and the history of Christ, where our pulpits utter dogmatic and arbitrary decisions, condemning as infidels and accursed all such as disagree therewith, be their life never so godly. These things are notorious. Still more, it may be set down as quite certain, that if Jesus could return from the other world, and bring to New England that same boldness of inquiry which he brought to Judea; that same love of living truth, and scorn of dead letters; could he speak as he then spoke, and live again as he lived before, he also would be called an infidel by the church; be abused in our newspapers, for such is our wont, and only not stoned in the streets, because that is not our way of treating such men as tell us the truth.

"Such is the Christianity of the church in our times. It does not look *forward* but *backward*. It does not ask truth at first hand from God; seeks not to lead men directly to Him, through the divine life, but only to make them walk in the old paths trodden by some good, pious

Jews, who, were they to come back to earth, could as little understand our circumstances as we theirs. The church expresses more concern that men should walk in these peculiar paths, than that they should reach the goal. Thus the means are made the end. It enslaves men to the Bible; makes it the soul's master, not its servant; forgetting that the Bible, like the Sabbath, was made for man, not man for the Bible. It makes man the less and the Bible the greater. The Saviour said, search the Scriptures; the Apostle recommended them as profitable reading; the church says, Believe the Scriptures, if not with the consent of reason and conscience, why without that consent or against it. It rejects all attempts to humanize the Bible, and separate its fictions from its facts; and would fain wash its hands in the heart's blood of those who strip the robe of human art, ignorance, or folly, from the celestial form of divine truth. It trusts the imperfect Scripture of the Word, more than the Word itself, writ by God's finger on the living heart.

"The church itself worships not God, who is all in all, but Jesus, a man born of woman. Grave teachers, in defiance of his injunction, bid us pray to Christ. It supposes the Soul of our souls cannot hear, or will not accept a prayer, unless offered formally, in the church's phrase, forgetting that we also are men, and God takes care of oxen and sparrows, and hears the young ravens when they cry, though they pray not in any form or phrase. Still, called by whatever name, called by an idol's name, the true God hears the living prayer. And yet perhaps the best feature of Christianity, as it is now preached, is its idolatrous worship of Christ. Jesus was the brother of all. He had more in common with all men, than they have with one another. But he, the brother of all, has been made to appear as the master of all; to speak with an authority greater than that of Reason, Conscience, and Faith;—an office his sublime and Godlike spirit would revolt at. But yet, since he lived divine on the earth, and was a hero of the soul, and the noblest and largest hero the world has ever seen, perhaps the idolatry that is paid him is the nearest approach to true worship, which the mass of men can readily make in these days. Reverence for heroes has its place in history; and though worship of the greatest soul ever swathed in the flesh, however much he is idolized and represented as incapable of sin, is without measure below the worship of the ineffable God; still it is the purest and best of our many idolatries in the nineteenth century. Practically speaking, its worst feature is, that it mars and destroys the highest ideal of man, and makes us beings of very small discourse, that look only backward.

"The influence of real Christianity is to disenthral the man; to restore him to his nature, until he obeys Conscience, Reason, and Religion, and is made free by that obedience. It gives him the largest liberty of the Sons of God, so that as faith in truth becomes deeper, the man is greater and more divine. But now those pious souls who accept the church's Christianity are, in the main, crushed and degraded by their faith. They dwindle daily in the church's keeping. Their worship is not Faith, but Fear; and Bondage is written legibly on their forehead, like the mark set upon Cain. They resemble the dwarfed creed they accept. Their mind is encrusted with unintelligible dogmas. They fear to love man, lest they offend God. Artificial in their anxiety, and morbid in their self-examination, their life is sickly and wretched. Conscience cannot speak its mother tongue to them; Reason does not utter its oracles; nor love cast out fear. Alas, the church speaks not to the hearty and the strong; and the little and the weak, who accept its doctrines, become weaker and less thereby. Thus woman's holier heart is often abased and defiled, and the deep-thoughted and true of soul forsake the church, as righteous Lot, guided by an angel, fled out of Sodom. There will always be wicked men who scorn a pure church, and perhaps great men too high to need its instructions. But what shall we say when the church, as it is, impoverishes those it was designed to enrich, and debilitates so often the trusting souls that seek shelter in its arms?

"Alas for us, we see the Christianity of the church is a very poor thing; a very little better than heathenism. It takes God out of the world of nature and of man, and hides him in the church. Nay it does worse; it limits God, who possesseth heaven and earth, and is from everlasting to everlasting, restricting his influence and inspiration to a little corner of the world, and a few centuries of history, dark and uncertain. Even in this narrow range, it makes a deity like itself, and gives us not God, but Jehovah. It takes the living Christ out of the heart, and transfigures him in the clouds, till he becomes an anomalous being, not God, and not man; but a creature whose holiness is not the divine image, he has sculptured for himself out of the rock of life, but something placed over him entirely by God's hand, and without his own effort. It has taken away our Lord, and left us a being whom we know not; severed from us by his prodigious birth, and his alleged relation to God, such as none can share. What have we in common with such an one, raised above all chance of error, all possibility of sin, and still more surrounded by God at each moment, as no other man has been? It has transferred him to the clouds. It makes Christianity a Belief, not a Life. It takes religion out of the world, and shuts it up in old books, whence, from time to time, on Sabbaths, and fast-days, and feast days— it seeks to evoke the divine spirit, as the witch of Endor is fabled to have called up Samuel from the dead. It tells you, with grave countenance, to believe every word spoken by the Apostles,—weak, Jewish, fallible, prejudiced, mistaken as they sometimes were—for this reason, because forsooth Peter's shadow, and Paul's pocket handkerchief, cured the lame and the blind. It never tells you, Be faithful to the spirit God has given; open your soul and you also shall be inspired, beyond Peter and Paul it may be, for great though they were, they saw not all things, and have not absorbed the Godhead. No doubt the Christian church has been the ark of the world. No doubt some individual churches are now free from these disgraces; still the picture is true as a whole.

"The Christianity of the Church is a very poor thing; it is not bread, and it is not drink. The Christianity of Society is still worse; it is bitter in the mouth and poison in the blood. Still men are hungering and thirsting, though not always knowingly, after the true bread of life. Why shall we perish with hunger? In our Father's house is enough and to spare. The Christianity of Christ is high and noble as ever. The religion of Reason, of the Soul, the Word of God, is still strong and flame-like, as when first it dwelt in Jesus, the chiefest incarnation of God, and now the pattern-man. Age has not dimmed the lustre of this light that lighteneth all, though they cover their eyes in obstinate perversity, and turn away their faces from this great sight. Man has lost none of his God-likeness. He is still the child of God, and the father is near to us as to him who dwelt in his bosom. Conscience has not left us. Faith and hope still abide; and love never fails. The Comforter is with us; and though the man Jesus no longer blesses the earth, the ideal Christ, formed in the heart, is with us to the end of the world. Let us, then, build on these. Use good words when we can find them, in the church or out of it. Learn to pray, to pray greatly and strong; learn to reverence what is highest; above all learn to live; to make Religion daily work, and Christianity our common life. All days shall then be the Lord's day; our homes the house of God, and our labour the ritual of Religion. Then we shall not glory in men, for all things shall be ours; we shall not be impoverished by success, but enriched by affliction. Our service shall be worship, not idolatry. The burthens of the bible shall not overlay and crush us; its wisdom shall make us strong, and its piety enchant us. Paul and Jesus shall not be our masters, but elder brothers, who open the pearly gates of truth, and cheer us on, leading us to the Tree of Life. We shall find the Kingdom of Heaven and enjoy it now, not waiting till death ferries us over to the other world. We shall then repose beside the rock of ages, smitten by divine hands, and drink the pure water of life as it flows from the Eternal, to make earth green and glad. We shall serve no longer a bond-slave to tradition, in the leprous host of sin, but become freemen, by the law and spirit of life. Thus like Paul shall we form the Christ within; and, like Jesus, serving and knowing God directly, with no mediator intervening, become one with him. Is not this worth a man's wish; worth his prayers; worth his work, to seek the living Christianity; the Christianity of Christ? Not having this we seem but bubbles,—bubbles on an ocean, shoreless and without bottom; bubbles that sparkle a moment in the sun of life, then burst to be no more. But with it we are men, immortal souls, heirs of God and joint heirs with Christ."

MOMIERS.

By this name certain religionists of the so-called Evangelical party have been designated in Switzerland, and some parts of France and Germany, since 1818. They appear originally to have borne a considerable resemblance to the Methodists of Great Britain; for like the latter, they at first embraced no tenets distinct from those of the Established Church, and were only distinguished from its members by a more habitual indulgence in devotional contemplation and religious exercise. But they did not long continue to harmonize with the preachers of the establishment. One of the most vehement of the party, in a pamphlet published in 1818, accused the latter of denying the divinity of our Saviour, and of a thorough backsliding from the doctrines of Calvinism; and the Geneva clergy (*la venerable compagnie*) having, in the view of allaying asperities, passed a resolution prohibiting any theories of the doctrinal points of religion from being propounded in the pulpit, and having counselled the clergy to avoid disputed points as much as possible in their discourses, the smouldering embers of their hostility to the Established Church burst into a flame. They now began to attack the clergy in the pulpit and in pamphlets, accusing them of having abandoned all gospel truth, and denying their right to be regarded as ministers of the establishment. But all their efforts to bring the latter into contempt were unsuccessful: the Genevese remained faithful to their pastors; and in the year 1835, the Momiers possessed only about two hundred adherents.

In the other parts of Switzerland, however, and more especially in the canton de Vaud, the zeal of these sectaries was attended with more success. After a few years' toleration of their preaching and proselytising, during which it was alleged that the Momiers had sown the greatest discontent among the inhabitants of the canton, the government at last saw the necessity of interference, and in the year 1824 promulgated some vigourous ordinances to put them down. These enactments, as might have been expected, failed of their effect. The enthusiasm of the Momiers was redoubled: they were now surrounded with the glory of martyrdom; and many who had before viewed their zeal with indifference or contempt, now deeply sympathised in what they could not but regard as an undisguised attack upon the liberty of conscience. In consequence of the general disgust that ensued on their promulgation, these ordinances were at first gradually relaxed, then suffered to be dormant, and at last repealed in 1831. Since that period the number of Momiers has gradually diminished; and in 1839, the clergy of this canton resolved by a large majority to revert to the ancient *regime* of the church.

CHAPTER XVII.

CONCLUDING REFLECTIONS IN BEHALF OF CHRISTIAN MODERATION

"There is nothing in the world more wholesome or more necessary for us to learn than this gracious lesson of Moderation, without which, in very truth, a man is so far from being a Christian that he is not himself! This is the centre wherein all both divine and moral philosophy meet—the rule of life—the governess of manners—the silken string that runs through the pearl chain of all virtues—the very elliptic line under which reason and religion move without any deviation, and therefore most worthy our best thoughts—of our most careful observance."—*Bishop Hall.*

"May we all of us, in our respective stations, become more disposed to provoke one another unto love and good works, and less disposed to backbite and devour one another for our opinions—may Christianity have its root in our hearts rather than in our heads—may it shew forth its fruit in the purity and integrity of our lives, rather than in the vehemence and subtlety of our disputes. In a word, may the time at length come when every individual in the church and out of the church, Trinitarian and Unitarian, may love his own heresy less than Gospel charity."—*Bishop Watson.*

First, Since the best and wisest of mankind, thus differ on the speculative tenets of religion, let us modestly estimate the extent of the human faculties.

A modest estimate of the human faculties is an inducement to moderation. After laborious investigations, probably with equal degrees of knowledge and integrity, men arrive at opposite conclusions. This is a necessary consequence of imperfection. Human reason, weak and fallible, soars with feeble, and often with ineffectual wing, into the regions of speculation. Let none affirm that this mode of argument begets an indifference to the acquisition and propagation of religious truth. To declare that all tenets are alike is an affront to the understanding. The chilling hesitation of scepticism, the forbidding sternness of bigotry, and the delirious fever of enthusiasm, are equally abhorrent to the genius of True Christianity. Truth being the conformity of our conceptions to the nature of things, we should be careful lest our conceptions be tinctured with error. Philosophers suppose that the senses convey the most determinate species of information: yet these senses, notwithstanding their acuteness, are not endued with an instinctive infallibility. How much greater cause have we to mistrust the exercise of our rational powers, which often from early infancy, are beset with prejudices!

Our reason, however, proves of essential use to us in ascertaining the nature of truths, and the degrees of evidence with which they are severally attended. This induces a modesty of temper, which may be pronounced the ground-work of charity. Richard Baxter, revered for his good sense as well as fervent piety, has these remarkable expressions on the subject:—" I am not so foolish as to pretend my certainty to be greater than it is, merely because it is dishonour to be less certain; nor will I by shame be kept from confessing those infirmities which those have as much as I, who hypocritically reproach me with them. My certainty that I am a man, is before my certainty that there is a God; my certainty that there is a God, is greater than my certainty that he requireth love and holiness of his creatures: my certainty of this is greater than my certainty of the life of reward and punishment hereafter; my certainty of that is greater than my certainty of the endless duration of it, and the immortality of individual souls; my certainty of the Deity is greater than my certainty of the Christian faith in its essentials, is greater than my certainty of the perfection and infallibility of all the Holy Scriptures; my certainty of that is greater than my certainty of the meaning of many particular texts, and so of the truth of many particular doctrines, or of the canonicalness of some certain books. So that you see by what gradations my understanding doth proceed, as also my certainty differeth as the evidence differs! And they that have attained to a greater perfection and a higher degree of certainty than I, should pity me, and produce their evidence to help me." This paragraph should be written on a tablet in letters of gold. Like the Roman laws of old, it ought to be hung up in public, and every means taken of directing towards it the attention of professors of Christianity. This accurate statement of the nature and degrees of belief duly impressed on the mind, would prevent an ignorant and besotted bigotry.

Reason, though imperfect, is the noblest gift of God, and upon no pretence must be decried. It distinguishes man from the beasts of the field, constitutes his resemblance to the Deity, and elevates him to the superiority he possesses over the lower creations. By Deists it is extolled, to the prejudice of revelation; and by enthusiasts depreciated, that they may the more effectually impose on their votaries the absurdities of their systems. Yet, strange inconsistency! even these enthusiasts condescend to employ this calumniated faculty in pointing out the conformity of their tenets to scripture, and in fabricating evidence for their support. But beware of speaking lightly of reason, which is emphatically denominated "the eye of the soul!" Every opprobrious epithet with which the thoughtless or the designing dare to stigmatize it, vilifies the Creator.

From the perusal of the preceding pages it will be seen how prone men are to extremes in the important affairs of religion. The evil principally arises from the neglect of reason, denominated by an inspired writer, "the candle of the Lord," and which must be the best guide in the interpretation of the New Testament. And the epithet "carnal" with which professors are too apt to stigmatise it, is never once applied to it in the Holy Scriptures. It is there attached not to reason, but to the ceremonial commandments of the former dispensation. But Mr. Locke justly remarks, "Very few make any other use of their half-employed and undervalued reason but to bandy against it. For when, by the influence of some prevailing head, they all lead one way, truth is sure to be borne down, and there is nothing so dangerous as to make any inquiry after her, and to own her for her own sake is a most unpardonable crime." Thus it appears that the neglect of reason in matters of religion is a long standing evil, and probably will never be altogether eradicated in the present imperfect condition of humanity. But far from fettering the human mind, Christianity allows it free and vigorous exercise. By coming in contact with sacred subjects it is refined and invigorated. It will be sublimed and perfected in a better world.

Circumscribed, indeed, are the operations of reason, and fallible are its decisions. That it is incompetent to investigate certain subjects which our curiosity may essay to penetrate, is universally acknowledged. Its extension, therefore, beyond its assigned boundaries has proved an ample source of error. Thus Mr. Colliber, an ingenious writer, (often referred to by Dr. Doddridge in his Lectures,) imagines in his treatise, entitled "The Knowledge of God," that the Deity must have some form, and intimates it may probably be spherical!" Indeed the abuse of reason has generated an endless list of paradoxes, and given birth to those monstrous systems of metaphysical theology, which are the plague of men, and the idol of fools. Upon many religious topics, which have tried and tortured our understandings, the sacred writers are respectfully silent. Where they cease to inform us we should drop our inquiries; except we claim superior degrees of information, and proudly deem ourselves more competent to decide on these intricate subjects. "The modesty of Christians," says Archbishop Tillotson, " is contented in divine mysteries, to know what God has thought fit to reveal concerning them, and hath no curiosity to be wise above what is written. It is enough to believe what God says concerning these matters, and if any man will venture to say more —every other man surely is at liberty to believe as he sees reason."

The primitive Christians, in some of their councils, elevated the New Testament on a throne; thus intimating their concern that by that volume alone their disputes should be determined. The President De Thou used to remark, " that the sword of the word of God ought to be he sole weapon—and those who are no longer to be compelled, should be quietly attracted by moderate considerations and amicable discussions." *

---

*" In all persuasions, the bigots are persecutors; the men of a cool

Secondly, The diversity of religious opinions implies no reflection upon the sufficiency of Scripture to instruct us in matters of faith and practice, and should not, therefore, be made a pretence for uncharitableness.

Controversies are frequently agitated concerning words rather than things. This is to be ascribed chiefly to the ambiguity of language, which has been a fertile source of ecclesiastical animosities. A common gazer at the starry firmament conceives the stars to be innumerable; but the astronomer knows their number to be limited—nay, to be much smaller than a vulgar eye would apprehend. On the subjects of religion, many men dream rather than think —imagine rather than believe. Were the intellect of every individual awake, and preserved in vigorous exercise, similarity of sentiment would be much more prevalent. But mankind will not think, and hence thinking has been deemed " one of the least exerted privileges of cultivated humanity." It unfortunately happens that the idle flights indulged by enthusiasts, the burdensome rites revered by the superstitious, and the corrupt maxims adopted by worldly-minded professors, are charged on the Scriptures of truth. Whereas, the inspired volume is fraught with rational doctrines, equitable precepts, and immaculate rules of conduct. Fanciful accommodations, distorted passages, false translations and forced analogies, have been the means employed to debase the Christian doctrine. A calm and impartial investigation of the word of God raises in our minds conceptions worthy of the perfections of Deity, suitable to the circumstances of mankind, and adapted to purify our nature.

The Catholics deprive their laity of the Scripture, by restraining its use, and denying its sufficiency. The same

---

and reasonable piety are favourers of toleration; because, bigots not taking the pains to be acquainted with the grounds of their adversaries' tenets, conceive them to be so absurd and monstrous, that no man of sense can give in to them in good earnest. For which reason, they are convinced that some oblique bad motive induces them to pretend to the belief of such doctrines, and to the maintaining them with obstinacy. This is a general principle in all religious differences, and it is the corner-stone of all persecution."—*Burke.*

reason also was assigned to vindicate the necessity of an infallible head to dictate in religious matters. Notwithstanding these devices to produce unanimity of sentiment, they were not more in possession of it than the Protestants. The sects which at different periods sprang up in the bosom, and disturbed the tranquillity, of the Catholic church, are proofs that they failed to attain the desired object. Pretences, therefore, however specious, should be rejected, if they tend to invalidate the sufficiency, or disparage the excellence of holy writ. Least of all should diversity of sentiment be alleged; for it does not originate in the Scriptures themselves, but in the imbecility of the understanding, in the freedom of the will, in the pride of passion, and in the inveteracy of prejudice. Deists, nevertheless, who are expert in observing what may be construed into an objection against revealed religion, declaim loudly on this topic. On account of the diversity of sentiment which obtains, they charge the Bible with being defective in a species of intelligence it never pretended to communicate. Unencumbered with human additions, and uncontaminated with foreign mixtures, it furnishes the believer with that information which illuminates the understanding, meliorates the temper, invigorates the moral feelings, and improves the heart. All Scripture given by inspiration, is profitable for doctrine, for reproof, for correction, for instruction in righteousness, that the man of God may be perfect, thoroughly furnished unto all good works. "Heaven and hell are not more distant," says Lord Lyttleton, " than the benevolent spirit of the gospel and the malignant spirit of party. The most impious wars ever made were called holy wars. He who hates another man for not being a Christian, is himself not a Christian! Christianity breathes love, and peace, and good will to men." *

---

* The Emperor Charles V., we are told, retired at the close of life to a monastery, and there, says Dr. Robertson, " he was particularly curious with regard to the construction of clocks and watches, and having found, after repeated trials, that he could not bring any two of them to go exactly alike, he reflected, it is said, with a mixture of surprise as well as regret, on his own folly, in having bestowed so much time and

Thirdly, Let not any one presume to exempt himself from an attention to religion, because some of its tenets seem involved in difficulties.

Upon articles which promote the felicity and secure the salvation of mankind, the Scripture is clear and decisive. The curiosity of the inquisitive, and the restlessness of the ingenious, have involved some subjects of theological disquisition in obscurity. Dr. Paley, speaking of the disputes which distract the religious world, happily remarks " that the rent has not reached the foundation." Incontrovertible are the facts upon which the fabric of natural and revealed religion is reared; and the gates of hell shall not prevail against it! He who searches the Scriptures, must confess that they teach, in explicit terms, that God rules over all—that man has fallen from his primeval rectitude—that the Messiah shed his blood for his restoration—and that in a future state rewards await the righteous, and punishments will be inflicted on the wicked.

From the preceding sketch of the different opinions of Christians, it appears that controversies have been chiefly agitated concerning the person of Christ, the subject of the divine favour, and the article of church government. But what was the specific matter of disputation? Not whether Christ has actually appeared on earth to introduce a new dispensation; nor whether God is disposed to shew grace or favour towards fallen man; nor whether the professors of religion ought to submit themselves to certain regulations, or church government, for mutual benefit. These are truths revered by every denomination, and the only point of contention has been, what particular views are to be entertained of these interesting facts. The *Trinitarian*, the *Arian*, and the *Socinian*, equally acknowledge the divinity of Christ's mission, or that he was the Messiah predicted by the ancient prophets; and the chief point of dispute is, whether this Messiah be a man highly inspired, or one of the angelic order, or a being

---

labour in the vain attempt of bringing mankind to a precise uniformity of sentiment concerning the intricate and mysterious doctrines of religion!"

possessed of the attributes of Deity. The *Calvinist*, the *Arminian*, and the *Baxterian* also, each of them firmly believes that the grace of God hath appeared, and differ only respecting the wideness of its extent, the mode of its communication. Similar observations might be transferred to the subject of church government, and the administration of ceremonies. But sufficient has been said to shew that the differences subsisting between the majority of Christians do not affect the truth of Christianity, nor hazard the salvation of mankind.

Faint indeed is the light thrown by revelation on certain subjects. Yet no lover of righteousness need distress himself, whether he be mistaken in leading a life of virtue and piety. Practical religion lies within a narrow compass. The sayings of Christ embrace almost every part of human conduct, though his disciples have been lamentably deficient in paying them a proper attention. Jesus Christ assures us, that " to love the Lord our God with all our hearts, is the first and great commandment—and that the second is like unto it—to love our neighbour as ourselves." They entertain mistaken views of the glorious gospel, who consider it inimical to the prosperity of the human race. Descending from a God of love, and presented to us by his only begotten Son—every mind should have opened for its reception. Wrangling should have been prevented by the clearness of its fundamental doctrines, hesitation about obedience precluded by the justice of its precepts, and the beauty of its examples should have captivated the most indifferent hearts.

The perplexity in which some religious tenets are involved, instead of alienating us from the practice of righteousness, should quicken our inquiries after truth. Indeed, upon a serious and intelligent individual, it produces this effect. Having in his eye the Scripture as the only standard, he is the more alive to free inquiry, when he contemplates the diversity of religious systems; and more accurately scrutinizes their nature, examines their foundations, and ascertains their tendencies. This mode of arriving at truth is attended with advantages. Our knowedge is enlarged, our candour established, and our belief founded on the basis of conviction. Such a believer reflects an honour upon the denomination with which he connects himself. For feeling the difficulties of religious investigation, he presumes not to charge with heresy those of his fellow Christians who differ from him; nor is he such a stranger to the perfections of the Deity, and to the benign spirit of his religion, as to consign them over to the regions of future misery! Of Mr. Gouge, an eminent Nonconformist minister, it is thus honourably recorded by Archbishop Tillotson:—" He allowed others to differ from him even in opinions that were very dear to him, and provided men did but fear God, and work righteousness, he loved them heartily, how distant soever from him in judgment about things less necessary; in all which he is very worthy to be a pattern to men of all persuasions."*

Fourthly, Let us reflect with pleasure in how many important articles of belief all Christians are agreed.

Respecting the origin of evil, the nature of the human soul, the existence of an intermediate state, and the duration of future punishments, together with points of a similar kind, opinions have been, and in this imperfect state will ever continue to be, different. But on articles of faith, far more interesting in themselves, and far more conducive to our welfare, are not all Christians united? We all believe in the perfections and government of one God, in the degradation of human nature through transgression, in the unspeakable efficacy of the life, death, and sufferings of Jesus Christ, in the assurance of the divine aid, in the necessity of exercising repentance and of cultivating holiness; in a resurrection from the dead, and in a future state of rewards and punishment. Cheerfully would I

---

* " Were one religion only to exist in a country, probably the people would soon become either indifferent about its tenets or superstitious in supporting them, and from the history of mankind, were two systems only of religion to prevail, zeal would be perpetually exercised to the destruction of each other; but variety which divides attention tends to lessen bigotry and arrest persecution—and hence seems best calculated to promote zeal without intolerance, virtue void of hypocrisy, and the general happiness of the community."

enter into a minute illustration of this part of the subject; but the devout and intelligent Dr. Price has discussed it, in his first Sermon on the Christian Doctrine, to which discourse I refer the reader, and recommend it to his repeated perusal. Many Christians are more anxious to know wherein their brethren differ from them, than wherein they are agreed. This betrays a propensity to division, and bears an unfavourable aspect on mutual forbearance, one of the highest embellishments of the Christian character. An enlightened zeal is compatible with religious moderation, which is more particularly opposed to the furious spirit of uncharitableness, the gangrene of genuine Christianity! From the shy and distant deportment of men of different persuasions towards each other, a stranger to them all would with difficulty be brought to believe that they looked up to the same God, confided in the same Saviour, and were bending their steps towards the same state of future happiness. The Christian world has the appearance of a subdued country, portioned out into innumerable districts, through the pride and ambition of its conquerors, and each district occupied in retarding each other's prosperity. Alas! what would the Prince of Peace say, were he to descend and sojourn among us! Would he not reprove our unhallowed warmth, upbraid us with our divisions, chide our unsocial tempers, and exhort to amity and concord? "This antipathy to your fellow Christians," would he say, "is not the effect of my religion, but proceeds from the want of it. My doctrines, precepts, and example, have an opposite tendency. Had you learned of me, you would never have uttered against your brethren terms of reproach, nor lifted up the arm of persecution. The new commandment I gave unto you was—That you love one another."

Were the professors of the Gospel once fully sensible how they coincide on the fundamental facts of natural and revealed religion, they would cherish with one another a more friendly intercourse, unite more cordially to propagate religion both at home and abroad, and a superior degree of success would crown their combined exertions for the purpose. Much it is regretted that disputes have generally been agitated concerning unessential points, and with an acrimony diametrically opposite to the Gospel of Jesus Christ. That controversy is in itself injurious to truth, no intelligent individual will insinuate. When conducted with ability and candour, light has been struck out, errors have been rectified, and information, on interesting subjects, has been communicated to the public. But alas! controversy has been perverted. To many who have engaged in theological discussion, victory, not truth, has been the object of pursuit. Seduced by unworthy motives, they swerved from the line of conduct prescribed by an apostle, and contended boisterously, rather than earnestly, for the faith once delivered to the saints. Fiery controversialists, hurried away by impetuousness of temper, or exasperated by the opposition of an acute and pertinacious adversary, have disgraced polemic pages by ungenerous insinuations. Thus are infidels furnished with an additional objection to revealed religion—the investigation of interesting truth terminates in mutual reproaches; and Christians of different sentiments, driven still farther from each other, are the less fitted to associate together in the common mansions of the blest! To this pernicious mode of agitating disputes, there are, however, exceptions; and instances of this kind might be adduced. In the defence of Christianity, and in the support of its particular doctrines, writers have stood forth, whose temper and liberality breathe the genuine spirit of the Christian Religion. Doddridge's Letters to the Author of Christianity not founded in Argument, Bishop Watson's Apologies, and Campbell's Answer to Hume on Miracles, are examples of the candour with which religious controversies should be conducted. In an enlightened age like the present, this conciliating spirit was to be expected; and we indulge the pleasing hope, that times still more auspicious to truth are approaching, when the amicable discussion of every doctrine shall obtain an universal prevalence Surely nothing can be more unphilosophical and pitiful than that morose spirit of bigotry, which is evinced in the tone of some writers calling themselves " evangelical." The time is gone by when the claim of any man or any sect to infallibility can be respected by the good and wise. Let us remember the counsel of one of the truest Christians that ever wrote:

> " Seize upon truth where'er 't s found,
>   Among your friends—among your foes,
> On Christian, or on Heathen ground;
>   The flower's divine where'er it grows;
> Neglect the prickles and assume the rose."—*Watts.*

" No way whatsoever," says the immortal Locke, " that I shall walk in against the dictates of my conscience, will ever bring me to the mansions of the blessed. I may grow rich by an art that I take no delight in—I may be cured of some disease by remedies I have no faith in; but I cannot be saved by a religion that I distrust, and a worship that I abhor. It is vain for an unbeliever to take up the outward shadow of another man's profession; faith only and sincerity are the things that procure acceptance with God."

Truth, indeed, moral and divine, flourishes only in the soil of freedom. There it shoots up and sheds its fruit for the healing of the nations! Civil and religious liberty are two of the greatest earthly blessings which Heaven can bestow on man. Thrice happy are the people who experience the benefits of good government, unburdened by oppression, and who enjoy the sweets of liberty, unembittered by licentiousness!

Fourthly, We should allow to others the same right of private judgment in religious matters, which we claim and exercise ourselves.

It is replied—" We forbid not the sober use of this privilege." But who can estimate the sobriety of another man's speculations? And by reprobating the opinions which a serious brother may happen to entertain in consequence of free investigation, we tacitly condemn that operation of his mind which induced him to take up such tenets. This is the spirit of popery in disguise. Cautiously exercising his reason, and devoutly examining the sacred records, let every man be fully persuaded in his own mind. This was the advice of Paul to the primitive Christians, and no substantial reason has been, or ever will be given, for its being abandoned. For a Protestant, who demands and exercises the right of private judgment, to deny it to his brother, is an unpardonable inconsistency. It is also an act of injustice, and, therefore, contrary to reason, condemned by revelation, and prejudicial to the best interests of mankind. He who insults your person steals your property, or injures your reputation, subjects himself to the punishment which the law denounces What then can we think of the man who attempts to rob you of the right of private judgment—a jewel of inestimable price—a blessing of the first magnitude! Were we once to relinquish thinking for ourselves, and indolently to acquiesce in the representations of others, our understandings might soon groan beneath the absurdities of other men's creeds, and our attention be distracted by the perplexed nature of our religious services. Hitherto, persons have never been wanting unreasonable enough to impose on their brethren articles of faith. The late Mr. Robinson, of Cambridge, an avowed foe to ecclesiastical tyranny, has traced its sources with his usual acuteness, and pronounces them to be power, law, patronage, office, the abuse of learning, and mistaken piety. These pretences for domination over conscience are plausible, and by their speciousness millions have been deceived. But explain to a man of common sense the nature and foundation of religious liberty, and the infatuation ceases. He must perceive that the Father of Spirits hath authorized no man to dictate to another what he is to believe, much

---

* William Penn has, in a letter to Archbishop Tillotson, these memorable words—"I abhor two principles in religion, and pity them that own them—The first is obedience upon authority, without conviction; and the other, destroying them that differ from me, for God's sake. Such a religion is without judgment though not without teeth—union is best if right—else charity."

less to impose his dogmas under pain of eternal punishment:

> "Let Cæsar's dues be ever paid
> To Cæsar and his throne;
> But consciences and souls were made
> To be the Lord's alone!"—*Watts.*

To use the language of the illustrious Washington, speaking of the United States,—" It affords edifying prospects indeed to see Christians of different denominations dwell together in more charity, and conduct themselves in respect to each other with a more Christian-like spirit, than ever they have done in any former age!"

Dr. Prideaux (a learned clergyman of the church of England) in his Life of Mahomet, speaking of the dissensions of the sixth century, remarks—" Christians having drawn the abstrusest niceties into controversy, did thereby so destroy peace, love, and charity among themselves, that they lost the whole substance of religion, and in a manner drove Christianity quite out of the world; so that the Saracens, taking advantage of the weakness of power and distractions of councils, which those divisions had caused, soon over-ran with terrible devastation all the Eastern provinces of the Roman empire; turned every where their churches into mosques, and forced on them the abominable imposture of Mahometanism."

Why even of yourselves judge ye not what is right? was the language in which Christ reproached the Pharisees; and prove all things, was Paul's exhortation to the church at Thessalonica. These passages alone shew, beyond the possibility of dispute, that both Christ and Paul were patrons of free inquiry. Free inquiry, in its fullest extent, has been found serviceable to the interests of religion. Hereby error ceases to be perpetuated, and truth emerges from those shades of darkness with which she has been enveloped. Survey the page of ecclesiastical history—mark the intervals of languor when the right of private judgment lay dormant—then was the church of Christ debilitated and pestered with an heterogeneous mass of errors. Excellently it is remarked in a periodical publication:—"No man can write down truth. Inquiry is to truth what friction is to the diamond. It proves its hardness, adds to its lustre, and excites new admiration." The ablest advocates for Christianity confess, that by the attacks of its enemies provoking examination, it has been benefited. To infidel writers we are indebted for Butler's profound Analogy, Law's Theory of Natural and Revealed Religion, Campbell's Dissertation on Miracles, Newton's Work on the Prophecies, Watson's admirable Apologies, and other performances, which reflect as much honour on the names of their respective authors, as they have rendered service to the cause they espoused. "Every species of intolerance," says Archdeacon Paley, "which enjoins suppression and silence, and every species of persecution which enforces such injunctions, is averse to the progress of truth, forasmuch as it causes that to be fixed by one set of men at one time, which is much better, and with much more probability of success, left to the independent and progressive inquiries of separate individuals. Truth results from discussion and from controversy, is investigated by the labour and researches of private persons; whatever therefore prohibits these, obstructs that industry and that liberty, which it is the common interest of mankind to promote."

Sixthly. Let us be careful to treat those who differ from us with kindness.

Believing those who differ from us to be the disciples of error, they have a claim on our compassion. And as a further incentive to a lenient conduct, it should be remembered, that we differ from them just as much as they do from us. By either party, therefore, no anathema should be hurled, and a proneness to persecution should be eradicated. The Quakers, in their address to James II. on his accession, told him, that they understood he was no more of the established religion than themselves:—"We therefore hope (say they) that thou wilt allow us that liberty which thou takest thyself." The terms schism and heresy are in the mouths of many, and it is no unfrequent case to find that those who use them most, least understand their real import. Dr. Campbell, who favoured the public with an excellent translation of the four Gospels, thus concludes a learned dissertation on the subject:— "No person who in the spirit of candour and charity adheres to that which to the best of his judgment is right, though in this opinion he should be mistaken, is in the scriptural sense either schismatic or heretic; and he, on the contrary, whatever sect he belongs to, is most entitled to those odious appellations who is most apt to throw the imputation upon others." Would to God that this observation were inscribed on the front of every place of worship and engraven on the memory of every individual in Christendom!

Upon the advantages arising from Christian moderation we might largely expatiate, and to detail the evils which have flown from an unenlightened and furious zeal, would be to stain my page with blood. Bishop Hall, in the last century, wrote a treatise on moderation, and has discussed the subject with that ability which is peculiar to all his writings. But this great and good man, towards the close of the same treatise, forgetting the principles which he had been inculcating, devotes one solitary page to the cause of intolerance. This page he concludes with these remarkable expressions:—"Master Calvin did well approve himself to God's church, in bringing Servetus to the stake at Geneva!" Blessed Jesus, how art thou wounded in the house of thy friends! After this deplorable instance of human inconsistency, should not the most eminent of the followers of Christ beware, lest, by indulging even in the slightest degree a spirit of intolerance, they be insensibly led either to adopt or applaud practices which, under the specious mask of an holy zeal, outrage the first principle of humanity? To love our own party only, is (to use the words of the excellent Dr. Doddridge) nothing else than self-love reflected. The most zealous partizans are revelling in self-gratification

And Mr. Jay, of Bath, in his excellent Sermons, remarks, that " the readiest way in the world to thin heaven and replenish the regions of hell, is to call in the spirit of bigotry. This will immediately arraign and condemn, and execute all that do not bow down and worship the image of our idolatry. Possessing exclusive prerogatives, it rejects every other claim—'Stand by, I am sounder than thou. The temple of the Lord, the temple of the Lord, the temple of the Lord are we!' How many of the dead has this intolerance sentenced to eternal misery, who will shine like stars in the kingdom of our Father!—how many living characters does it not reprobate as enemies to the cross of Christ, who are placing in it all their glory! No wonder, if under the influence of this consuming zeal, we form lessening views of the number of the saved. I only am left—yes, they are few, indeed, if none belong to them who do not belong to your party—that do not see with your eyes—that do not believe election with you, or universal redemption with you—that do not worship under a steeple with you, or in a meeting with you—that are not dipped with you, or sprinkled with you! But hereafter we shall find that the righteous were not so circumscribed; when we shall see—many coming from the east, and from the west, from the north, and from the south, to sit down with Abraham, Isaac, and Jacob, in the kingdom of heaven!" Were these truly evangelical sentiments more prevalent among professors of every description, the ravages of infidelity would cease—Christians themselves become more united, and rapid advances would be thus making towards their moral and religious improvement.

Christians, indeed, of almost every denomination, appear at times to have forgotten, that harshness widens rather than closes the breaches which diversity of sentiment may have occasioned. Coercive measures reach not the mind, and the issuing edicts to extort assent to speculative tenets, is the bombast of civil authority. Truth rests on evidence. But what has evidence to do with exertions of power, implements of torture, and scenes of devastation? From the commencement of the fourth century, down to that illustrious æra of the reformation, wide and unmolested was the empire of ignorance over the human mind. At Rome, for a series of ages, the chair of infallibility was filled by a succession of intolerant and domineering pontiffs. Systems of cruelty were devised and practised, for the support of their 'most holy' faith. Out of that once respectable capital of the world, the demon of persecution rushed forth, brandishing his torch, and deluged the church of Christ with the blood of her martyrs! Impatient for the destruction of the human race, he flew into different regions of the earth, framed racks, fixed stakes, erected gibbets, and, like a pestilence, scattered around him consternation and death! Shall the mild and evangelical genius of Protestanism countenance a temper which incites to such execrable deeds, and enrols the names of the perpetrators in the calendar of the saints? In this twilight state of being, to expostulate is our province—to inveigh and persecute is forbidden. The glorious Gospel of the blessed God prohibits rash accusations, cruel surmises, and malignant anathemas. Had a regard been paid to the golden rule—Do unto others as ye would they should do unto you, intolerance would never have reared its ensanguined crest to affright the children of men. "Ye know not what manner of spirit ye are of"—was our Saviour's reprimand to the disciples, who, in the plenitude of their zeal, would have called down fire from heaven to consume the deluded Samaritans. Too often does a portion of this accursed spirit reign in the breasts of Protestants. Hence censures are poured forth, hatreds are engendered, and a preparation for heaven is retarded. Instead, therefore, of usurping the seat of judgment, which the Almighty has exclusively reserved to himself, and of aiming to become the dispensers of the divine vengeance, let us wait the issue of all things in deep and reverential silence. A wise and a good God will solemnly decide the business, when he judges the world in righteousness!

Seventhly, Let us not repine because perfect unanimity of religious sentiment is unattainable in this present state.

A repining spirit is the source of ill temper towards those who dissent from us; but it seems to be the intention of the Divine Being, that we should think differently concerning certain points of faith and practice. Variety marks the works of God. It is impressed throughout the circumference of the natural, the animal, and the intellectual world. Above us we behold the dazzling brightness of the sun, the pale splendour of the moon, the mild twinkling of the stars, and the variegated colours which adorn the firmament of heaven! Around us the surface of the earth is diversified into a thousand beautiful forms, and in the animal, the vegetable, and the fossil kingdoms, no two individual productions are perfectly alike! Within us, upon the slightest examination, we discern our minds stamped with an original peculiarity. From senseless idiotism, up to the sagacity of Newton, how numerous are the gradations of intellect! Minds are of various sizes. Their capacities, habits, and views, are never in strict conformity with each other. In some degree, therefore, diversity of opinion flows from the structure of our understanding. To fall out with this branch of the dispensations of God, is to arraign his wisdom. Doubtless he might have shed upon us such a degree of light, that we should have seen as with one eye, and have been altogether of one mind. But the Supreme Being has otherwise ordered it, and with becoming resignation let us acquiesce in the propriety of the appointment. Lord Mansfield, that ornament of the law, declares that " There is nothing certainly more unreasonable, more inconsistent with the rights of human nature, more contrary to the spirit and precepts of the Christian religion, more iniquitous and unjust, more impolitic, than persecution! It is against natural religion, revealed religion, and sound policy!"*

---

* The biographer of Bishop Burnett tells us, that when making his Tour on the Continent, this great and good prelate " there became acquainted with the leading men of the different persuasions tolerated in that country, particularly Calvinists, Arminians, Lutherans, Baptists, Brownists, Papists, and Unitarians, amongst each of which, he

Innumerable and unavailable have been the attempts made in the successive ages of the Church to produce unanimity of sentiment. For this purpose legislatures have decreed acts, poured forth torrents of blood, and perpetrated deeds at which humanity sickens, shudders, and turns away with disgust. Francis I., king of France, used to declare, "that if he thought the blood in his arm was tainted with the Lutheran heresy, he would have it cut off, and that he would not spare even his own children, if they entertained sentiments contrary to the Catholic Church." Pride in one person, passion in a second, prejudice in a third, and in a fourth, investigation, generates difference of opinion. Should diversity be deemed an evil, it is incumbent on rational beings, and congenial with the dignity of the Christian profession, to improve it to valuable purposes. It is a fact, that different denominations have, in every age of the church, kept a jealous eye over each other; and hereby the Scriptures, the common standard to which they appealed for the truth of their respective tenets, have been preserved in greater purity. It may also be added, that diversity of opinion quickens our inquiries after truth, and gives scope for the exercise of our charity, which in one passage of the sacred writings is pronounced superior to faith and hope, and in another passage termed the bond of perfectness. Much improvement have good men extracted from the common evils of life, by these evils giving rise to graces and virtues which otherwise, perhaps, would have had no existence; or at least, would have been faintly called forth into action. To perceive the justice of this observation, it is not necessary that we be profound contemplators of human affairs.

Under the accumulated difficulties of faith and practice, by which we are embarrassed in this sublunary state of imperfection, we should meditate on the doctrine of a Providence, which administers the richest consolation. The dominion exercised by the Supreme Being over the works

used frequently to declare, he met with men of such unfeigned piety and virtue, that he became fixed in a strong principle of universal charity."

of his hands, is neither partial as to its objects, narrow in its extent, nor transitory in its duration. Unlike earthly monarchs, who expire in their turn, and who are successively born into the tombs of their ancestors, the King of Saints liveth and reigneth for ever and ever! Evils, indeed, have entered the world, and still continue to distress it. But these evils have not crept into the system unknown to its great author; and the attributes of Deity ensure their extirpation. Our rejoicing is—the Lord God omnipotent reigneth! Glorious, therefore, must be the termination of the divine dispensations. The august period is predicted in sacred writ, and lies concealed in the womb of time. Distant may be its arrival, but its blessings once realized, will compensate the exercise of your faith, and the trial of your patience:

> "One part, one little part, we dimly scan,
>   Thro' the dark medium of life's fev'rish dream,
> Yet dare arraign the whole stupendous plan,
>   If but that little part incongruous seem.
> Nor is that part, perhaps, what mortals deem;
>   Oft from apparent ills our blessing rise---
> O! then renounce that impious self-esteem,
>   That aims to trace the secrets of the skies;
> For thou art but of dust---be humble and be wise."
>   BEATTIE.

THE END.

www.ingramcontent.com/pod-product-compliance
Lightning Source LLC
Chambersburg PA
CBHW032110230426
43672CB00009B/1690